D0085413

Studies in Moral, Political, and Legal Philosophy

GENERAL EDITOR, MARSHALL COHEN

DAVID JOHNSTON

The Rhetoric of *Leviathan*

THOMAS HOBBES AND THE POLITICS OF CULTURAL TRANSFORMATION

✲ ✲ ✲ ✲ ✲ ✲ ✲ ✲ ✲

PRINCETON UNIVERSITY PRESS

Published by Princeton University Press, 41 William Street,
Princeton, New Jersey 08540
In the United Kingdom: Princeton University Press, Guildford, Surrey

Library of Congress Cataloging in Publication Data will be found on the last printed page of this book

ISBN 0-691-07717-7

This book has been composed in Linotron Garamond

Clothbound editions of Princeton University Press books
are printed on acid-free paper, and binding materials are
chosen for strength and durability

Printed in the United States of America by Princeton University Press
Princeton, New Jersey

DESIGNED BY LAURY A. EGAN

This Book Is Dedicated to Wendy

IN APPRECIATION FOR A SPLENDID DECADE AND

IN ANTICIPATION OF MANY MORE TO COME

Contents

Preface

THIS BOOK grew out of the observation that in both method and content Hobbes's *Leviathan* owes at least as much to modes of thought that were dominant in the sixteenth century as it does to the scientific outlook of the seventeenth century and beyond with which we usually associate his name. For a number of years now, interpreters have been intent upon portraying Hobbes as a forerunner of liberalism and spokesman of the emerging bourgeoisie. There is much to be learned from this forward-looking perspective, but its dominance in the field of Hobbes studies has had the unfortunate side effect of pre-forming the perceptions of his readers in ways that have tended to obscure some of the most important elements in his thought. The aim of this book is to help correct this distortion by restoring an awareness of the roots of Hobbes's thinking in the humanist and polemical traditions of the Renaissance and by showing how these elements shaped his argumentation in *Leviathan*. In pursuing this aim I have been led to emphasize what Hobbes was attempting to *do* in that work as well as, in a narrow sense, what he was trying to say. The notion that speech and the written word are forms of action, which is so frequently forgotten when political philosophy is made into an object of academic study and assimilated to the tendency toward quiescence in modern philosophy, was a commonplace to Hobbes and his Renaissance forebears. By dwelling upon this notion I hope to bring some light to a dimension of his work that is far less clearly understood than it ought to be.

The origin of this study can be traced back to a seminar led by Sheldon Wolin in which I was privileged to have an opportunity to articulate some arguments against Quentin Skinner's interpretation of Hobbes and receive the benefit of Professor Skinner's response. Although their respective concepts of political theory as a "thought deed" and "speech act" have very different philosophical roots, both have helped shape my own thinking, and in some ways this work is an attempt to come to terms with these concepts by examining their applicability to Hobbes.

Under the supervision of Professors Wolin and Dennis Thompson, I prepared the first version of the study that ultimately became this book. Without their inspiration, advice, criticism, and encouragement this work would have been impossible. I am deeply grateful to David Mayhew and Frank Turner, whose support during these past several years has been of inestimable value, and wish also to thank Zbigniew Pelczynski for his consistent encouragement and hospitality. Terence Ball, David Gauthier, Joseph Hamburger, Charles E. Lindblom, James Scott, Ian Shapiro, and Rogers Smith all read the initial draft of this book, and I owe a very great deal to their comments for any improvements I have been able to achieve in the final version. I am especially indebted to Nannerl O. Keohane, now President of Wellesley College, and David Smith for stimulating my interest in political philosophy.

I wish to thank the American Council of Learned Societies and Yale University for financial support that enabled me to compose this book. Some of my early research was supported by a grant from the A. Whitney Griswold Fund at Yale. The initial draft was written in the pleasant and helpful atmosphere of the Social Studies Faculty Centre of Oxford University in the spring of 1984. I am also grateful to Pembroke College for making me a temporary Member during this period. Sanford Thatcher of Princeton University Press has been immensely encouraging and helpful throughout the process that has turned the manuscript he first read into a book. Finally, for their tireless patience in typing and retyping this book through two complete drafts, I am thankful to Ruth Muessig and Roberta Dulong.

New Haven, Connecticut
December 1985

A Note on References

THE TITLES of works by Hobbes referred to in this book have been shortened to the forms given below. Works that are divided into numbered sections or paragraphs are cited accordingly. Thus *Elements* I.1.1 refers to *The Elements of Law, Natural and Politic*, part I, chapter 1, section 1. Works that are not so divided are cited by chapters, where appropriate, and page numbers in the editions listed below. For *Leviathan* I have provided the page numbers of both the Macpherson edition and the original edition of 1651. Thus *Leviathan*, ch. 43, p. 626 [331], refers to p. 626 of the Macpherson edition and p. 331 of the original. All emphases in quotations are in the original texts cited unless otherwise noted.

Answer "The Answer of Mr. Hobbes to Sir Will. D'Avenant's Preface before Gondibert," in *Sir William D'Avenant's Gondibert*, David E. Gladish, ed. (Oxford: Clarendon Press, 1971).

Anti-White *Thomas White's De Mundo Examined*, Harold Whitmore Jones, trans. (London: Bradford University Press, 1976).

Behemoth *Behemoth; or, The Long Parliament*, 2nd ed., Ferdinand Tönnies, ed. (London: Frank Cass and Co., 1969).

Considerations *Considerations upon the Reputation, Loyalty, Manners, and Religion of Thomas Hobbes*, in *EW* 4.

De Cive *De Cive*, The English Version, vol. 3 of *Philosophical Works of Thomas Hobbes*, Howard Warrender, ed. (Oxford: Clarendon Press, 1983).

De Corpore *Elements of Philosophy Concerning Body*, in *EW* 1.

NOTE ON REFERENCES

De Homine *De Homine*, as translated in *Man and Citizen*, Bernard Gert, ed. (Garden City, New York: Doubleday, 1972).

Elements *The Elements of Law, Natural and Politic*, 2nd ed., Ferdinand Tönnies, ed. (London: Frank Cass and Co., 1969).

EW *The English Works of Thomas Hobbes of Malmesbury*, 11 vols., Sir William Molesworth, ed. (London: John Bohn, 1839-1845).

Leviathan *Leviathan; or, The Matter, Forme, and Power of a Commonwealth, Ecclesiasticall and Civill*, C. B. Macpherson, ed. (Harmondsworth, Middlesex: Penguin, 1968).

Thucydides Hobbes's translation of Thucydides' *History of the Peloponnesian War*, in *EW* 8.

Introduction

WHEN *Leviathan* first appeared in 1651 it was immediately recognized as a work of extraordinary scope. Whatever their opinions of it, all readers of Hobbes's book saw it as the expression of a comprehensive vision of the world, which united metaphysical, theological, and political arguments into a single distinctive outlook. At the center of this outlook lay mechanical materialism, the doctrine that the universe consists of nothing more than matter in motion. For most of his readers Hobbes's materialism sufficed to establish him as an atheist as well. His political theory seemed likewise to be a natural extension of these materialistic and atheistic views. To his critics, Hobbes's skepticism about man's natural capacity for goodness appeared to flow from his lack of faith in a beneficent God. Hobbes's admirers interpreted the links between his metaphysics and his politics in more generous terms. But critics and admirers alike were convinced that the political theory of *Leviathan* was intimately connected with the metaphysical and theological views expressed in the same book.

As his teachings became increasingly acceptable during the two centuries that followed his death, this perception of the unity of Hobbes's philosophy gradually broke down. His theology came to be seen as an historical curiosity. His metaphysics, though loosely compatible with the philosophical materialism that became popular during the Enlightenment, was superseded by views based upon the Newtonian conception of the universe. At the same time, however, his political doctrines seemed to retain their relevance. While they never lost their controversial edge, these doctrines gained acceptance as one of the main currents in modern political thought and, in the nineteenth century, acquired orthodox status within the movement toward legal positivism in England. Hobbes's establishment as a leading figure in the history of political philosophy was accompanied by the erection of a partition between his political doctrines on the one hand and his metaphysics and theology on the other.

This partition of his work generated a question that has haunted Hobbes studies for the past hundred years: is his philosophy the architectonic structure derived by deduction from first principles he sometimes claimed it to be? More generally stated the question is whether Hobbes's philosophy possesses the inward unity of a genuine system. The usual answer to this question has been no. Robertson's observation a century ago that "the whole of his political doctrine . . . has little appearance of having been thought out from the fundamental principles of his philosophy"[1] is typical. Most interpreters since then have agreed that the systematic pretensions of his philosophy are little more than a veil designed to disguise the cracks in an essentially syncretic amalgamation of ideas.

This dominant view has been challenged from time to time. Some critics have argued that Hobbes's system is united by "the continuous application of a doctrine about the nature of philosophy"[2] or by a concept of method that is applied consistently in all its parts. Others have noted that the theology of *Leviathan* complements its political doctrine,[3] and some have even claimed that that theology is the foundation of his politics. Surprisingly, however, these claims have almost never

[1] George Croom Robertson, *Hobbes* (Edinburgh and London: William Blackwood and Sons, 1910; first published 1886), p. 57.

[2] Michael Oakeshott, *Hobbes on Civil Association* (Berkeley and Los Angeles: University of California Press, 1975), p. 16.

[3] E.g. Alan Ryan, "Hobbes, Toleration, and the Inner Life," in David Miller and Larry Siedentop, eds., *The Nature of Political Theory* (Oxford: Clarendon Press, 1983), pp. 197-218, esp. p. 201.

been supported by any systematic examination of the relevant portions of his work. With one or two notable exceptions those few interpreters who have taken the trouble to examine his metaphysics and theology have accepted the prevailing orthodoxy that a rigid wall separates his treatment of these topics from his political philosophy as such.

The inability of his interpreters to resolve this problem arises mainly from the fact that, apart from a few efforts to situate his doctrine in relation to the civil war in England, they have assumed that this doctrine must be treated as an abstract, timeless scheme of equal applicability to every time and place. This assumption has had two effects. First, it has led interpreters to define the content of Hobbes's argument from the outset in ways that exclude from consideration much of what he actually said. Arguments deemed to be of merely local and transitory interest are considered unworthy of serious discussion, which should be reserved for Hobbes's enduring theoretical contributions. The fact that the line separating these two categories of statements has shifted from time to time has not deterred his interpreters from continuing to draw it. Second, the political qualities of Hobbes's work itself—as distinct from the subject of that work—have consistently been neglected. The statement that *Leviathan* is an intensely political book will surprise no one, but the implications of this observation have never been carried to their conclusion in the critical literature. The *Leviathan* that occupies a place in the pantheon of great political literature is in some ways as dead as the gods contained in the original.

This study is an attempt to overcome some of these difficulties. The methodological goal of this book is to emancipate Hobbes from the shackles imposed by an idea of philosophical activity that owes more to contemporary preconceptions about philosophy than to any genuine appreciation of his own philosophical premises. My point of departure is provided by the perception of unity with which *Leviathan* was greeted by its original readers. What follows from this point is that each of Hobbes's statements must be taken seriously, however transitory some of them may at first appear. The fact that his original readers perceived his argument as a unity does not prove that it is so, but to rule certain of his statements out of court *a priori* because of their alleged lack of enduring significance must almost inevitably lead to the conclusion that that argument is syncretic. By taking seriously the text of *Leviathan* as a whole, I hope to avoid the obvious artificiality of this conclusion.

Secondly, the political aims of Hobbes's work will be given much more careful consideration than is ordinarily conferred upon them. Simply to accept his own statement that his work was "occasioned by the disorders of the present time"[4] and to conclude that the work can be understood adequately against the backdrop of his understanding of the civil war is not enough. It is a premise of this book that the aims of Hobbes's work must be determined by investigation, not by some arbitrarily imposed assumption. The extent to which those aims are timeless and speculative, on the one hand, or determined by reference to problems raised by the civil war, for example, on the other cannot be stipulated in advance.

A further aim of this study is to view the argumentation of *Leviathan* against the background of its own genesis. It is now widely accepted that a break in Hobbes's thinking occurred at some point during his middle age and that this break had a decisive impact upon the formulation of his political philosophy. In some respects this picture is correct, but its dominance has had the consequence of inducing most interpreters to overlook the importance Hobbes attached to the effective expression and transmission of ideas. This concern was an inheritance from the rhetorical tradition with which he became deeply familiar during the first four decades of his life. A re-examination of the genesis of his thought will enable us to demonstrate that this

[4] *Leviathan*, Review and Conclusion, p. 728 [395].

legacy played a central role in bringing together elements of his philosophy which in their initial form bore little relation to one another.

My suggestion, then, is that we examine the genesis and structure of *Leviathan* without dismissing from the outset vast stretches of the text and without taking for granted an understanding of Hobbes's aims the validity of which has not been demonstrated. When this suggestion is pursued it can be seen that the argumentation of this work is the product of a synthesis that was achieved over a period of time. In its initial form, as Robertson observed, Hobbes's political argument was connected at most by a slim thread with his materialist metaphysics. Hobbes envisaged a grand deductive system of which his civil philosophy would be the final and crowning component, but the actual relationship between his metaphysics and his political philosophy was no more than one of analogy. In time, however, a different and more intimate relationship between these initially diverse aspects of his philosophy was established. The basis of this relationship was not logical deduction, but polemical effect. Hobbes came to the conclusion that both theology and metaphysics were of direct political importance, that political consequences flowed from the widespread adoption of certain theological and even metaphysical views. The integration of theological and metaphysical argumentation with his political doctrine was accomplished in connection with a return to some of the ideas he had imbibed from the rhetorical tradition and with a consequent reorientation in his conception of the aims of political philosophy. The argument of *Leviathan* is united by a single political aim that underlies the entire work. The various components of this argument are tied together as the constituent elements of a single political act.

The political character of this act must not be construed in too narrow a sense. *Leviathan* is an intensely political work in that its guiding thread is provided by an overriding political aim, but Hobbes does not attempt to achieve that aim by attending only to the set of institutions and practices that nowadays are usually called "political." To a great extent his efforts are focused upon a transformation in the popular culture of his contemporaries. The stimulus behind these efforts was provided by the perception that certain features in the imaginative world of his contemporaries were inherently antagonistic to the establishment of political authority upon any rational basis. Hobbes's book attacks those features and attempts to replace them with doctrines he considered both more enlightened and more compatible with a rational political society. What knits together the seemingly disparate threads of his theology and metaphysics with those of his political doctrine (in the narrow sense) is the aim of initiating a cultural transformation through which Hobbes hoped to lay the foundations required for any truly rational polity to come into being.

In *Leviathan*, then, Hobbes's political philosophy in the narrower sense—his demonstration of the basis, generation, and institutions proper to a commonwealth—came to be couched within a larger polemical framework. This framework is designed to initiate a transformation in the culture of his time, to undermine a set of popular beliefs he considered inimical to political authority and replace them with "enlightened" views of God, the universe, and the self. Hobbes regarded his own time as the first real opportunity for many centuries to initiate a cultural transformation of the kind and scope needed. *Leviathan* is the product of a determined effort to take advantage of this opportunity. It is the aim of my book to trace the genesis of this effort and bring out its implications for the structure of Hobbes's political philosophy.

The Rhetoric of *Leviathan*

CHAPTER ONE ✲

Historiography and Rhetoric

HOBBES AND THE RHETORICAL TRADITION

HOBBES'S TRANSLATION of Thucydides, which he completed in 1628 at the age of forty, is conventionally regarded as the product of an early, humanistic period of his life. As such, it is argued, this translation is to be sharply distinguished from the works of his later, philosophical period. Even those interpreters who claim to discern some of the substance of his later views on moral and political subjects in Hobbes's introduction to this work agree that from a methodological standpoint, at least, the scientific and philosophical products of his later years are utterly different from the small literary output of his humanistic period. This interpretation, while not simply false, is extremely misleading, and has on occasion induced its defenders to distort Hobbes's thinking in curious ways.

Consider the following line of argument. In the introduction to his translation, Hobbes advocates a very particular and restricted conception of the scope of historical writing. The historian should confine himself simply to the narration of events, using observable actions as his basic data. He should not waste words by speculating about motives, since these are by nature unknowable. As Hobbes himself puts it, "the inward motive . . . is but conjectural." But since he believed motives to be the causes of human actions, their exclusion from history amounts to an acknowledgment that history cannot teach us about causation. This limitation, we are told, explains why Hobbes later came to identify history with "prudence" as opposed to "science." Causation, in his view, is the principal or sole concern of science. There can therefore be no common ground between this early conception of history as mere narrative and Hobbes's later idea of philosophy or science.[1]

This argument drastically oversimplifies Hobbes's historiographical views. Hobbes did argue that an element of conjecture is always involved in the interpretation of motives. But his conclusion was that historians should be cautious and shrewd in attributing motives to historical actors, not that they should be barred from doing so altogether. Hence he says that in some histories

> there be subtle conjectures at the secret aims and inward cogitations of such as fall under their pen; which is also none of the least virtues in a history, where conjecture is thoroughly grounded, not forced to serve the purpose of the writer in adorning his style, or manifesting his subtlety in conjecturing. But these conjectures cannot often be certain, unless withal so evident, that the narration itself may be sufficient to suggest the same also to the reader.[2]

This argument is a counsel of caution as well as a reproach to historians who invent interpretations of men's thoughts and motives out of whole cloth. It is similar in kind to Hobbes's

[1] Richard Ashcraft, "Ideology and Class in Hobbes' Political Theory," *Political Theory* 6 (1978), p. 39. The quotation is from *Thucydides*, pp. xxvii-xxviii.

[2] *Thucydides*, p. viii.

criticism of cartographers who adorn their maps with imaginary islands and coastlines.[3] But it is also a commendation of historians whose conjectures about the secret thoughts and aims of men are thoroughly grounded. Hobbes is as far from wishing to bar all consideration of motives from history as he is from desiring to eliminate all islands and coastlines from maps.

Indeed, the quality that makes Thucydides such an outstanding historian—"in whom . . . the faculty of writing history is at the highest," Hobbes says—is his extraordinary shrewdness as an interpreter of the thoughts and motives of other men. His acuity as an observer and analyst of the human character is so great as to make him occasionally appear obscure. But

> the obscurity that is, proceedeth from the profoundness of the sentences; containing contemplations of those human passions, which either dissembled or not commonly discoursed of, do yet carry the greatest sway with men. . . .

As Hobbes puts it simply in his letter of dedication, "No man better discerned of men."[4]

Hobbes is also absolutely clear that one of the principal aims of historical writing should be to lay bare the causes of events. This understanding emerges most emphatically in the course of his defense of Thucydides against the charges of a critic, Dionysius Halicarnassius. Dionysius objected to several aspects of Thucydides' history, including the order of his presentation, which Hobbes calls his "method." The basis of some of these objections was his view that Thucydides should have been more careful in his history to enhance the glory of Athens. In choosing the points at which to begin and end his history, in reporting the blunt language of the Athenians in the Melian Dia-

[3] *Thucydides*, p. x.

[4] *Thucydides*, pp. vii, xxix, iv.

logue, and in a variety of other decisions, Thucydides had actually harmed the reputation of his city.

Hobbes attacks these objections as utterly inconsistent with the true purposes of history. Dionysius seeks to "delight more the ear with fabulous narrations, than satisfy the mind with truth"; he "makes the scope of history, not profit by writing truth, but delight of the hearer, as if it were a song." Truth, and especially true causes, should be the historian's overriding concern, regardless of whether their revelation might tend to blemish the image of one's own city. Thus "it was the duty of him that had undertaken to write the history of the Peloponnesian war, to begin his narration no further off than at the causes of the same, whether the Grecians were then in good or in evil estate." Furthermore, the presentation of these causes should be carefully designed to reveal their true comparative importance. Thus Thucydides was right, in spite of Dionysius' perverse objections, to begin his explanation by stating the pretexts upon which the war was begun, only afterward going on to explain "the true and inward motive of the same." For on the one hand pretexts, however slight, are always necessary to the instigation of war; while on the other, their comparative insignificance should be demonstrated by distinguishing them from underlying causes.[5]

It is therefore impossible to concur with the view that the break between Hobbes's early conception of history and his later idea of philosophy or science occurred over the issue of causation, if it occurred at all. Hobbes was already deeply concerned about causation in 1628. Far from considering causal explanation beyond the scope of history, he actually viewed the construction of such explanations as the principal duty of any historian. He did not assume that this duty could always be fulfilled easily. One of the hardest of all the historian's tasks is to reconstruct the thoughts and motives of his protagonists. No

[5] *Thucydides*, pp. xxiv, xxvi, xxv, xxvii.

human being has direct access to the thoughts and motives of any other, and these are thus easily disguised. But this difficulty merely tells us what quality should be most highly prized in an historian. Above all else, an historian should be a shrewd observer and judge of human nature.

The view that the issue of causation was central to Hobbes's break with his own early, humanistic outlook is not the only interpretation of this alleged event. Perhaps the most famous account of it, and certainly the most subtle and interesting interpretation of Hobbes's writings on Thucydides, occurs in Leo Strauss's well-known book on Hobbes. His argument runs along the following lines. The introduction to Hobbes's translation of Thucydides rests upon the assumption that history is an adequate source of political knowledge. As his thinking developed, however, Hobbes began to distinguish between what is and what should be, between fact and right. As this development proceeded, history lost its special significance for him. The reduced standing of history in his thinking is evident in *Leviathan* in his emphasis on the problematic nature of all historical knowledge, an emphasis that undermines his original assumption about the adequacy of historical knowledge. Hobbes's thinking continued to develop in this same direction even after he had finished *Leviathan*. Ultimately he came to blur the distinction between history, conceived as a serious search for truth, and poetry or fiction. This lack of interest in the distinction between history and fiction as articulated in Hobbes's *De Homine* of 1658 is the "most precise expression" of his "turning away from history."[6]

This argument contains an important element of truth, but that truth must be disentangled from some serious distortions. In the first place, the suggestion that Hobbes came progressively to consider historical knowledge problematic is an error. Strauss cites the following passage from *Leviathan* in evidence:

[6] Leo Strauss, *The Political Philosophy of Hobbes* (Chicago: University of Chicago Press, 1952; first published 1936), ch. 6, esp. pp. 96-98.

> For he that hath seen by what courses and degrees, a flourishing State hath first come into civil warre, and then to ruine; upon the sights of the ruines of any other State, will guesse, the like warre, and the like courses have been there also. But this conjecture, has the same incertainty almost with the conjecture of the Future; both being grounded onely upon Experience.[7]

This passage certainly suggests that historical knowledge can be problematic, but it does so in a way that is entirely consistent with the views Hobbes had already expressed in 1628. Even then, as we have seen, he had argued that historians must build their accounts of events partly by a process of conjecture, even when trying to explain contemporary events. The *Leviathan* passage refers to the situation of an observer attempting to reconstruct distant historical events by examining artifacts, not that of an historian seeking to explain events he has observed personally. It is neither surprising nor very significant that Hobbes considered the knowledge attainable by such an observer less reliable and more conjectural than that of an historian like Thucydides. There is thus no reason to believe that he ever came to view historical knowledge in general as more conjectural than he had already considered it in 1628. And it is worth noticing that when he came to write his own history of the English civil war, although he re-emphasized the difficulty of interpreting men's motives at several points, he never regarded his account of the causes of the war—an event at which he, like Thucydides in the Peloponnesian War, had been close at hand—as the slightest bit infected with uncertainty.[8]

The notion that Hobbes demonstrates his rejection of history as a source of political knowledge by blurring the distinction

[7] *Leviathan*, ch. 3, p. 98 [11].

[8] *Behemoth*. See pp. 29, 37, 72, and 169, for his reservations about the difficulty of deciphering motives, and pp. 15, 45 for his insistence on the causal nature of his history.

between history and fiction must also be corrected, for fiction had played an important role in his original conception of historiography. One of the practices in Thucydides' history he commends is the use of fictitious speeches or "*deliberative orations*" to convey the "grounds and motives" of actions to the reader.[9] Because thoughts and motives are inaccessible to direct observation, they must be explained by some device apart from the simple narration of events. And since our knowledge of these thoughts and motives is always to some extent conjectural, any device used to explain them will necessarily involve a certain element of contrivance or fiction, as do the Thucydidean speeches. It is arguable, in fact, that Hobbes considered the invention of fictions essential to any genuinely causal understanding of historical events, since he regarded thoughts and motives as decisive elements of causation in human affairs.[10] At the very least it is clear that he saw no conflict between the use of fiction for such purposes and the requirements of historical truth.

Nor did Hobbes actually blur the distinction between history and poetry or fiction in his later writings. One of the pieces of evidence cited to support this view is the preface to Hobbes's translation of Homer, a work he completed near the end of his life. An heroic poem, as Hobbes describes it, is very similar to and may sometimes even be a sort of history, since its aim is to raise admiration for great deeds and men, who may be historical figures. But it is far from true to say that he does not even distinguish history from poetry in this preface, for he compares these two arts at more than one point, sometimes to distinguish between them, sometimes to establish a point they share in

[9] *Thucydides*, p. xxi.

[10] Cf. Wesley Trimpi's very interesting discussions of this general issue in "The Ancient Hypothesis of Fiction: An Essay on the Origins of Literary Theory," *Traditio* 27 (New York: Fordham University Press, 1971) and "The Quality of Fiction: The Rhetorical Transmission of Literary Theory," *Traditio* 30 (New York: Fordham University Press, 1974).

common.[11] History may even be written in verse, in which case the two arts are combined; but the fact that Hobbes approved the combination does not show that he failed to distinguish them.

The other piece of evidence cited to support this view is particularly interesting. It is a passage from the *De Homine* of 1658 in which Hobbes says:

> Letters are . . . useful, too, especially histories; for these supply in abundance the evidence on which rests the science of causes; in truth, natural history for physics and also civil histories for civil and moral science; and this is so whether they be true or false, provided that they are not impossible.[12]

This passage, represented to us as the "most precise expression" of Hobbes's rejection of history, shows nothing of the kind. It is a forceful argument for the usefulness of history to science, which says nothing to imply the inferiority of the former to the latter. It does place false "histories" on a par with true ones, thus seeming to blur the distinction between history and fiction. But the noteworthy fact is that it treats history and fiction equally only insofar as it regards both as equally suitable raw materials for science. Hobbes considered hypothetical constructions, even when false, useful to science in much the same way as he had earlier argued that contrived orations can be useful in historical explanation.[13]

Hence the argument that Hobbes turned away from history because he came increasingly to consider it a problematic and unreliable source of political knowledge is also flawed. Still, it remains true that by 1640 at the very latest he had begun to

[11] *EW* 10, pp. v, vi.

[12] *De Homine*, p. 50. Strauss cites this passage in the original Latin.

[13] For an interesting discussion of this methodological continuity in Hobbes's thought, see Miriam M. Reik, *The Golden Lands of Thomas Hobbes* (Detroit: Wayne State University Press, 1977), pp. 47-50.

draw a very strong distinction between history and science. He calls science "knowledge of the truth of propositions," and considers it capable of attaining universal conclusions. History, on the other hand, is "nothing else but sense, or knowledge original," otherwise called simply "experience"; and "Experience concludeth nothing universally." What ultimately divides history from science is that the former can never be concerned with anything more than the particulars of experience, whereas the latter is capable of delivering universal knowledge.[14]

This distinction is commonly regarded as the most important sign of the gulf that divides the scientific and philosophical outlook of Hobbes's later years from the humanistic viewpoint of his earlier period. The reason Hobbes turned away from history is neither that he considered it incapable of causal explanation nor that he began to distrust its reliability. Instead, Hobbes turned away from history because he had discovered a different source of political knowledge, science, which is more powerful than history because it makes universal statements possible.

There is considerable truth in this interpretation. Hobbes praises philosophy and science—words he uses interchangeably—highly in many works from 1640 onward, sometimes in extravagant terms. His own proud claim to have written the first genuine civil philosophy of all time assumes a very high estimation of the importance of that art.[15] And the following observation, extracted from a discussion of political knowledge in *Leviathan*, can probably be regarded as an expression of his preference for philosophy over history as a source of such knowledge:

> When for the doing of any thing, there be Infallible rules, (as in Engines, and Edifices, the rules of Geometry,) all

[14] *Elements* I.6.1, I.4.10. Hobbes draws the distinction between history and science (or philosophy) in a slightly different way in *De Corpore* I.1.8, but he continues to maintain a very rigid distinction between them.

[15] *De Corpore*, Epistle Dedicatory.

> the experience of the world cannot equall his Counsell, that has learnt, or found out the Rule.[16]

Yet we must be careful not to overgeneralize. Hobbes certainly considered philosophy more powerful in an explanatory sense than history, since he regarded philosophy as capable of discovering rules of general or even universal validity. But explanatory power of this kind was not the only facet of these arts that interested him. Perhaps the best way to demonstrate this fact will be to examine some of the more explicit and extensive discussions in which these two arts are compared with one another.

One of the fullest discussions occurs in a manuscript, on Thomas White's *De Mundo*, that Hobbes composed in the early 1640's. White's book, which appeared in 1642, was an attempt to reconcile the new cosmology of Descartes and Galileo with the Catholic faith. Hobbes's refutation begins with what he probably takes to be the most fundamental tenet of his criticism: the contention that philosophy must be treated with the methods of logic alone and that, by implication, philosophy does not mix well with faith. In the course of this discussion, he takes pains to differentiate logic (the discursive method of philosophy) from "the other arts by which we expound, and discourse upon, any kind of subject." There are four of these arts altogether, Hobbes declares: logic, history, rhetoric, and poetry. Each art has its own distinct, legitimate end. The end of logic is to demonstrate the truth of something universal. The aim of history is to narrate some sequence of particular facts. Rhetoric aims to move the listener to perform something, and poetry—in a formulation that reveals Hobbes's special regard for heroic poetry as the archetype of this genre—exists in order to glorify great deeds and to transmit a knowledge of them to posterity.[17]

Each of these aims is best pursued by its own, distinct type

[16] *Leviathan*, ch. 25, p. 308 [135].
[17] *Anti-White* I.1, 2.

of elocution. Logic must avoid "tropes or figure," since these introduce equivocation and ambiguity, which are opposed to the aims of "those who proceed from definitions." History, on the other hand, may make use of metaphors, but only those that do not excite emotions of hatred or sympathy, since its aim is not to move the mind, but to "shape" it. It also should not contain aphorisms (or precepts), whether in the form of ethical theorems or universal dictates on "manners," since its end is to narrate singular facts, not to make universal assertions. In rhetorical style, however, aphorisms and metaphors are equally admissible, since each of these has a substantial capacity for exciting emotions, which is the main aim of rhetoric. Finally, poetic style admits metaphors, since it is designed to give ornament to deeds in order to glorify them; but it should exclude aphorisms, which detract from its beauty, measure, and harmony.[18]

In 1650, some eight years later, Hobbes echoes these views in a short essay he composed on epic poetry:

> But the subject of a Poeme is the manners of men, not naturall causes; manners presented, not dictated; and manners feyned (as the name of Poesy importes) not found in men. They that give entrance to Fictions writ in Prose, erre not so much, but they erre. For Poesy requireth delightfulnesse, not onely of fiction, but of stile; in which if Prose contend with Verse it is with disadvantage and (as it were) on foot against the strength and winges of *Pegasus*.[19]

These comments are consistent with the conceptions of philosophy, history, and poetry we have already seen expressed in Hobbes's earlier writings. He begins by contrasting poetry with the arts that are concerned with causes, such as history and philosophy. He then appears to contrast poetry with philosophy alone, which treats "manners dictated" (that is, rules); and

[18] *Anti-White* I.2.
[19] *Answer*, p. 46

then to contrast poetry with history alone, distinguishing a treatment of "manners feyned" from one of "manners found in men." Finally, Hobbes once again points to the importance of "delightfulnesse" in poetry, a quality necessary to maintain a grip on the reader's attention; for as he said many years later, "all men love to behold, though not to practise virtue,"[20] and the teaching of virtue through heroic example is one of the purposes of heroic poetry.

Two features in these discussions are especially noteworthy. First, Hobbes treats philosophy, history, and poetry, as well as rhetoric in the earlier discussion, as four arts of discourse, each with its own distinct aims. He does not rank these arts in order of value, importance, or usefulness, but simply compares them with one another, arguing that each is adapted to its own given ends. In particular, he does not say that philosophy is superior to the other arts, or to history alone, as he might easily have done. Second, in both discussions Hobbes devotes a good deal of attention to the forms of elocution or style appropriate to each of these arts. This fact is hardly surprising in the later discussion, the main aim of which is to elaborate on the purposes and qualities of epic poetry. But it is equally true of his earlier remarks, which are intended to lay out his own views on the subjects of logic and philosophy. Hobbes was keenly interested in and had thought a great deal about elocution and style. His interest in these considerations was not confined to their application in poetry and rhetoric, but extended to their use in philosophy and history as well.

In fact, elocution and style had been the principal topics in Hobbes's treatment of Thucydides' writings many years before these discussions. He distinguishes two things that have to be considered in historical writing, truth and elocution: "For in *truth* consisteth the *soul*, and in *elocution* the *body* of history. The latter without the former, is but a picture of history; and the

[20] *EW* 10, p. iii.

former without the latter, unapt to instruct." But instruction is the ultimate aim for which history should be designed. "For the principal and proper work of history [is] to instruct and enable men, by the knowledge of actions past, to bear themselves prudently in the present and providently towards the future."[21] In short, we must assess the qualities of a history by examining it from two quite distinct angles. History must be considered, first, as a form of inquiry, a way of *acquiring* a knowledge of truth. And second, it must be viewed as a kind of pedagogy, a means by which that knowledge is *transmitted* to others. Hobbes's discussion of Thucydides' writings from the first of these angles is perfunctory. The balance of his treatment is tipped overwhelmingly toward a consideration of Thucydides' elocution and style, those qualities which most forcefully affect its worth as a means of transmitting knowledge.

The rather striking degree of concern Hobbes displays for matters of elocution and style is in part a reflection of the intellectual atmosphere in which he wrote. Throughout the Renaissance it had been widely assumed that the bulk of all human wisdom was contained in the writings of the ancients. Aristotle was called *the* philosopher because it was believed that the art of philosophy had reached its height in him. Demosthenes was considered the greatest of rhetoricians, toward whom the Roman theorists of that art, Cicero and Quintilian, had turned to master its intricacies. On practically every subject the works of ancient writers were considered authoritative. By the early seventeenth century this view was beginning to give way. The most spectacular instance of its downfall was in astronomy, where the authoritative status of Ptolemy's system had been challenged and, from the viewpoint of many scientists, beaten by the new Copernican theory. This and other events led some philosophers to question the authoritative status of ancient

[21] *Thucydides*, pp. xx, vii.

learning in general. Yet this attitude of doubt remained a minority view; few voices had dared to assert it in public.[22]

This assumption was extremely important for the way in which scholars like Hobbes thought about knowledge. Knowledge was not, as we are likely to assume, something waiting to be discovered. Most if not all of it *had* been discovered, by the ancients. The central problem of knowledge was not how to discover it, but how to recover those truths that had already been known to the ancients. Many of those truths had been lost or obscured during the two thousand years or more since they had first become known. Manuscripts had been lost or corrupted, arguments had been misinterpreted. The most important methods of inquiry were accordingly those of scholarship and textual criticism, and the most important problems of knowledge had to do with its preservation and transmission, not its discovery. Hobbes's emphasis upon elocution and style—upon the rhetoric of Thucydides' history—is partly a reflection and extension of this broad concern with the transmission of knowledge.

Yet there are signs in Hobbes's argument that his keen interest in Thucydides' rhetoric has even more specific grounds. Hobbes pointedly remarks upon Thucydides' rhetorical training at the feet of one of the great practitioners of the art.[23] He repeatedly cites Cicero and Lucian, two of the acknowledged masters of the rhetorical tradition. And in introducing his subject he notes that

> Homer in poesy, Aristotle in philosophy, Demosthenes in eloquence . . . do still maintain their primacy . . . And in the number of these is justly ranked also our Thucyd-

[22] Descartes, the most famous philosopher to do so, did not publish his *Discourse Concerning the Method* until 1637, nine years after Hobbes published his translation.

[23] *Thucydides*, p. xv.

> ides; a workman . . . in whom the faculty of writing history is at the highest.[24]

In setting history alongside philosophy, poetry, and rhetoric in this way—as Hobbes continued to do in later years—he was giving voice to a prescriptive formula for the humane studies that was rooted in Cicero's classic discussions of the rhetorician's art. These discussions had acquired canonical status as the founding works of the rhetorical tradition, and Hobbes's own observations on historiography take place within this Ciceronian framework.

This framework had for many years set the terms for a venerable debate about the relative merits of philosophy, history, and poetry for teaching. Aristotle had compared these different arts in his *Poetics* (1451b), and his discussion was certainly highly regarded. But in its Renaissance form this debate was shaped more decisively by Cicero and Quintilian, who was probably the most influential representative of the rhetorical tradition in England.

Each of these three arts had famous and persuasive advocates. Early in the sixteenth century, Erasmus had argued that "philosophy teaches us more in one year than our own individual experience can teach us in thirty, and its teaching carries none of the risks which the method of learning by experience of necessity brings with it."[25] His defense of teaching through philosophical precepts emphasizes the intensive character of philosophical instruction, the capacity of a precept to transmit a great deal of knowledge in only a few words. Later, however, this kind of argument began to decline in favor. Perhaps as a result of the Ramist movement for educational reform, which got underway toward the middle of the century, later partici-

[24] *Thucydides*, p. vii.

[25] *De Pueris Statim ac Liberaliter Instituendis* (1529), translated by W. H. Woodward in *Desiderius Erasmus Concerning the Aim and Method of Education* (Cambridge: Cambridge University Press, 1904), pp. 191-192.

pants in the debate began to emphasize the plainness, simplicity, and forcefulness of their preferred forms of discourse and instruction.[26] Thus Thomas Blundeville, for example, argued in 1574:

> The way to come to that peace whereof I speake, is partly taught by the Philosophers in generall precepts and rules, but the Historiographers doe teache it much more playnlye by perticular examples and experiences, and speciallye if they be written with that order, diligence, and iudgement, that they ought to be.[27]

Probably the most famous of all the works produced by this debate, however, was Sir Philip Sidney's *Defense of Poetry*. In contrast to his predecessors, Sidney argues that poetry combines the best of both philosophy and history by presenting the universal content of precepts cloaked in the more striking and effective form of a fictitious narration. Poetry, especially heroic poetry, is superior to philosophy because it is able to give a more "perfect picture" than the latter by not being bound to imperfect reality. The philosopher's method of teaching by precept is weak, he claims, because it "bestoweth but a wordish description, which doth neither strike, pierce, nor possess the sight of the soul so much as that other doth." Teaching, the essential aim of poetry, requires the forcefulness transmitted by visual impressions, but lacking in precepts. Hence the philosopher's wisdom must be "illuminated or figured forth by the speaking picture of poesy." History possesses this forcefulness because it too gives pictures, but it is deficient in ethical content, since it is limited to reporting actual events. Poetry com-

[26] For accounts of this movement see Wilbur S. Howell, *Logic and Rhetoric in England, 1500-1700* (New York: Russell and Russell, 1961; first published 1956) and Walter J. Ong, *Ramus, Method, and the Decay of Dialogue* (Cambridge, Mass.: Harvard University Press, 1958).

[27] "The True Order and Methode of Wryting and Reading Hystories," published by Hugh G. Dick in *Huntington Library Quarterly* 3 (1940), p. 161.

bines the best of both these arts by its latitude in designing a "perfect pattern."[28]

Sidney's argument rests upon the premise that effective teaching requires the transmission of forceful impressions to the mind (or "soul") together with the thesis that the visual image, even if conveyed in words as a "speaking picture," is capable of making a far deeper, more striking impression than any merely verbal argument or precept. In effect his argument is that the visual is far more powerful than the merely conceptual, that the image is more forceful and effective than the proposition. And Hobbes, in his own discussion of elocution and style, concurs absolutely. Borrowing from Plutarch, he argues that Thucydides excels in perspicuity, for he

> aimeth always at this; to make his auditor a spectator, and to cast his reader into the same passions that they were in that were beholders . . . these things, I say, are so described and so evidently set before our eyes, that the mind of the reader is no less affected therewith than if he had been present in the actions.[29]

Perspicuity, intimately associated by its etymology with the faculty of sight, is for Hobbes the first and most important of all the elements of style. A perspicuous discourse is also, he implies, an efficacious one, because it creates the kind of forceful impression that does not quickly fade.[30] This argument was expressed in classic form by Quintilian:

> There are certain experiences which the Greeks call *fantasia*, and the Romans *visions*, whereby things absent are presented to our imagination with such extreme vividness that they seem actually to be before our very eyes. It is the

[28] Sir Philip Sidney, *A Defense of Poetry*, J. A. Van Dorsten, ed. (Oxford: Oxford University Press, 1966), pp. 32-34.

[29] *Thucydides*, p. xxii.

[30] *Thucydides*, p. viii.

> man who is really sensitive to such impressions who will have the greatest power over the emotions. . . . From such impressions arises that *energeia* which Cicero calls *illumination* and *actuality*, which makes us seem not so much to narrate as to exhibit the actual scene, while our emotions will be no less actively stirred than if we were present at the actual occurrence.[31]

This emphasis upon the power of the visual is a vital element in Hobbes's thought. It lies at the heart of the comparison between philosophy and history he draws in his discussion of Thucydides. Commending Thucydides once again, he points out that

> [d]igressions for instruction's cause, and other such open conveyances of precepts, (which is the philosopher's part), he never useth; as having so clearly set before men's eyes the ways and events of good and evil counsels, that the narration itself doth secretly instruct the reader, and more effectually than can possibly be done by precept.[32]

The obvious interpretation of this passage is that it constitutes Hobbes's contribution, in 1628, to the ancient debate about the relative merits of philosophy and history (poetry and rhetoric being omitted here) described above.[33] This interpretation is not wrong, but it is important to understand both the scope of Hobbes's comparison and the reasons for his argument. Hobbes is comparing philosophy with history primarily as means of instruction, media for the transmission of knowledge, rather than as forms of inquiry. His main interest here is in their comparative pedagogical values. And his argument is that

[31] *Institutio Oratoria*, 4 vols., trans. H. E. Butler (Cambridge, Mass.: Harvard University Press, 1953), vol. 2, pp. 433-437.

[32] *Thucydides*, p. xxii.

[33] Strauss, *Political Philosophy of Hobbes*, pp. 79-85. The passage in question is cited on p. 80, n. 1.

the visual image is more powerful for this purpose than the precept, the merely conceptual argument.[34]

Two points about this comparison are noteworthy. First, Hobbes's comparison here, which implies the superiority of history over philosophy, is despite appearances perfectly compatible with the comparison he drew much later in *Leviathan*, which seems to imply the reverse. The two discussions take place on different planes. In 1628 Hobbes concluded that history is more forceful than philosophy as a means for the transmission of knowledge. In his discussion of some twenty years later, he concludes that philosophy is more powerful than history as a mode of inquiry, that philosophy has greater explanatory power than history. Hobbes rigorously distinguished between inquiry and transmission (or between "truth" and "elocution"). Hence these remarks do not in themselves demonstrate any shift in his evaluation of the relative merits of these two arts. He valued history for its pedagogical or instructional qualities in 1628, and philosophy for its explanatory power—its capacity for identifying general or universal rules—in 1651; but whether a shift in his evaluation had taken place in the interim cannot be determined from these passages alone.

Second, while Hobbes is ostensibly comparing the relative merits of history and philosophy in his passage on Thucydides, the real weight of his comparison lies in the contrast he draws between the visual image and the precept. What makes Thucydides' discourse so powerful is the way in which he has "clearly set before men's eyes" the events as well as the deliberations leading up to them. Hobbes dwells at some length upon this extraordinarily visual quality of Thucydides' history, for it is this quality that enables the history to create such vivid mental impressions, so much deeper and more effective than

[34] Cf. Murray Wright Bundy, "The Theory of Imagination in Classical and Medieval Thought," *University of Illinois Studies in Language and Literature* 12, nos. 2-3 (1927).

those created by more purely conceptual forms of discourse. Indeed, by arguing that the narration "doth secretly instruct the reader" Hobbes seems to suggest that these visual impressions constitute a channel for the transmission of knowledge in unconscious or subliminal ways. Hobbes's argument is a commendation of history by comparison with philosophy. But it is even more importantly a recognition of and tribute to the power of the visual image for creating mental impressions. Though in one sense more primitive and less rational than the precept or general rule, which involves conceptual thought, the visual image is nonetheless a more powerful means for the transmission of ideas. This contrast between the visual and the conceptual, between the image and the precept, is the basic theme of Hobbes's argument, easily overshadowing in importance the more superficial comparison between philosophy and history with which it is linked in this passage.

The conventional view of Hobbes's development, which breaks his life into an early humanistic period and a later scientific one, contains one very important element of truth. It captures the fact that Hobbes became fascinated with a form of reasoning that had previously been unknown to him very soon after he had completed and published his translation of Thucydides. This was the axiomatic method of reasoning commonly associated with geometry. What drew him to this mode of reasoning—which had been in common use by late scholastic philosophers for some years before Hobbes discovered it—was its seemingly immense explanatory power. By attending carefully to the definition of his axioms and to the rules of logic used to combine them with one another, Euclid had constructed a system of universal propositions that Hobbes considered the first and still most highly developed science in the world. This achievement exercised an almost magnetic attraction over Hobbes's imagination. He had never known anything of its kind. The "precepts" he had associated with philosophy in 1628 were no more than loose generalizations, rules of thumb drawn from experience. Now he was confronted with a form of reasoning that seemed to offer the prospect of genuinely universal conclusions, based less upon experience than upon rigorous definitions. The prospect clearly excited him, and gave him an entirely new view of the explanatory potential of philosophy. This new view underlies his observation in *The Elements of Law* that "[e]xperience concludeth nothing universally" as well as his commendation of those who have "learnt, or found out the Rule" in *Leviathan*.

In this sense Hobbes's discovery did indeed lead him to re-evaluate his original opinion concerning the adequacy of history as a source of political knowledge. This re-evaluation was not based upon fresh doubts about the reliability of historical knowledge. It was rooted instead in the idea that the axiomatic method of reasoning, which Hobbes came increasingly to associate with science, might provide a different and, in an explanatory sense, more powerful source of political knowledge than history could ever hope to be. But this new fascination with the axiomatic method and its explanatory potential did not in any sense constitute a rejection of the rhetorical tradition that had shaped Hobbes's thinking during the first forty years of his life. The ideas and interests he had inherited from that tradition continued to contribute to the formation of his political thought throughout the rest of his life.[35]

[35] This argument should not be confused with Strauss's claim that Hobbes derived much of his "anthropology" from a series of studies of Aristotle's *Rhetoric* (see *Political Philosophy of Hobbes*, pp. 35-43). Strauss actually asserts that Hobbes grew less and less interested in rhetoric with the passage of time (p. 41, n. 1). This assertion is true only insofar as we equate his interest in rhetoric with his interest in the formal study of rhetoric. It is worth pointing out that the shorter of the two digests commonly attributed to Hobbes and included in the nineteenth-century edition of his works (*EW* 6, pp. 511-536) was actually the work of another writer, Dudley Fenner, as was pointed out in 1951 by both Walter J. Ong, "Hobbes and Talon's Ramist Rhetoric in English," *Transactions of the Cambridge* [England] *Bibliographical Society* 1, pt. 3 (1951), pp. 260-269, and Wilbur S. Howell (*Logic and Rhetoric*, p. 263ff.).

The aspect of this inheritance that remained of greatest importance to Hobbes's later political philosophy was his keen interest in and sensitivity for the transmission of ideas, as opposed to their original acquisition, in "instruction" (broadly conceived) as opposed to inquiry. His fascination with inquiry, as exhibited in the new philosophy of Descartes and the new science of Galileo as well as in the axiomatic method itself, is obvious. Less obvious, but no less important, is the fact that he was also deeply interested in the transmission of ideas in ways that later came to affect his very conception of philosophy, especially political philosophy. The theme that dominated his thinking about transmission, as developed in his writings on Thucydides in 1628, was the contrast between the power of the visual image or "speaking picture" and the powerlessness of the merely conceptual proposition for creating mental impressions. While his views on this topic did not remain entirely static, Hobbes never abandoned his conviction that the more conceptual forms of expression, the precept and proposition, are weak media for the transmission of ideas. This conviction, together with his keen interest in the problem of transmission itself, constitute the legacy handed down from the rhetorical tradition to Hobbes's political philosophy.

Hobbes set this concern about transmission to one side during the composition of the first manuscript version of his political philosophy, *The Elements of Law*, in 1640. This manuscript is thus the most exclusively "scientific" version of his political philosophy. It is concerned above all with the elaboration of a set of propositions about politics modeled loosely upon the axiomatic method of reasoning. It is far from free of rhetoric and polemic, but its main design is essentially scientific as opposed to rhetorical, guided by an ideal of inquiry rather than by a con-

Strauss had no way of knowing this fact, but it has also been overlooked in recent work on Hobbes, e.g. William Sacksteder, "Hobbes: Philosophical and Rhetorical Artifice," *Philosophy and Rhetoric* 17 (1984), pp. 30-46.

cern for transmission. During the decade that followed this work, however, these rhetorical concerns returned to the forefront of Hobbes's political thinking, leaving their mark not only upon the substance of his arguments, but upon Hobbes's idea of political philosophy as well. Their impact reaches its height in *Leviathan*, in which Hobbes attempts to synthesize the new science's methods of reason as applied to politics with the older lessons of the rhetorical tradition, as I will seek to demonstrate in the following chapters.

CHAPTER TWO ✫

The Elements of Law

REASON VERSUS RHETORIC

THE ASSERTION that *The Elements of Law* is essentially scientific as opposed to rhetorical in design is by no means a self-evident truth. Formidable objections can be raised. The manuscript was first circulated in the spring of 1640, a time of great political excitement and impending upheaval. Toward the beginning of the year, King Charles I, pressed by a need for funds to conduct his war against the Scots, had decided to convene Parliament for the first time in more than a decade. Royal policies on taxation and religious practice had been controversial for years and were bound to be hotly debated. Hobbes took an extremely keen interest in these issues. He even stood for election to the House of Commons,[1] and the fact that he failed

[1] Writing to his son toward the beginning of 1640, Sir John Coke says: "Mr. Fulwood telleth me that Derbymen are resolved to give no way to the election of Mr. Hobs; and he thinketh your brother may be introduced. But I shall not persuade him to put himself in contestation against my lord [presumably the Earl of Devonshire, who must have sponsored Hobbes's candidacy]. Only if you find that Hobs cannot prevail, do what you can for your brother, and write speedily how they stand affected, that we may co-operate also from hence." [Great Britain] Historical Manuscripts Commission, *Twelfth Report, Appendix, Part Two: The Manuscripts of the Earl Cowper, K. G.*,

to win a seat did nothing to dampen his enthusiasm for participation in the ongoing debate. His own later reflections on this period suggest that his manuscript was composed specifically to contribute to this debate.[2] These reflections are corroborated by the letter of dedication, in which Hobbes observes that "it would be an incomparable benefit to commonwealth, if every man held the opinions concerning law and policy here delivered" and goes on to speak of the "ambition . . . of this book . . . to insinuate itself with those whom the matter it containeth most nearly concerneth. . . ." In short, Hobbes's manuscript was a work of persuasion and political engagement, not a merely academic treatise. Any interpretation that failed to take note of its role in the contemporary political debate would be highly misleading.

Yet Hobbes's manuscript is also very far from being an ordinary political tract. It is clearly intended to persuade, to alter the opinions of its readers, and by so doing to have an impact upon contemporary politics. But the means Hobbes uses to accomplish these aims are, principally, the scientific ones of logic and rational demonstration. And he characterizes the aims of his treatise in scientific terms as well. Thus he argues, again in his dedication, that his aim is to "reduce this doctrine [of justice and policy] to the rules and infallibility of reason," and goes on to claim to have presented "the true and only foundation of such science." However boastful this claim may be, there is no reason not to accept it as an accurate indicator that Hobbes himself thought he was constructing a true, logically demonstrated science of politics.

It might be argued that these two aims, far from being in tension with one another, are entirely compatible, or even mutually reinforcing. The scientific aspirations of his manuscript

preserved at Melbourne Hall, Derbyshire (London: Her Majesty's Stationery Office, 1888), p. 251. I am grateful to Conrad Russell for this citation.

[2] *Considerations*, p. 414.

contribute toward its political ambitions because Hobbes believed he could persuade his readers to adopt his conclusions about "law and policy" by proving the truth of those conclusions scientifically, by logical demonstration. On this view it would be misleading to suggest that either of these aims predominates over the other. *The Elements of Law* cannot be called "essentially scientific" any more than it can be said to be "essentially political" in design. The scientific and political aims of this manuscript are simply two complementary aspects of a larger whole, and any attempt to disentangle these aims from one another must be artificial and contrived.

This interpretation is appealing because of the way in which it appears to reconcile Hobbes's two great passions—for science and for politics—with one another. Yet on closer examination it proves to be extremely questionable. The obstacle to this reconciliation lies in Hobbes's view of the impotence of the philosophical proposition. Success in political persuasion hinges upon an ability to transmit ideas forcefully, to create deep and striking mental impressions. But according to the views Hobbes had held some years earlier, philosophical propositions, and the more conceptual forms of expression in general, are poor media for the creation of such impressions. We cannot simply assume that there is no tension between the scientific and political aims of this manuscript, for Hobbes's earlier views would not have permitted such an easy reconciliation between the aims of scientific demonstration and political persuasion.

It is true that the work in which Hobbes first expresses his conviction about the weakness of the philosophical proposition was written twelve years earlier than *The Elements of Law*. During these years he had discovered geometry and developed an entirely new conception of philosophy. One can easily imagine that these events might have led him to abandon his conviction about the weakness of philosophical propositions. But the facts do not support this surmise. In *The Elements of Law*, Hobbes continued to contrast the power of rhetoric and its capacity to evoke images with the impotence of conceptual reasoning for the purpose of creating mental impressions and shaping opinion.[3] It would be as wrong to suggest that this manuscript is simply a work of scientific demonstration as it would be to argue that it is simply an effort of political persuasion. It is obviously both. But it would also be a mistake to overlook the inherent tension between these two aims, especially in view of Hobbes's explicit recognition of the source of that tension.

Hence the problem of the main design of *The Elements of Law* cannot be escaped by applying a simple formula that pretends to reconcile its diverse aims. Hobbes's manuscript is both a work of science and a contribution to political debate, but these two dimensions of the manuscript are at least partially heterogeneous rather than complementary. Each of these two aims played a role in the formulation of this work. The exact extent and nature of these respective roles cannot be determined *a priori*, or in isolation from Hobbes's argument as a whole. The following pages will begin, then, by sketching that argument in a skeletal way. Once this sketch is complete we will be in a position to consider the status of Hobbes's theory, the idea of a theory of politics it seems to embody; with this idea in mind, we will be prepared to return to the question of the main design of the manuscript.

The Political Argument

The Elements of Law consists of two parts. The first of these is a treatise on human nature ("Concerning men as persons natural"), while the second concerns government and politics ("Concerning men as a body politic"). When it was finally published, some ten years after being written, it was broken up into two separate treatises, *Human Nature* and *De Corpore Politico*.

[3] *Elements* II.8.14; cf. *Anti-White* I.1.2, *Answer*, pp. 49-50.

Human Nature was intended to underpin the political argument of the latter work by providing the psychological premises upon which it rests. While he was composing the manuscript, Hobbes considered this underpinning, together with the logical presentation of his argument as a whole, to be the most important innovations of his political theory. He says at the outset that a knowledge of human nature is essential to his subject, the "true and perspicuous explication of the elements of laws, natural and politic."[4] Many earlier writers had incorporated assertions about human nature into their political theories. Yet in a letter written in 1635 Hobbes argues that no one has yet succeeded in explaining the "facultyes and passions of the soule." While acknowledging that progress on this subject was being made by others, he goes on to claim proficiency in it for himself and to boast that if no one else should produce an adequate theory soon, then "I hope to be the first."[5] Hobbes had already been working in this direction for several years, going back perhaps as far as 1630.[6] Thus *Human Nature* was the product of an ambition to "make sense" of psychology that had been percolating for perhaps a decade. Unlike the views of his predecessors, Hobbes's theory of politics would be true and perspicuous in part because it would be based upon an adequate psychology.

Human Nature develops two main arguments. The first is that human beings tend by nature to be offensive to one an-

[4] *Elements* I.1.1.

[5] Letter of August 25, 1635, in [Great Britain] Historical Manuscripts Commission, *Thirteenth Report, Appendix, Part Two: The Manuscripts of His Grace the Duke of Portland* preserved at Welbeck Abbey, vol. 2 (London: Her Majesty's Stationers, 1893), pp. 125-126. Hobbes uses the word "soule" here in a psychological rather than a spiritual sense.

[6] When he apparently composed "A Short Tract on First Principles," an intriguing work in the history of science, dealing with (among other topics) the "two discerning facultyes, in generall, of the Soul; sense and understanding." See *Elements*, Appendix I, p. 210, as well as the extremely important discussion of this work by Frithiof Brandt in *Thomas Hobbes' Mechanical Conception of Nature* (Copenhagen: Levin and Munksgaard, 1928), pt. 1.

other. Left to their own devices, they will almost inevitably clash. This argument is later taken up in *De Corpore Politico* as an important component in Hobbes's description of "the condition of men in mere nature." The second argument is that there are elements in human nature that can be tapped to overcome this mutual offensiveness. The most important of these elements are fear of death, which Hobbes portrays as a passion shared by all human beings, and reason.

Hobbes cites two principal causes of the "offensiveness of man's nature one to another."[7] The first is that all men have appetites that are, by nature, insatiable. Hobbes provides a physiological argument to support this contention. All of our perceptions and ideas, he argues, are really nothing but "motion in some internal substance of the head."[8] This motion continues onward from the head to the heart, where it encounters that "vital" motion which sustains life. By this vital motion he appears to mean the circulation of blood, which had been discovered in relatively recent times by William Harvey, who had subsequently become friendly with Hobbes. Hobbes's basic argument was that when the motion set underway by any perception arrives at the heart and encounters the vital motion, it must necessarily either quicken or hinder that vital motion. Experiences that quicken the vital motion cause pleasure, while those that slow it cause pain. But there is no natural limit to the extent to which the vital motion can be augmented. Hence there is no such thing as an utmost or ultimate pleasure. Nor is there any pleasure to be found in rest or withdrawal from experience. "FELICITY," he argues, "consisteth not in having prospered, but in prospering."[9]

These physiological ideas provide an interesting justification for Hobbes's view that men's appetites are insatiable, but they

[7] *Elements* I.14.11.
[8] *Elements* I.7.1.
[9] *Elements* I.7.7.

are almost certainly not the original source of that view. Similar notions had been expressed by earlier moralists, including Bacon. Indeed, the author of *Horae Subsecivae*, a work published anonymously in 1620 that some scholars ascribe to Hobbes's own pupil, William Cavendish, had made this argument about the very significant appetite for ambition:

> It is an unlimited desire never satisfyed; a Continual proiectinge without stop: an indefatigable search of those thinges wee wish for though want not: no Contentment in a present state eyther fortunate or prosperous.[10]

Hobbes did not derive his view from a physiological argument, but he probably believed that this argument lent support to that view.

The second principal cause of men's natural offensiveness to one another is their vanity or, as Hobbes usually calls it, vainglory. Vainglory is only one form of the more general passion of glory, which is "that passion which proceedeth from the imagination or conception of our own power, above the power of him that contendeth with us." The common, subjective term for this passion is pride. Sometimes a degree of glory or pride is justified, as when our "imagination of our power and worth" is based upon "an assured and certain experience of our own actions." But most men are inclined to overrate their own power and importance, either because the opinions and flattery of

[10] From the manuscript version published in Friedrich O. Wolf, *Die Neue Wissenschaft des Thomas Hobbes* (Stuttgart–Bad Canstatt: Friedrich Frommann, 1969), p. 139. The authorship of this work is disputed, and it has sometimes been attributed to Hobbes himself, though the arguments presented in favor of this view are weak. This debate goes back to Strauss, *Political Philosophy of Hobbes*, p. xii, n. 1. Recent contributions to the debate have been made in Wolf's book and by Arlene W. Saxonhouse in "Hobbes and the *Horae Subsecivae*," *Polity* 13 (1981), pp. 541-567, both of whom argue the case for Hobbes's authorship; and in James Jay Hamilton, "Hobbes's Study and the Hardwick Library," *Journal of the History of Philosophy* 16 (1978), pp. 445-453, who argues against it.

others lead them to do so or because of "the fiction . . . of actions done by ourselves, which never were done," sometimes derived from reading too many romantic stories. When men indulge their own imaginations in this way they are suffering from vainglory.[11]

Vainglory is a very common passion. All men believe themselves to be at least as capable as anyone else; to believe merely this much is, in Hobbes's view, to be "moderate." As he argues at one point, men "do every one naturally think himself as able, at the least, to govern another, as another to govern him."[12] Many men go beyond moderation and consider themselves superior to most others. When carried to extremes this excessive vainglory can lead to madness. Hobbes cites the example of "one that preached in Cheapside from a cart there, instead of a pulpit, that he himself was Christ, which was spiritual pride or madness."[13]

Hobbes's interest in vanity or pride goes back at least to his introduction to Thucydides. There he constructs an argument against democracy on the premise that that form of government encourages this passion.[14] Vanity also plays a large role in the theory worked out in *The Elements of Law*, but it plays a very different role in that theory from the one it had performed in Hobbes's earlier work. Together with the natural insatiability of men's appetites in general, vainglory is used by him to explain why men are mutually offensive by nature. For "some are vainly glorious, and hope for precedency and superiority above their fellows, not only when they are equal in power, but also when they are inferior." This hope for superiority makes even those who are moderate and ask for nothing more than recognition of their equal standing with other men "obnoxious to the

[11] *Elements* I.9.1.

[12] *Elements* I.17.1; cf. I.14.3.

[13] *Elements* I.10.9.

[14] *Thucydides*, pp. xvi-xvii.

force of others, that will attempt to subdue them."[15] Even if men's appetites were not insatiable, their vanity would lead them into conflict with one another, and it would do so even if there were some men who were neither vain nor immoderate of appetite. Thus, "the greatest part of men, upon no assurance of odds, do nevertheless, through vanity, or comparison, or appetite, provoke the rest, that otherwise would be contented with equality."[16]

The destructive consequences of this natural offensiveness would be inevitable were it not for the existence of countervailing elements in human nature. The first of these is fear of death. Hobbes argues that "necessity of nature maketh men to will and desire *bonum sibi*, that which is good for themselves, and to avoid that which is hurtful; but most of all that terrible enemy of nature, death."[17] The contention that men must by their nature seek to avoid death is crucial to the political theory of *The Elements of Law* as a whole. Given his premise about the natural offensiveness of men, it was essential for Hobbes to find a motive that was powerful enough to counteract the insatiability and vanity that lay behind that offensiveness. The contention that fear of death is such a motive is a central postulate of his theory.

Hobbes's claim that fear of death is the most powerful of all motives can be broken down into two more fundamental premises. The first of these is that men are essentially egoistic beings. His statement that "every man by natural necessity desireth his own good"[18] is a mild and vague formulation of this premise to which few observers of human behavior would object. But he also formulates this principle in much more rigorous terms when he says, "For by necessity of nature every man doth in all his voluntary actions intend some good unto him-

[15] *Elements* I.14.3.

[16] *Elements* I.14.5.

[17] *Elements* I.14.6.

[18] *Elements* I.14.12.

self."[19] This is a strong and apparently universal statement. It suggests that literally all human actions must be motivated by the intention of procuring some good for the actor. Actions that seem to be set in motion by some other consideration, such as acts of apparent altruism, must actually rest upon some egoistic motive that is not readily apparent.

It is important to distinguish sharply Hobbes's premise that all men are egoistic by nature from his view that most men are vainly glorious. He considered vanity a passion to which all men are susceptible, but he did not believe that all men actually succumb to it. Indeed vanity, for Hobbes, is an obstacle to the successful pursuit of one's own good, since it is based upon a mistaken estimate of one's power and is likely to lead to ambitious undertakings that have very little chance of success. Egoism, according to Hobbes's premise, is a motivational principle that lies behind all human actions. Vanity is a source of misinformation and confusion, which tend to hinder the successful operation of this egoistic principle.

The second fundamental premise behind Hobbes's postulate about the power of fear of death is that death is the greatest evil that can befall any man. As we have seen, he calls death "that terrible enemy of nature," and argues that men seek to avoid it more than anything else. The main significance of the physiological theory examined above lies in the grounding it provides for this premise. Hobbes's argument, that the motion set underway within the body by any experience must necessarily either help or hinder the vital motion that sustains life, implies that there can be no such thing as an utmost pleasure, since there is no limit to the extent to which the vital motion can be helped. But there is a natural limit to the extent to which that motion can be hindered, which is reached when the vital motion stops at death. Hence for Hobbes, who defines good and

[19] *Elements* I.16.6.

evil with reference to pleasure and pain,[20] the greatest evil any man can experience is his own death.[21] While this physiological theory is not the only route by which Hobbes could have reached his view that death is the greatest of all evils, he seems to have believed that it provided a scientific basis for that view.

The final basic element of Hobbes's psychology is the contention that reason gives human beings the means required to avoid the greatest of all evils, death. It is, he says, "the work of reason" to direct men toward their own good, and it is *a fortiori* the work of reason to enable men to avoid their greatest enemy, death. Thus he argues that "[it] is not against reason that a man doth all he can to preserve his own body and limbs, both from death and pain," and goes on to point out that "[r]eason therefore dictateth to every man for his own good, to seek after peace . . . and to strengthen himself. . . ."[22]

There are, then, two basically opposed kinds of elements that can be discovered in human psychology. The appetites, which are by nature insatiable, make men offensive to one another, and the common tendency toward vanity or vainglory compounds this mutual offensiveness. The destructive consequences of this offensiveness can be counteracted, however, by fear of death, especially if this fear is guided carefully by reason free of the misperceptions and confusions vanity tends to promote. The juxtaposition of these two kinds of elements in *Human Nature* provides Hobbes with the psychological premises that underlie his political argument in *De Corpore Politico.*

These psychological premises provide the basis for a set of

[20] *Elements* I.7.3. Hobbes emphasizes that these definitions are subjective, since each man relates these terms to his own "constitution." His point is that each man defines his own ultimate evil in exactly the same way as all other men.

[21] J.W.N. Watkins gives a more extensive discussion of the significance of Hobbes's physiological theory in *Hobbes's System of Ideas*, 2nd ed. (London: Hutchinson, 1973), pp. 75-84.

[22] *Elements* I.15.1, I.14.6, I.14.14.

observations on human behavior and interaction that play an important role in this political argument. These observations are causal or predictive in nature. They purport to describe the consequences of various human actions and conditions. But the causal or behavioral language in which they are framed forms only one dimension of Hobbes's political argument. A second dimension of this argument is constructed out of concepts drawn from the language of ethics and the law. This language is used to describe rights and obligations, and in general to characterize human situations in juridical terms. Hobbes's psychology does not draw upon this second, juridical language, but it is essential to the argument of *De Corpore Politico*. While he almost never brings his movements between these two kinds of language to the attention of his readers—a fact that has spawned a host of vexing problems for his interpreters and probably led Hobbes himself to adopt confused positions on some issues—he did draw a clear distinction between them in principle.[23] The political argument of his manuscript as a whole is constructed by interweaving behavioral propositions drawn from the language of causation with juridical propositions formulated in the language of ethics and law.

Hobbes begins this argument by describing "the condition of men in mere nature," who lack the benefit of political bonds. Any man in this condition, he argues, enjoys a "*right of nature*" to "preserve his own life and limbs, with all the power he hath."[24] By a right he does not mean an entitlement that other men have a duty to respect. Hobbes means only that men have no obligations that could interfere with their efforts to preserve themselves. In his usage a right, though a juridical concept, is merely a particular type of freedom: namely, freedom from obligation. Possession of a right by one man implies nothing about either the rights or the duties assignable to others.

[23] Hobbes seems to draw this distinction more clearly in *Leviathan* than in *Elements*. For examples, see ch. 15, p. 213 [78], and ch. 20, p. 261 [107].

[24] *Elements* I.14.6.

This freedom or right to preserve oneself implies a right to all the means necessary to this end. Furthermore, it presupposes that every man is to be allowed to judge for himself what those means may be. This complete freedom to use all the means necessary for one's self-preservation and to judge for oneself what those means may be amounts to a completely unrestricted right to all things: "Every man by nature hath right to all things, that is to say, to do whatsoever he listeth to whom he listeth, to possess, use, and enjoy all things he will and can."[25] But the possession of this unrestricted right or freedom is of very little use to anyone because of the natural offensiveness of men suggested by Hobbes's arguments in *Human Nature.* Since men are naturally offensive, and since each one possesses the same unrestricted right to all things, the almost inevitable result will be a condition of mutual hostility Hobbes calls "the estate of war."[26] For if some men might be willing to restrain their actions to those really necessary for their own preservation, others would for various reasons exceed those bounds, placing all into a condition of great insecurity and mutual hostility.[27]

The further consequence of this unfortunate set of circumstances is that "irresistible might in the state of nature is right."[28] This conclusion seems to follow from Hobbes's discussion of the right of nature. Since the right of nature enjoyed by all men in the state of nature extends to "all things," it must extend as far as any man's strength or might in that condition can carry it. If a man in the state of nature is capable of conquering a whole city, he would not exceed his right of nature by doing so. This does not mean that his right of conquest must be respected by others. It means only that he is not wrong to conquer, if he can.

Hobbes supports his inference that the condition of man in

[25] *Elements* I.14.10.

[26] *Elements* I.14.11.

[27] *Elements* I.14.5.

[28] *Elements* I.14.13.

mere nature is one of war by appealing to examples from history as well as his own time. "[T]he histories of our ancestors, the old inhabitants of Germany and other now civil countries," he argues, show that their populations were sparse and that life was short and bereft of the comforts that can usually be procured in a settled, peaceful society. These same disadvantages are apparent in "the experience of savage nations that live at this day."[29] In short, the state of war is not the figment of a wayward philosophical imagination. It is a real condition, from which people who are denied the benefits of political community must suffer.

This portrait of man's natural condition is bleak, but not absolutely desperate. It eludes despair because of the existence of certain laws of nature that point the way to escape from its calamitous consequences. Hobbes begins his account of these laws by insisting that their sole basis can be nothing other than man's natural reason. "WHAT it is we call the law of nature," he points out, "is not agreed upon by those that have hitherto written."[30] Some have attempted to base the law of nature on the consent of all nations. Others base it upon the practice of the wisest and most civilized nations. Still others argue that it is founded upon the consent of all mankind. None of these formulae is adequate, and the last is literally absurd, since it implies that no man could ever offend against the natural laws. The only acceptable way of deriving those laws is by a careful application of the ability to reason shared by all men.

The argument that reason provides the sole basis for deriving the laws of nature was not original with Hobbes. But his relentless application of this principle, and the distinctive interpretation he gave to it, were without precedent. Hobbes defined reason as an ability to calculate, to construct syllogisms that would allow us to proceed by deduction from given prem-

[29] *Elements* I.14.12.

[30] *Elements* I.15.1.

ises to certain conclusions. It is not, for him, a transcendent faculty enabling men to peer into the nature of things, as Plato along with many other classical philosophers believed. It is simply an instrument that can be applied to principles that are "found indubitable by experience."[31] It has no power to reveal the mysteries of nature to us, but it can help us make our own experience more intelligible and suggest ways of making our future lives more pleasant.

Hobbes's essential argument is that the laws of nature can be derived by applying this instrument to a principle with which all men may be presumed to agree. "[A]ll men agree," he argues, "to be directed and governed in the way to that which they desire to attain, namely their own good."[32] And what they desire most of all is to preserve themselves from "that terrible enemy of nature, death."

Most of the results that flow from this application of reason to the principle of self-preservation were absolutely conventional. Hobbes insists that reason dictates that for our own good we should do everything possible to attain peace with our fellow men. The state of war presents a constant threat to the self-preservation all men desire. The best way to surmount that threat is by escaping this condition altogether. This is the single most important conclusion of the law of nature, of which he says at one point that its "sum . . . consisteth in making peace."[33]

The greater part of his exposition of the laws of nature is a discussion of the rules he believes should be followed by all men in their efforts to pursue this aim. The first two of these rules are the ones he considers essential. These are "*that every man divest himself of the right he hath to all things by nature*"; and "*[t]hat every man is obliged to stand to, and perform, those covenants which he maketh*."[34] The rationale for the first of these rules is obvious.

[31] *Elements* I.5.12; cf. I.5.11 and II.10.8.

[32] *Elements* I.15.1.

[33] *Elements* I.15.2.

[34] *Elements* I.15.2, I.16.1.

Men are miserable in the state of nature because all of them have a right to all things. If they can mutually agree to accept restraints upon this right, the cause of their insecurity will have been overcome. The second rule is a corollary of the first. For this mutual agreement to achieve the desired effect, it must be binding upon all parties to it. Men can escape the miseries of the state of nature by agreeing to accept obligations that restrict their natural right to all things.

All the rest of the particular laws of nature flow from this same general principle. There is no reason to discuss them in detail. Hobbes prescribes that men should be charitable, accommodating, and forgiving; that they should not be vengeful, nor harbor contempt or hatred for others, and so forth. These laws are perfectly conventional rules of social behavior, very few of which would have been disputed by his predecessors in the theory of natural law.

The other result of his theory was more unusual. This was Hobbes's conclusion that in the absence of any binding, enforceable agreement among men to lay down their natural right to all things, each man should "strengthen himself with all the help he can procure, for his own defence against those, from whom such peace cannot be obtained."[35] This principle dictates that men in the state of nature should do everything within their power to build up their defensive strength. Hobbes acknowledges that pursuit of this principle will intensify the hostile and insecure character of human relations in the state of nature. Men who attempt to procure maximum protection from others in that state will naturally be led to seek power over those others, who will react by attempting to gain power for themselves. The mutual distrust and fear from which men suffer in the state of nature is partly a paradoxical consequence of this struggle for security.[36]

This conclusion was highly provocative. Since man's natural

[35] *Elements* I.14.14; cf. I.15.1.
[36] *Elements* I.14.3.

condition is a state of war, his first and overriding aim must always be to secure his own preservation. But the result of his efforts to do so is necessarily to intensify the insecurity of that condition. It is true that there are a few precepts of the natural law that can be observed even in time of war. Gratuitous cruelty, for example, cannot possibly contribute to any man's security, and the law proscribing it can be adhered to without danger.[37] On the whole, however, the laws of nature tending to promote peace are of little consequence in the absence of a general agreement among men to lay down their natural right to all things, backed by a power capable of enforcing that agreement. The starkly contrasting courses of action toward which Hobbes's doctrine of the law of nature points are crystallized in his own characteristically pithy formula: "to be sociable with them that will be sociable, and formidable to them that will not."[38]

Since the laws of nature have little practical force in man's natural condition, the central message of Hobbes's formula is that we should do everything we possibly can to escape that condition. Hobbes lays the groundwork for this escape in a discussion that follows his formulation of the first law of nature. This discussion describes the conditions under which men may transfer their rights. The most important concept developed in this discussion is that of a covenant.

A covenant, for Hobbes, is a specific form of contract. Contracts in general are agreements between two or more persons in which each of those persons transfers a right he already possesses in return for some benefit he does not yet possess. When such a contract includes a promise by at least one of those agreeing to it to perform his part of the bargain at some future time, it is an agreement based upon trust. This is the form of agreement Hobbes calls a covenant.[39]

[37] *Elements* I.19.2.

[38] *Elements* I.17.15.

[39] *Elements* I.15.8, 9.

An escape from the state of nature can be effected by a specific form of covenant in which, in accordance with the prescription laid down in the first law of nature, everyone agrees to divest himself of the right to all things he has by nature. What each party to this covenant gives up is his natural right to all things. What each receives in return is the security that flows from the fact that all others have likewise given up their natural rights to all things. Each party to this covenant accepts an obligation to restrain his actions within certain bounds that are artificially created; this is what it means for them to give up their original natural rights.

In order to secure their escape from the state of nature, however, men must do more than give up their natural right to all things. They must create "some common power, by the fear whereof they may be compelled both to keep the peace amongst themselves, and to join their strengths together, against a common enemy."[40] For in divesting themselves of their natural right to all things, men do not discard the qualities of human nature that make them naturally offensive to one another. These qualities are permanent attributes of human psychology. In the absence of a power great enough to check them, they would inevitably lead men to clash with one another, and these clashes could easily result in destruction of the covenant. The only way to ensure against this calamity is to appoint some man or council to adjudicate in any disputes that may arise and to give that man or council the power to enforce its decisions.[41] Such a grant of power is a condition without which no agreement of the kind envisaged by Hobbes would be possible. For without it no party to the convenant would be guaranteed that the others will keep their end of the bargain. The covenant would be a mere, ineffective juridical form. And, Hobbes observes, "such covenants are of none effect."[42]

[40] *Elements* I.19.6.
[41] *Elements* I.19.4, 6-7.
[42] *Elements* I.15.10.

By creating such a common power or sovereign, men constitute themselves into a commonwealth. Their chief aim in doing so is to secure themselves against the dangers of death and bodily harm. This aim determines the scope of the powers that must be invested in the sovereign as well as the extent of all its members' subjection to that power: "How far therefore in the making of a commonwealth, a man subjecteth his will to the power of others, must appear from the end, namely security."[43]

Hobbes argues that these powers must be very broad.[44] To protect his subjects adequately a sovereign must have, first, the power of coercion, which Hobbes also calls by its traditional name, the sword of justice. Second, he must have the sword of war, which also entails the right to command all the resources that might be necessary to prosecute a war. Third, he must have the power of judicature, so that he may settle all controversies that might arise among his subjects, either personally or through his deputies. Fourth, he must have the right to set down rules by which relations between the members of the commonwealth can be regulated. These are ordinarily called the civil laws. Hobbes lays special emphasis upon those laws designed to control the distribution and exchange of property. Fifth, he must be able to appoint magistrates and ministers to assist him in his work. Finally, the sovereign must be immune from the application of his own or any other laws against himself. As the power by which it is unified, the sovereign cannot be attacked without attacking the commonwealth itself. Taken together, Hobbes explains, these powers "make the sovereign power no less absolute in the commonwealth, than before commonwealth every man was absolute in himself to do, or not to do, what he thought good."[45]

For Hobbes this statement, which is the culmination of his

[43] *Elements* II.1.5.

[44] *Elements* II.1.6-12.

[45] *Elements* II.1.13.

entire political argument, has two dimensions of meaning, corresponding to the two languages out of which he constructs that argument as a whole. It means both that the *rights* of sovereignty must be unlimited and that a sovereign must be able to exercise effectively absolute *power* over the actions of his subjects. Hobbes uses the terms "right" and "power" in this section of his manuscript almost interchangeably, but his argument is absolutely clear that a sovereign must have the "means and strength" to enforce his decisions as distinct from, and in addition to, the juridical right to make them.[46]

Thus Hobbes's argument moves simultaneously along two lines, which intersect in his doctrine of sovereignty. His key juridical idea is that the absolute right to all things possessed by all human beings in the state of nature is converted by means of a covenant into the absolute right of a sovereign to adjudicate disputes, declare war, make laws, and do all other things he deems essential for the protection and contentment of his subjects. Some of the details of this idea are fuzzy and obscure. The most important of these obscurities has to do with whether or not the subjects of a commonwealth retain a right to resist their sovereign under certain circumstances. This issue was of (sometimes literally) capital importance to many of Hobbes's contemporaries, but his statements about it are slippery and sometimes appear to be mutually contradictory.[47] There is no ambiguity, however, in his account of the rights of sovereignty. These rights are absolute, and extend as far as the sovereign considers necessary.

The key behavioral proposition that accompanies this juridical line of Hobbes's argument is that fear of death, guided by rational knowledge of the causes of death, is such a powerful motive that it is capable of causing men to curb their natural

[46] *Elements* I.19.7.

[47] Cf. *Elements* I.17.2, I.19.10, II.1.5, II.1.7. Richard Tuck discusses Hobbes's account of this issue in his *Natural Rights Theories: Their Origin and Development* (Cambridge: Cambridge University Press, 1979), ch. 6.

appetites, vanity, and contentiousness in order to subject themselves in obedience to a common sovereign. By subjecting themselves in this way the members of a commonwealth give their sovereign the power to enforce his laws, judgments, and other actions and decisions. This proposition is the indispensable motivational foundation of Hobbes's political argument, without which the juridical line of that argument, which declares the rights of sovereignty to be absolute, would be "of none effect." As he argues in the final paragraph of part I of *The Elements of Law*, "The *cause* in general which moveth a man to become subject to another, is (as I have said already) the fear of not otherwise preserving himself."[48] Hobbes's juridical argument describes the legal and ethical consequences of the creation of a commonwealth. But the behavioral dimension of his argument accounts for the true causes of that creation.

The Idea of a Scientific Theory

As the letter of dedication prefixed to his manuscript makes clear, Hobbes understood *The Elements of Law* to be a work of science. He equates science with "knowledge of the truth of propositions." Such propositional knowledge may be universal in scope, as is that knowledge embodied (for example) in the theorems of geometry. A sharp distinction must therefore be drawn between science and history (including natural history), which is based upon direct "experience of the effects of things that work upon us from without." For we can perceive or experience things only as discrete particulars, never as universals; hence "we cannot from experience conclude . . . any proposition universal whatsoever. . . ." History, as characterized in this manuscript, consists of a series of discrete statements of fact. The basic units of science, by contrast, are universal prop-

[48] *Elements* I.19.11, emphasis added; cf. I.15.13.

ositions. Unlike ordinary statements of fact, these universal propositions can be joined into larger networks of knowledge through ratiocination or reasoning. Here again the pattern Hobbes appears to have had in mind was provided by geometry and its axiomatic method of reasoning. A whole science, then, consists of a network of universal propositions joined together by ratiocination.[49]

It is sometimes argued that this view of science presupposes a radically nominalistic conception of truth and a deep skepticism about the notion that there is any real relationship between scientific knowledge, on the one hand, and nature or reality, on the other. Since "there is nothing universal but names," and names are the arbitrary creations of the founders of knowledge, it follows that all truth for Hobbes must be analytic: "for, truth, and a true proposition, is all one."[50] Science is a purely linguistic artifact, a system of discourse consisting of propositions that are analytically meaningful and analytically true or false. There can be no real relationship between such a linguistic artifact and reality. Even Hobbes's doctrine of evidence, which at first glance seems to anchor science in reality, actually confirms the diremption between them. Evidence, according to Hobbes, is "the concomitance of a man's conception with the words that signify such conception in the act of ratiocination."[51] But these conceptions are only the phantasms, or motions in the mind, produced by the motions of other bodies acting on the senses, and Hobbes neither asserts nor implies

[49] *Elements* I.6.1, I.4.11, I.5.11. In his much later *De Corpore* (IV.25.1) Hobbes distinguishes between two branches of science or philosophy, one of which proceeds from knowledge of causes to knowledge of effects and consists of universal propositions, while the other proceeds from knowledge of effects to knowledge of their possible causes and consists of "single and particular" propositions. One example of the first kind of science is geometry; an example of the second is physics.

[50] *Elements* I.5.6, I.5.10.

[51] *Elements* I.6.3.

that they correspond to realities. Thus, it is argued, Hobbes is a metaphysical nominalist according to whom neither our words and propositions nor our conceptions and ideas themselves bear any knowable relation to the underlying nature of things.[52]

A strong streak of nominalist skepticism does indeed run throughout Hobbes's thinking and leave a mark upon his idea of science, but the importance of that mark is not as great as this interpretation suggests. Several of the early chapters of *The Elements of Law* are devoted largely to an attempt to work out the relationship between experience on the one hand and scientific propositions on the other. In one passage, for example, Hobbes argues:

> Knowledge, therefore, which we call SCIENCE, I define to be evidence of truth, from some beginning or principle of sense. For the truth of a proposition is never evident, until we conceive the meaning of the words or terms whereof it consisteth, which are always conceptions of the mind; nor can we remember those conceptions, without the thing that produced the same by our senses.[53]

The exact meaning of this passage is obscure, but it is at least clear that Hobbes is attempting to relate the propositions of science to the objects of knowledge, and not merely to "conceptions of the mind." His efforts, too, to discriminate carefully between "whatsoever accidents or qualities our senses make us think there be in the world . . . but are seemings and apparitions only," and the "things that really are in the world without us"—to distinguish, that is, between subjective qualities imposed by the mind and the objective properties of things—make sense only if we assume that he considered it important

[52] Dorothea Krook, "Thomas Hobbes's Doctrine of Meaning and Truth," *Philosophy* 31 (1956), pp. 3-22.

[53] *Elements* I.6.4.

for science to be anchored in a faithful transcription of reality.[54] Hobbes's account of the relationship between science and reality may not be entirely clear at all points, but it is plain that he considers it necessary for the propositions of science to be firmly rooted in experience, as his remark that no reliable science can be constructed "without beginning anew from the very first grounds of all our knowledge, sense" also suggests.[55]

In *The Elements of Law*, then, Hobbes conceived of science as a network of universal propositions joined together by ratiocination and grounded, though in a way he was unable to define clearly, in experience.[56] But an important question about this conception of science remains. J.W.N. Watkins has suggested that the propositions of Hobbes's science should be considered empirical hypotheses. One of the principal benefits of Hobbes's attempt to construct a demonstrable science of politics, he argues, was that it led him to shape his (personal and subjective) thoughts about politics into an (objective) system of interconnected ideas. The ideas that constitute such a system transcend the thinking out of which they first arose, and can be examined from a variety of viewpoints, many of which their creator might

[54] *Elements* I.2.10; cf. I.2.4-9, I.5.12. Hobbes considered this distinction essential for science, and had discussed it as early as 1630 in "A Short Tract on First Principles" (*Elements*, Appendix I), sec. 3. In later arguments, he implied that this discussion was a milestone in the history of science. Cf. Brandt, *Thomas Hobbes' Mechanical Conception, passim.*

[55] *Elements* I.5.14.

[56] Hobbes's important discussion of the method of resolution and composition in his much later work, *De Corpore*, ch. 6, is in part an effort to define the relationship between scientific propositions and the perceptions of experience clearly. It is noteworthy, however, that he offers no similar discussion in any earlier work, including his *Anti-white*, where such a discussion might have been expected. It is a plausible inference that this method had far less impact upon Hobbes's thought than several interpreters have recently argued. For examples of this argument see Watkins, *Hobbes's System*, chs. 3, 4, and Isabel C. Hungerland and George R. Vick, "Hobbes's Theory of Signification," *Journal of the History of Philosophy* 11 (1973), pp. 459-482.

not have anticipated. By shaping these ideas into a system interconnected by relations of deduction and logical implication, Hobbes rendered them eminently criticizable, even falsifiable. For Watkins, then, the propositions that constitute Hobbes's science are empirical hypotheses, predictive statements that can be scrutinized in the light of experience and cast away if experience shows them to be false.[57]

This interpretation may suggest possibilities for reconstructing some of Hobbes's arguments, but it cannot be squared with his own idea of science. One supposed example of an empirical hypothesis in Hobbes's system is his contention that men must by their nature seek to avoid death. This statement has been systematically falsified, Watkins argues, by evidence from several primitive tribes of circumstances under which death is passively and routinely accepted.[58] But Watkins need not have turned to such exotic sources for his evidence, for in *The Elements of Law* itself Hobbes acknowledges that there are some circumstances under which men will accept death as the preferable of two alternatives. In fact he specifies at least two motives that can be sufficiently powerful to induce men to accept death. The first of these is the desire to escape humiliation:

> REVENGEFULNESS is that passion which ariseth from an expectation or imagination of making him that hath hurt us, to find his own action hurtful to himself, and to acknowledge the same; and this is the height of revenge. For though it be not hard, by returning evil for evil, to make one's adversary displeased with his own fact; yet to make him acknowledge the same, is so difficult, that many a man had rather die than do it.[59]

The second is fear of damnation and hell: "For why should a

[57] *Hobbes's System*, pp. 8-11, 121-125.

[58] *Hobbes's System*, pp. 122-123.

[59] *Elements* I.9.6; cf. his remarks on courage at I.9.4.

man incur the danger of a temporal death, by displeasing of his superior, if it were not for fear of eternal death hereafter?"[60] Hobbes was perfectly aware that people sometimes face death willingly. Yet he shows no sign of believing that this fact undermines his contention that men must by their nature seek to avoid death.

It might be argued that Hobbes's contention about fear of death is a conditional proposition, and that these two cases are exceptions in which the conditions for its applicability are violated. Hobbes says nothing about the conditional character of scientific knowledge in *The Elements of Law*, but in *Leviathan* he does observe that "*Science* . . . is *Conditionall*." It would be a mistake, however, to assume that he meant science is conditional upon the possibility of falsification by experiment or experience. For he goes on to suggest that science has to do with the "Consequences of one Affirmation, to another."[61] In observing that science is conditional Hobbes seems to be arguing that the truth of a scientific proposition is a function of the logical relationships between it and the other propositions and theorems of science, not that scientific knowledge is conditional upon the possibility of falsification by experience. We know, in fact, that Hobbes took almost no interest in the possibility of experimental falsification or verification, even in physical science.[62] And the notion that the propositions of Hobbes's science are conditional, empirical hypotheses is extremely difficult to reconcile with the decidedly absolute tone in which he often formulated them, as, for example, in his statement that "*necessity of nature* maketh men . . . to avoid that which is hurtful; but most of all that terrible enemy of nature, death."[63]

[60] *Elements* II.6.5.

[61] *Leviathan*, ch. 9, pp. 147-148 [40].

[62] Cf. Brandt, *Thomas Hobbes' Mechanical Conception*, chs. 9, 10, and M. M. Goldsmith, *Hobbes's Science of Politics* (New York and London: Columbia University Press, 1966), p. 242.

[63] *Elements* I.14.6, emphasis added; cf. I.16.6.

The best analogy through which to understand Hobbes's idea of science proves, once again, to be that which he himself was most inclined to draw. The propositions and theorems of science in general for him are identical in kind to the propositions and theorems of geometry. Like geometrical propositions, those of any other science are universal and abstract. Their truth is dependent upon the logical interconnections between them, not upon the extent to which they "fit" or correspond to empirical reality. They are conditional in the sense in which any deductive inference is conditional upon the truth of its premises. Hobbes would have found the notion that such a scientific proposition should be subject to empirical testing or falsification absurd. One cannot empirically test the proposition that a straight line is the shortest distance between two points, or that two parallel straight lines can never intersect one another. Nor is empirical investigation any means for testing the Pythagorean Theorem, the truth of which can be confirmed over and over again by experience, but proved (or disproved) only by deductive reasoning. The propositions of science, as Hobbes conceives them, are absolutely not to be confused with empirical hypotheses.

Does this conclusion mean that we must revert to the view that there is no real relationship for Hobbes between scientific propositions and the things of reality? No. For in the first place, the definitions and axioms upon which any science in his view ultimately rests must be drawn from experience. "Sense," as we have seen above, provides us with "the very first grounds of all our knowledge." Scientific propositions are abstract, but they are abstracted *from experience.* And in the second place, while the *truth* of such propositions is dependent only upon the logical interconnections between them, there is a sense in which the *validity* of any science as a whole is dependent upon its connection with reality. For Hobbes this connection need not, however, be one of simple representation. Geometry is validated for him not by being an accurate representation of reality (which it is not), but by the fact that it can be used to control and change reality. The science of geometry is the ultimate source of our skills of navigation, geography, astronomy, architecture, and in general of "all those excellences, wherein we differ from such savage people as are now the inhabitants of divers places in America."[64] The final "proof" of its validity as a whole, though not of the truth of its individual propositions, lies in these practical achievements.

The provocative implication of this idea of science was that it left open the question of the way in which disparities between scientific theory, on the one hand, and reality, on the other, should be resolved. Talk about the degree of correspondence or disparity between theory and reality is undeniably meaningful in Hobbes's view. But as we have already seen through the example of his contention about fear of death, the existence of disparity is not necessarily sufficient reason to question either the truth or the validity of a scientific theory. For the truth of such a theory rests upon the logical interconnectedness of its propositions, and its validity is a function of its capacity to be put to practical use. There is no presumption that disparities between theory and reality should always be resolved by adjusting theory to "fit" or represent reality more accurately. After all, the fact that there are no perfectly straight lines in nature does not constitute a criticism of geometry. When we respond at all to the discrepancy between the perfectly straight lines of geometric theory and the imperfect lines found in nature, we do so by striving to bring those imperfect lines more fully into accord with the perfection of geometry, as every architect clearly understands. There is no necessary reason to expect that we should respond differently to a discrepancy between the theory of politics and political reality.

The behavioral propositions of *Human Nature*, and of Hobbes's political argument generally, describe a model of hu-

[64] *Elements* I.13.3.

man action. They are causal or predictive in nature; but taken individually, at least, they are not subject to direct verification (or falsification) by experience. Nor are they purely linguistic constructs that bear no real relationship to the things of reality. The model of human behavior they collectively describe is dependent for its validity upon its connection with reality. But that connection is an approximate one, and the approximation between model and reality may be more or less close. This model provides some of the most crucial premises out of which Hobbes constructs his political theory as a whole. It is drawn from experience, but the portrait of behavior it constitutes is an idealized and "perfected" one that neither pretends nor aspires to complete descriptive accuracy. And there is no presumption that any discrepancies between this model and the realities of behavior should be resolved by alterations to the model, since it cannot be assumed that the model, rather than reality, is flawed.

Reason

The most significant determinant of the extent to which actual human behavior resembles Hobbes's model is reason. For Hobbes, as we have seen, reason is essentially an instrument. It is used to guide men in the way toward their ends. But the degree to which men are capable of applying reason to their ends can vary enormously:

> Every man by natural passion, calleth that good which pleaseth him for the present, or so far forth as he can foresee; and in like manner that which displeaseth him evil. And therefore he that foreseeth the whole way to his preservation (which is the end that every one by nature aimeth at) must also call it good, and the contrary evil. And this

> is that good and evil, which not every man in passion calleth so, but all men by reason.[65]

Some men are capable of much greater foresight than others. Every man is egoistic by nature and aims at his own preservation, but many men mistake the means to this end. The varying degrees of success with which men are able to bring reason to bear upon their ends accounts for the difference between a confused, misdirected egoism and a clear understanding of the pathways to one's own preservation dictated by nature.

This foresight is not identical with what Hobbes calls prudence, which in this manuscript he equates with the knowledge of particulars drawn from experience, also called history: "PRUDENCE is nothing else but conjecture from experience, or taking of signs from experience warily."[66] It does give men a capacity to make rough guesses about the way to their own good, but Hobbes emphasizes that these guesses can never be more than rough and imperfect:

> This taking of signs from experience, is that wherein men do ordinarily think, the difference stands between man and man in wisdom, by which they commonly understand a man's whole ability or power cognitive. But this is an error; for these signs are but conjectural; and according as they have often or seldom failed, so their assurance is more or less; but never full and evident.[67]

As we have already seen, Hobbes draws a very strict distinction between conclusions drawn from experience alone and those produced by ratiocination or reasoning. The genuine foresight that men need to see the "whole way" to their own preservation cannot be provided by the conjectures made possible from experience alone. It is a product of "right reason," of reckoning

[65] *Elements* I.17.14.

[66] *Elements* I.4.10.

[67] *Elements* I.4.10.

from "principles that are found indubitable by experience, all deceptions of sense and equivocation of words avoided."[68]

Although reason puts a knowledge of the way to their own preservation within men's reach, it also poses great dangers. In itself reason is infallible, but men's application of it is not. When men do misreckon, the results can be spectacular. For the conclusions of faulty reasoning are not merely mistakes; they are absurdities. Ratiocination leads men to "multiply one untruth by another," so that a very few simple errors become magnified into outrageously ridiculous conclusions.[69] Hobbes may have thought that this capacity for reason to mislead accounts for the extraordinary extent to which some people diverge from the way to their own preservation, the end that nature prescribes to every man. Even the fact that some men prefer to sacrifice life itself in order to avoid humiliation or the possibility of eternal damnation could be construed as one of the absurd results of the human ability to misreckon in spectacular fashion.

The main cause of misreckoning is the misuse of language. As Hobbes takes care to point out, language is the basis of all reason and all science. Reasoning consists in the construction of propositions and the linking of these propositions to one another through syllogisms. None of this would be possible, in his view, without language.[70] But language is also the basis for another human creation, the art of rhetoric. According to the view Hobbes adopted in *The Elements of Law*, rhetoric is the greatest and most insidious enemy with which reason has to contend. It is powerful because it plays upon men's passions, which he acknowledges to be "the beginning of speech." It is insidious because it imitates reason and is so easily confused with it: "*ratio*, now, is but *oratio*, for the most part, wherein

[68] *Elements* I.5.12.

[69] *Elements* I.5.12-13.

[70] *Elements* I.5.4, 11, 13; I.6.1.

custom hath so great a power, that the mind suggesteth only the first word, the rest follow habitually, and are not followed by the mind."[71] It is exceedingly easy to put on the show of a rational discourse, but it takes great mental effort to break the mold of habit and subject a chain of words to the scrutiny of reason. Most of what passes for reasoning is mere babbling.

The difference between reason and its bogus forms is vast in its implications, but difficult to detect. What most clearly distinguishes reason from rhetoric is that the words in which we reason are always accompanied by a clear grasp of the conceptions they represent. This clear grasp must accompany every link in any chain of reasoning. This is perhaps the most important implication of Hobbes's doctrine of evidence, which he considers vital to any knowledge of truth: "For if the words alone were sufficient, a parrot might be taught as well to know a truth, as to speak it. Evidence is to truth, as the sap is to the tree. . . . [W]ithout it truth is nothing worth."[72]

Rhetoric is an imitation of truth in the same way in which the mimicking of a parrot is an imitation of speech. Rhetoric begins and ends with mere opinions. It is unaccompanied by evidence. For Hobbes this does not merely mean that it makes assumptions which are accepted without proof. It means that rhetorical assertions do not correspond to thoughts or conceptions in the mind. Neither the rhetorician nor his listeners can have any idea, in the most literal sense, of what he is saying. They can and do begin with passions and opinions, which the art of rhetoric is designed to strengthen or dilute according to the aims of the speaker. What they do not have, and what cannot be raised by the art of rhetoric, is any clear conception of truth. Rhetoric, though difficult to distinguish from rational discourse, is in reality its antithesis.[73]

[71] *Elements* I.5.14.

[72] *Elements* I.6.3.

[73] *Elements* I.13.2, 4.

The political consequences of this opposition between reason and rhetoric are enormous. If rhetoric is so powerful that it is capable of diverting men from the pathway toward self-preservation dictated to them by nature, it is by this very fact also capable of calling the entire basis of sovereign power and political order into question. For Hobbes commonwealths are built upon the assumption that men will act rationally to preserve their own lives. Men agree to become members of a commonwealth to preserve life, and the power of their sovereign rests ultimately upon their continuing desire to avoid death. If this desire itself, or the ability to act rationally to secure it, is removed, the entire foundation of the commonwealth crumbles. In this sense, political order for Hobbes is intimately dependent upon linguistic order, because only by maintaining linguistic order can we be assured that the members of a commonwealth will remain mindful of the overriding importance of their own preservation, and hence also of the need to remain strictly obedient to their sovereign.[74]

The opposition between reason and rhetoric is posed in a variety of forms in *The Elements of Law*. It appears as a contrast between logic and rhetoric, *ratio* and *oratio*, teaching and persuasion, the *mathematici* and the *dogmatici*. This contrast runs throughout the entire work, from the very first line of Hobbes's dedicatory epistle onward. Some indication of its importance can be gathered from the fact that Hobbes makes it the subject

[74] The close connection between political order and linguistic order in Hobbes's theory has been emphasized by several interpreters, most notably Sheldon Wolin in *Politics and Vision* (Boston: Little, Brown, 1960), ch. 8, and Terence Ball in "Hobbes' Linguistic Turn," *Polity* 17 (1985), pp. 739-760. Both these interpreters argue that Hobbes saw a need for the members of a commonwealth to share a common political language. This argument is important, but my point is the different one that Hobbes saw a need for the members of a commonwealth to bear constantly in mind the importance of their own preservation, an end from which they could be diverted by the rhetorical distortion of "right reason."

of the culminating chapter of *Human Nature*, immediately preceding his discussion of the state of nature in the complete manuscript. The opposition between reason and rhetoric is the most fundamental theme of the entire work.

At first glance Hobbes's opposition between reason and rhetoric appears to constitute a wholesale attack upon the art of rhetoric in general, and thus a reversal of the views he had expressed some twelve years earlier in his introduction to Thucydides' history. The ideals of the rhetorical tradition pervade that introduction. Like its earlier representatives, Hobbes had seen rhetoric as a supreme art that brings the virtues of philosophical wisdom together with the benefits of political action. Rhetoric, for him, had been associated with the highest and most esteemed forms of political practice. The ideas expressed in his manuscript of 1640 seem to reject those earlier views. In this work rhetoric is depicted as the insidious impostor of reason. It leads men to embrace absurd conclusions and destroys their ability to distinguish between truth and falsehood. The insinuation of rhetoric into the place of reason has political consequences of the utmost importance. It causes men to become confused about the way to their own preservation, and by doing so strikes at the very foundations of political order.

This appearance of a reversal is illusory. Hobbes's seeming attack upon the art of rhetoric in fact develops a theme that had already occupied his attention in his introduction to Thucydides' history. In that work he had been extremely critical of rhetoricians who abuse their art to curry favor with the "multitude." He had linked this criticism with an attack upon the democratic government of Athens, in which "such men only swayed the assemblies, and were esteemed wise and good commonwealth's men, as did put them upon the most dangerous and desperate enterprizes."[75] This attack is echoed in *The Elements of Law*, and the reasoning behind it is in both cases essen-

[75] *Thucydides*, p. xvi.

tially the same. It is that rhetoric, especially when abused in public assemblies, obstructs men's abilities to think clearly and, most important, to perceive their own limitations.[76] The opposition between reason and rhetoric in Hobbes's manuscript extends this criticism by tying it into a larger theory of the use and misuse of language, but it is not an entirely new facet of his thought and does not constitute a reversal of his earlier views.

Indeed Hobbes remains as impressed by the power of rhetoric in this manuscript as he had been in his much earlier translation. Rhetoric is at its most powerful when it is used to whip up the passions of a crowd, "[f]or commonly truth is on the side of the few, rather than of the multitude." The absurdity of the opinions that rhetoric can generate and to which it appeals is no obstacle to its ability to hold the minds of gullible men in its grip. The most effective device enabling it to maintain this grip is—just as Hobbes had argued before—the image: "For not truth, but image, maketh passion." Once a clever rhetorician has succeeded in mesmerizing his listeners through the power of such images, he is in a position to manipulate their actions. For whatever men's ultimate ends may be, the immediate cause of their actions is always some opinion, "[i]n which sense they say truly and properly that say the world is governed by opinion."[77]

In evoking his old thesis about the power of the image and its rhetorical presentation, Hobbes is implicitly posing a question about the character and aims of his own political theory. Perhaps the clearest formulation of this question occurs in an observation he makes toward the end of his manuscript:

> Now to demonstration and teaching of the truth, there are required long deductions, and great attention, which is unpleasant to the hearer; therefore they which seek not truth, but belief, must take another way. . . . And such

[76] *Elements* II.2.5, II.5.8.

[77] *Elements* I.13.3, I.13.7, I.12.6.

> is the power of eloquence, as many times a man is made to believe thereby, that he sensibly feeleth smart and damage, when he feeleth none, and to enter into rage and indignation, without any other cause, than what is in the words and passion of the speaker.[78]

By contrasting the power of rhetoric and its capacity to evoke images with the impotence of conceptual or scientific reasoning for the purpose of shaping belief, Hobbes encapsulates the dilemma that confronted his own political theory. If the aim of theory is to present a true science of politics, as the opening line of his manuscript declares, then the very presentation of that science will inhibit rather than facilitate the inculcation of its conclusions in the form of opinion or belief. If, on the other hand, the aim of his theory is to induce men to hold "the opinions concerning law and policy here delivered," as his dedication suggests, then this aim can best be pursued by taking "another way" than that of "demonstration and teaching of the truth," by plainly drawing upon the power of language and eloquence to combat the distortions of reason caused by abuse of this power. Is political theory essentially a scientific enterprise or a political act? Should it rely upon the methods of rational demonstration and propositional argument, which are best suited for teaching truth, or upon the evocation of visual images and palpable emotions, which are far more adept at shaping opinion and belief? The fundamental dilemma confronting Hobbes's political theory can be reduced to the simple question: science or rhetoric?

In *The Elements of Law* Hobbes chose science. It would be far from true to say that he never indulges in the slightest rhetorical flourish, or that his argument is never punctuated by a striking visual image. The distinction between logical argument and rhetorical presentation was not so absolute as to preclude any intermingling of these two forms of discourse. But on the

[78] *Elements* II.8.14.

whole the method of argument upon which he relies comes much closer to that of strict rational demonstration than to any essentially rhetorical form. *The Elements of Law* is calculated to persuade by logical, not rhetorical, means. It was liable to appeal to those who took a lively scientific interest in the subjects with which it deals, but not to stir the imaginations of others, to whom it must have seemed, as Hobbes himself put it, "but dry discourse" indeed.[79] The claim in his letter of dedication that he "was forced to consult . . . more with logic than with rhetoric" may be slightly disingenuous, but as an overall characterization it is accurate. Hobbes's manuscript was essentially a work of science. In his own estimation it undoubtedly realized his early aim to make sense of the "facultyes and passions of the soule," and its second portion, *De Corpore Politico*, went well beyond this ambition. But it did not in any substantial way break out of the limits imposed by its scientific form.

There is no way for us to be certain why, in view of his observations on the limited usefulness of scientific reasoning for inculcating belief, Hobbes nonetheless confined his own exposition to an essentially scientific form, but it is not difficult to adduce plausible conjectures about his reasons for this decision. *The Elements of Law* was a manuscript treatise, which remained unpublished for a decade after its completion, and even then appeared with Hobbes's consent only after an unauthorized printing of a portion of the work. It was initially circulated among, and presumably intended for, a very restricted audience. It seems likely that he would have considered logic and scientific demonstration the best, most persuasive form of discourse for such an audience, even though he knew it would not be so suitable for a larger readership.[80] Time may have been a

[79] *Elements* I.5.11.

[80] As Howell points out, logic in the English Renaissance was thought of as a means for communicating with learned audiences, while rhetoric was considered a means for popular communication. This difference was conveyed through Zeno's metaphor, used by both Cicero and Quintilian, which com-

factor, too. Hobbes had been working on the topics discussed in *Human Nature* for several years, but in his *Considerations*, composed shortly after the Restoration of 1660, he explicitly suggests that the treatise was actually written during the first few months of 1640.[81] He may simply not have had enough time to act upon his own implied recommendation that a work of political persuasion must do more than demonstrate its conclusions by the relatively dry means of logical argument.

Other conjectures can also be suggested. In early 1640 Hobbes may not have considered the discrepancy between his model and the realities of English politics very great. The convening of the Long Parliament, which made drastic inroads into royal power, was still six months away when he dedicated the work, and civil war did not actually break out until 1642. The King had been challenged before, and had managed to weather all earlier crises. Hobbes thought it would prove profitable for people to understand and adopt his political principles, but there is no sign at this time that he was genuinely alarmed, or that he had yet foreseen that sovereign power in England was about to crumble. The political atmosphere was highly charged, but collapse did not yet appear imminent. Under these circumstances Hobbes may have deemed it potentially useful, but less than urgent, for his political principles to achieve widespread acceptance.

And in any case Hobbes, despite his complaints about the impotence of reason in comparison with rhetoric, displays considerable faith in reason in his manuscript. Reason is as real and essential an element of human nature as passion, or any other attribute:

> Reason is no less of the nature of man than passion, and is the same in all men. . . .

---

pared the relationship between logic and rhetoric to that between a closed fist and an open hand. See Howell's *Logic and Rhetoric*, esp. ch. 1.

[81] *Considerations*, p. 414.

> For these powers we do unanimously call natural, and are contained in the definition of man, under these words, animal and rational.
>
> [T]he whole nature of man . . . may all be comprehended in these four: strength of body, experience, reason, and passion.[82]

Though men are susceptible to the seductions of rhetoric, they have within themselves the power to resist those seductions. Hobbes sometimes gives the impression that he holds the intellectual powers of most men in low esteem. If he does so, it is not because he believes that they lack the capacity to understand. Even his own complex argument is well within the reach of most men, "for there be few men which have not so much natural logic, as thereby to discern well enough, whether any conclusion I shall hereafter make, in this discourse, be well or ill collected. . . ."[83] Logic and reason for Hobbes, in *The Elements of Law*, were natural gifts. They might be sharpened by exercise or dulled by disuse, but they are nonetheless essential attributes of human nature. Men are commonly susceptible to persuasion by crafty rhetoricians, but they have the natural capacity to resist and overcome this weakness.

Hence while Hobbes recognizes that great obstacles stand in the way of the perfection of reason, he nonetheless regards reason as an entirely natural capacity and considers rationality to be a perfectly natural state of mind. What causes men's reason to fail is the misuse of language. In politics at least, this distortion is caused primarily by the abuses to which rhetoricians, who are often moved by secret designs and private ambitions, subject language.[84] To restore men to their natural reason re-

[82] *Elements* I.15.1, I.1.4, I.14.1.

[83] *Elements* I.5.11.

[84] *Elements* II.8.12-15.

quires nothing other than the elimination of this distortion.[85] From a theoretical viewpoint this assumption was perhaps the most important factor behind Hobbes's decision to frame his argument essentially in the form of a scientific demonstration. The decision to rely upon the methods of propositional argument and logical demonstration, in spite of his own long-standing doubts about their ability to compete with more vivid and captivating means of persuasion, can in this sense be seen as an act of theoretical optimism based upon faith in human rationality. If such a faith did shine through the argument of this manuscript, however, it was soon to be banished from Hobbes's political universe.

[85] Richard Peters' charge that Hobbes had an "incredibly naive" faith in the efficacy of definitions for eliminating disorder might seem to be corroborated by this reasoning, but in fact that charge is extremely simplistic. Hobbes did not believe that definitions carry any force of their own, and much of my argument to this point has sought to show that he was extremely wary of the efficacy of logical demonstration for inducing belief in general. Hobbes did, however, believe that abuses of language could have seriously subversive political implications, and considered it worth his while to point out some of these abuses. Peters' argument is made in his *Hobbes* (Harmondsworth, Middlesex: Penguin, 1967), p. 56.

CHAPTER THREE ✲

Rhetoric Rediscovered

FROM DRY DISCOURSE TO SPEAKING PICTURE

DURING THE DECADE that followed his completion of *The Elements of Law*, Hobbes composed two additional works of political theory, the Latin treatise *De Cive*, which was first printed in April 1642, and the *Leviathan* of 1651. While the conclusions of these later works are broadly consistent with those of his original manuscript, Hobbes did make some important adjustments both in their precise formulation and in the arguments used to produce them. Some of those adjustments involved the clarification of conceptual ambiguities that had remained unresolved in his initial theory.[1] Others can be construed as attempts to adapt his doctrine to shifts of political circumstance.[2] But perhaps the most striking difference be-

[1] Cf. F. S. McNeilly, *The Anatomy of Leviathan* (London: Macmillan, 1968); David P. Gauthier, *The Logic of Leviathan* (Oxford: Clarendon Press, 1969); Richard Tuck, *Natural Rights Theories*, ch. 6.

[2] Hobbes himself suggests that he adapted his arguments in this manner. See his comments on capital punishment in *Leviathan*, Review and Conclusion, p. 722 [392], and on the mutual relation between protection and obedience in his *Considerations*, pp. 423-424. Cf. also Quentin Skinner, "Con-

tween *Leviathan* and the earlier versions of his political theory is the new language in which that theory was expressed. In his original manuscript Hobbes had framed his political argument essentially in the form of a logical demonstration. He had, in effect, chosen the "dry discourse" of science over the more evocative and powerful language of rhetoric. The expositional strategy adopted in *Leviathan* was almost diametrically opposed to that of this manuscript. The language is vastly more vigorous, vivid, and rhetorical in character throughout the work. Simile and metaphor are in constant use, as when Hobbes compares the papacy to a "Kingdom of Fairies," or when he compares the commonwealth itself to the great Leviathan mentioned in the ancient book of Job. The work is full of arguments by suggestion or insinuation, which contrast in a striking manner with Hobbes's earlier attempts to justify his views by strict logical demonstration. He indicts the Roman and Presbyterian churches by invoking a rule of legal presumption—borrowed, significantly, from Cicero himself—rather than by offering any positive proof of their guilt.[3] It would be wrong to suggest that *Leviathan* is *not* a work of science or philosophy, for it clearly is such a work. But it also goes much further beyond the bounds of propositional argument and logical demonstration than either of Hobbes's earlier works, especially his original manuscript of 1640, had done. *Leviathan* is a philosophical treatise, but it is also much more. It is an intensely polemical work with literary qualities comparable to those of the most esteemed works in the whole of English literature.

It is often assumed that there is no significant relationship between these changes in the literary form of his work and the substance of Hobbes's theory. The polemical cast assumed by his argument, it is claimed, was a product of relatively local and

quest and Consent: Thomas Hobbes and the Engagement Controversy," in G. E. Aylmer, ed., *The Interregnum* (London: Macmillan, 1972), pp. 79-78.

[3] *Leviathan*, ch. 47, pp. 704-706 [381-382].

transitory political concerns that left no genuinely enduring marks upon his political philosophy. Some critics have even argued that the rhetorical qualities of *Leviathan*, while enhancing its appeal as a work of literature, actually tend to make it more obscure than, and hence inferior to, his earlier writings as philosophy.[4] These arguments presuppose a radically disembodied conception of the nature of political philosophy, one that is essentially foreign to Hobbes's way of thinking. The fact is that this dramatic change in literary form was connected with important changes in the substance of his political theory, and ultimately was symptomatic of an underlying metamorphosis in his conception of the nature and aims of political philosophy.

These changes will be examined in the chapters that follow. It may be useful here to anticipate the way in which the argument of those chapters will unfold.

Hobbes's initial political theory, as we have seen, was constructed by interweaving two distinct kinds of language into a single argumentative structure. Behavioral propositions drawn from the language of causation were combined with juridical propositions formulated in the language of ethics and law. Hobbes's theory of the commonwealth, and his conclusions about the rights and obligations of subjects and sovereigns, required both languages. But the behavioral dimension of his argument accounts for the true causes of a commonwealth, and hence also for the distribution of rights and obligations that flows from its creation. The key behavioral proposition of this argument is that fear of death, guided by rational knowledge of its causes, is such a powerful motive that it is capable of causing men to curb their other passions and subject themselves to a common sovereign. This proposition, drawn from his analysis of human nature, is thus the essential foundation of Hobbes's political argument as a whole.

[4] M. M. Goldsmith, New Introduction to *Elements*, p. xxi; Bernard Gert, ed., Introduction to *Man and Citizen* (Garden City, N.Y.: Doubleday, 1972), p. 3. Cf. Oakeshott, *Hobbes on Civil Association*, pp. 14-15, 150-154.

This proposition, however, like those of his political argument generally, is drawn from a model of human behavior to which reality may approximate more or less closely. Hobbes was aware of the discrepancy between his model of behavior and reality in *The Elements of Law*, but he did not comment upon it directly. The one major source of discrepancy examined in that work was the misuse of language, which obscures men's reason and impairs their ability to foresee the way to the ends prescribed by nature. The opposition between reason, which guides men to their ends, and the rhetorical abuse of language, which obstructs their ability to pursue them, is the fundamental theme of this manuscript. But Hobbes appears neither to consider this opposition insuperable nor to be alarmed about the discrepancies between his model and the realities of human behavior.

In *Leviathan*, however, Hobbes appears far more troubled by these discrepancies than he had been in his earlier work. He had come to believe that their source was much more deeply ingrained in human nature than he had originally thought. This conviction led him to paint a new and more complicated portrait of man, one that emphasized over and over again the distance that separated his model of man (a rational egoist guided above all by fear of death) from the realities of human behavior. The outline of this portrait will be sketched in Chapter 4, below.

The new portrait of man led Hobbes to reconsider his original conception of the aims of his political philosophy. In his original manuscript, as we have seen, a tension can be detected between the two distinct aims of scientific demonstration and political persuasion. There are clear signs that Hobbes had both these aims in mind, but there are equally clear indications in the text that he did not feel capable of pursuing both equally, since scientific demonstration required "long deductions, and great attention," which are useless or even detrimental for the inculcation of opinions, the aim of a persuasive discourse. In choosing to frame his political doctrine essentially in the form of a logical demonstration, Hobbes was effectively subordinating the political aims of his work to its scientific aims. But there was nothing necessary about this choice, and it came to seem less and less satisfactory as Hobbes became increasingly troubled by the depth of the divergence between the prescriptions and premises of his theory, on the one hand, and the realities of human nature and politics, on the other. In the end he reversed the priorities evident in his original manuscript, and in *Leviathan* established the dominance of the political aims of his theory.

This reversal amounted to an acknowledgment that the problems confronting his political philosophy could be resolved only by changing reality itself. These problems, as Hobbes saw them, had less to do with any inadequacy of his own theoretical propositions than with the failure of reality to live up to his vision. Like the discrepancy between a perfect geometrical figure and the imperfect forms found in nature, that between Hobbes's theory and the imperfect realities of human nature and politics was not to be resolved by altering the theory. Theory, for Hobbes, was the measure of reality, not the reverse. The aim of political philosophy should be to change the world, not merely to explain it.

This conception of the nature and aims of political philosophy developed, as the above account has sought to suggest, out of seeds that were already present in the original version of Hobbes's political philosophy, *The Elements of Law*. But it was not yet fully formed when he composed that manuscript. Nor was it a product exclusively of what Raymond Polin has called the "internal maturation" of Hobbes's doctrine.[5] The conditions for its cultivation included the stimulation of political and social events as well as the time required for its gestation. Ul-

[5] Raymond Polin, *Politique et Philosophie chez Thomas Hobbes* (Paris: Presses Universitaires de France, 1953), p. 229ff.

timately, however, this conception of political philosophy shaped the argument of *Leviathan* decisively, manifesting itself equally in both the substance and the form of that work. The remainder of this chapter will begin to examine the course traversed in the transition from Hobbes's initial and more purely scientific conception of political philosophy to his later and more intensely political understanding of its aims.

The Problem of the Audience

The Elements of Law was written, the evidence suggests, with a very restricted audience in mind. In his letter of dedication Hobbes states plainly: "The ambition . . . of this book [is] . . . to insinuate itself with those whom the matter it containeth most nearly concerneth." The manuscript was aimed at people of some political importance, who were in positions that enabled them to make decisions about matters of "law and policy." In this respect the aim of this manuscript was very similar to that which Hobbes had envisaged for his translation of Thucydides' history some twelve years earlier. In the dedicatory epistle to that work, he had recommended Thucydides "for his writings, as having in them profitable instruction for noblemen, and such as may come to have the managing of great and weighty actions." Ordinary readers, who regarded history chiefly as a source of entertainment, were of no interest to him. Hobbes even went so far as to suggest that the true lessons of history, with their profound political implications, should be made inaccessible to such casual readers through the adoption of esoteric methods of writing: "for a wise man should so write, (though in words understood by all men), that wise men only should be able to commend him."[6] In *The Elements of Law*, he explicitly repudiated all such esoteric methods of writing by

[6] *Thucydides*, p. xxix.

adopting the Baconian dictum that the principles and reasoning of his science should be "evident even to the meanest capacity."[7] But his general conception of the audience for which his work was intended remained much the same as it had originally been. Both works were addressed to a political elite, and ordinary readers were of little or no interest to Hobbes.

This conception of the audience for political writing was traditional. Ever since the time of Plato the notion that political philosophy should be written essentially for use by a ruling elite, either actual or potential, had been extremely influential. It was very popular among Renaissance humanists, and was taken for granted in such extremely diverse works as Machiavelli's *The Prince*, Erasmus's *The Education of a Christian Prince*, Guillaume Budé's *De l'Institution du Prince*, and Sir Thomas Elyot's *The Boke Named the Gouvernor*. It also gave rise to a tradition of reflection on the problems of counseling rulers to which Sir Thomas More, Elyot, and Thomas Starkey all made important contributions in England during the sixteenth century. Within this tradition Hobbes's remarks upon esoteric writing were not the slightest bit idiosyncratic, for similar observations had been made by writers as diverse as Erasmus, Sir Philip Sidney, and even, in the seventeenth century, Francis Bacon himself.[8] Most political writers in the early sixteenth century, and many for a very long time afterward, thought of themselves primarily as educators and counselors of rulers or potential rulers. This self-image left a powerful mark upon the design of their writings. It remains very much in evidence both in Hobbes's translation of 1628 and in his manuscript of 1640.

[7] *Elements* I.13.3.

[8] Cf. Erasmus's letter of 1514 to Martin Dorp, in Desiderius Erasmus, *The Praise of Folly* (New Haven: Yale University Press, 1979), pp. 139-174; Sidney's *Defense*, p. 75, ll. 2-6; and Francis Bacon, *The Advancement of Learning* (Oxford: Clarendon Press, 1974), pp. 81-82. For a general account see Frances A. Yates, *Giordano Bruno and the Hermetic Tradition* (London: Routledge and Kegan Paul, 1964).

This self-image was conceived at a time when the dissemination of knowledge, in written form at least, was necessarily restricted to a very few people. Only a very few were literate in any case, and even those who were literate usually found it extremely difficult to obtain access to written works. These existed in manuscript form only, and were therefore both rare and extraordinarily expensive. But these circumstances began to change rapidly toward the end of the fifteenth century. The earliest beginnings of this change in England can be dated symbolically to the year 1476, when William Caxton brought the first printing press to Westminster. Even before this time the demand for reading matter had increased sharply, and the rate at which vernacular manuscripts were produced had been stepped up accordingly. The introduction of Caxton's press accelerated this development. A deliberate popularizer, Caxton divided his production between devotional works and romances, and did everything he could to encourage his market to grow. His efforts were extremely successful.[9] The volume of activity by English printers continued to expand rapidly throughout the sixteenth century and beyond. Forty-six titles were published in England during the year 1500. A century later this number had more than quintupled, to 259. By 1640 it had more than doubled again, to 577 entries.[10] Throughout this period the public appetite for printed works grew at a phenomenal pace, fundamentally transforming the conditions under which knowledge was disseminated.[11]

One of the factors that made this growth possible was a swift rise in the rate of literacy. There is no way to know what this

[9] Nellie S. Aurner, *Caxton: Mirrour of Fifteenth-Century Letters* (London: P. Allan, 1926), ch. 15.

[10] A. W. Pollard and G. R. Redgrave, eds., *A Short-Title Catalogue of Books Printed in England, Scotland, and Ireland and of English Books Printed Abroad, 1475-1640* (London: The Bibliographical Society, 1946).

[11] Cf. Elizabeth L. Eisenstein, *The Printing Press as an Agent of Change*, 2 vols. (Cambridge: Cambridge University Press, 1979).

rate was in the early sixteenth century. Contemporary estimates vary wildly.[12] A sustained expansion in the number of children attending schools, however, did get underway during the latter half of that century and continued until about the middle of the next. This expansion occurred in the philanthropically supported "petty" schools as well as the more elite grammar schools. These petty schools spread literacy beyond the reserve of the privileged, so that by the early seventeenth century basic literacy had become very common even among the poor. The education of women, while continuing to lag well behind that of men, was also becoming socially respectable, enhanced in part by the example of Elizabeth I. By the 1630's, perhaps as many as one-half of adult males, and one-third of all adults in England, could read. Together with a simultaneous wave of expansion in higher education, these developments probably made mid-seventeenth-century England the best-educated society the world had ever seen.[13]

One of the most novel and important inventions of this highly educated society was the newspaper. In the early sixteenth century the main source of written news was the broadside ballad (a form of commentary roughly equivalent to the modern political cartoon), which was printed and sold in large quantities. By the middle of that century handwritten newsletters, which reported events in a more detailed and factual manner, were becoming common. During the 1590's these began to give way to the *coranto*, a printed compendium of news from many places, usually covering a period of about a week.[14] In 1620 one of these newspapers, as they later came to be called, began appearing in London about twice a month, and within a

[12] See H. S. Bennett, *English Books and Readers: 1475 to 1557*, 2nd ed. (Cambridge: Cambridge University Press, 1969), p. 28.

[13] Lawrence Stone, "The Educational Revolution in England, 1560-1640," *Past and Present* 28 (1964), pp. 41-80.

[14] Matthias A. Schaaber, *Some Forerunners of the Newspaper in England, 1476-1622* (Philadelphia: University of Pennsylvania Press, 1929).

few years competitors had appeared and increased this frequency to once a week.[15] From this point onward the newspapers began to establish an increasingly firm role for themselves in English public life. The importance of this role is underscored by the actions of the crown, which banned them altogether in 1632 and allowed publication to resume six years later only under conditions of very strict censorship, as well as by the flood of newspapers that poured forth after the Long Parliament abolished all restrictions in late 1640. In the course of becoming highly educated, Englishmen had also developed an increasingly voracious appetite for news of and opinions about political affairs.

These developments created a new channel through which political writers could hope to communicate their ideas. Formerly such writers had to content themselves with a very limited audience, but printing technology and educational advances made it possible for them to begin composing for a much larger public. The first systematic attempt in England to make use of the printing press to shape public opinion occurred as early as the late 1530's, when Thomas Cromwell engineered an official campaign of political propaganda in support of King Henry VIII's break with Rome. Cromwell engaged prominent canon lawyers to compose treatises, extended protection to the anti-papal playwright John Bale, encouraged the rewriting of church history, and commissioned a series of political tracts—all designed to support Henry's decision to reject papal claims of authority over the English church and monarch.[16] None of the tracts and treatises generated by this campaign even approached the stature of a genuinely philosophical work. But in principle the channel of direct public appeal of which they had

[15] Joseph Frank, *The Beginnings of the English Newspaper, 1620-1660* (Cambridge, Mass.: Harvard University Press, 1961).

[16] Quentin Skinner, *The Foundations of Modern Political Thought*, vol. 2: *The Age of Reformation* (Cambridge: Cambridge University Press, 1978), pp. 93-108.

taken advantage was open to philosophers, too. They could choose to continue writing exclusively or primarily for a political elite, but another way was now open to them.

In 1628 Hobbes showed no interest whatsoever in this new route of direct public appeal. His translation is addressed exclusively—so he argues—to "the few and better sort of readers," and all others are deemed inconsiderable.[17] In his dedication of *The Elements of Law*, Hobbes continues to cling to this elitist conception of his audience, but there are also signs of change. Ultimately, he argues, the full benefit of his doctrine would be realized only "if *every man* held the opinions concerning law and policy here delivered."[18] His manuscript is not designed to shape public opinion directly. In fact the opposition between reason and rhetoric that runs throughout the work, along with the dilemma for his own political theory posed by this opposition, suggest that he regarded his own manuscript as diametrically opposed to any such design. But Hobbes did envisage an indirect channel through which his own political philosophy might be brought to bear upon public opinion. The universities, he argues, had in the past provided the "grounds and principles" out of which numerous false and seditious popular opinions had ultimately grown. If in the place of these old, corrupt doctrines his own, true political philosophy "were perspicuously set down, and taught in the Universities," Hobbes asserts, then

> there is no doubt . . . but that young men, who come thither void of prejudice, and whose minds are yet as white paper, capable of any instruction, would more easily receive the same, and afterward teach it to the people, both in books and otherwise, than now they do the contrary.[19]

[17] *Thucydides*, p. x.

[18] *Elements*, Epistle Dedicatory, emphasis added.

[19] *Elements* II.9.8.

Hobbes shows a great deal more interest in public opinion in *The Elements of Law* than he had shown in his earlier translation, in which he had summarily dismissed all but "the few and better sort of readers." While his treatise was addressed directly to a very restricted audience, he clearly entertained hopes of shaping public opinion indirectly by having his doctrines adopted in the universities and disseminated through the writing, teaching, and preaching of those influential intellectuals who had been taught there. Political philosophy could still be written for the few, but Hobbes now believed that its ultimate aim must be to shape public opinion at large, if only by educating the educators.

The Cultural Foundations of Political Power

Hobbes became increasingly impressed by the power of public opinion between this time and the late 1640's, when he was composing *Leviathan.* One sign of this change is a shift in his analysis of the causes of sedition or rebellion. In *The Elements of Law* he lists three major causes of sedition: discontent, pretense of right, and hope of success. Discontent was the first and most fundamental of these causes. It was, for him, a product of objective conditions, including deprivation, fear of want and bodily harm, and—more insidiously in his view—lack of power. Pretense of right, based upon subjective opinions, was an important but secondary cause. And Hobbes's account suggests strongly that he believed such opinions often to be no more than pretexts for, rather than genuine, underlying causes of sedition. He calls seditious opinions pretenses, and argues that they arise "when men have an opinion, *or pretend to have an opinion*: that in certain cases they may lawfully resist him or them that have the sovereign power. . . ."[20] This argument is strik-

[20] *Elements* II.8.1-4, emphasis added.

ingly reminiscent of the distinction he had drawn earlier between the pretexts and the genuine causes of the Peloponnesian War, and its general conclusion seems to be about the same. Pretexts are necessary for a war (or rebellion) to occur, but they are neither identical to nor as fundamental as the underlying causes of such an event.[21] The implication of this view is that objective conditions, rather than subjective opinions, are generally the more significant causes of sedition.

The account of these causes in *Leviathan* is very different. There the first item on Hobbes's list of "*things that Weaken, or tend to the* DISSOLUTION *of a Common-wealth*" is the willingness of some sovereigns to accept less power than is required by the absolute nature of the office of a sovereign. He traces the source of this weakness in England all the way back to William the Conqueror. Seditious opinions are again the second item on his list, but in causal importance Hobbes now appears to deem them primary. He calls seditious doctrines a form of "poyson," implying by this metaphor that they are of fundamental rather than superficial importance in making subjects disloyal.[22] In a later passage he develops a similar metaphor, calling such opinions a "subtile liquor," and arguing that it is by their effects rather than any previous discontent that certain subjects "were first seasoned, against the Civill Authority."[23] Objective conditions are now relegated to a distinctly secondary place in his account of the causes of rebellion, coming after those popular opinions that constitute "such Diseases of a Common-wealth, as are of the greatest, and most present danger."[24] Thus public opinion or ideology had replaced more objective conditions at the focus of Hobbes's account of the causes leading to civil war.

This same shift is also evident in his account of the duties or office of a sovereign. In *The Elements of Law* Hobbes argues that

[21] *Thucydides*, pp. xxvii-xxviii.

[22] *Leviathan*, ch. 29, p. 365 [168].

[23] *Leviathan*, ch. 30, p. 385 [180].

[24] *Leviathan*, ch. 29, p. 373 [173].

the duty of a sovereign is to promote both the eternal and the temporal good of his subjects.[25] Their eternal good is promoted by the establishment of such doctrines and rules as the sovereign deems conducive to salvation. Their temporal good consists of four things: multitude of population, commodity of living, internal peace, and external defense. After discussing the first two points, Hobbes goes on to consider the requirements of internal peace. Under this heading he discusses, first and at some length, ways of preventing the discontent that arises from oppression and, sometimes, from the excessive ambition of certain subjects. Only afterward and more briefly does he go on to consider ways of "rooting out from the consciences of men all those opinions which seem to justify, and give pretence of right to rebellious actions."[26] He regarded the shaping of favorable public opinion as an important duty of sovereigns, but it was near the bottom of his list of such duties, both in the order of his exposition and in order of importance.

In *Leviathan*, however, the shaping of favorable public opinion gets the lion's share of Hobbes's discussion of the office or duties of a sovereign. He begins by arguing that the first duty of a sovereign is to maintain the full rights of his office. But he then goes on to discuss, in elaborate detail and at considerable length, the need for "the grounds of these Rights, . . . to be diligently, and truly taught."[27] This discussion is clearly developed out of the paragraph devoted to this topic in *The Elements of Law*, but the fact that it is so much more lengthy and elaborate than that paragraph had been (coupled with its placement before rather than after his treatment of policies concerning taxation, public charity, laws, punishments, and other matters affecting the subjects' objective condition) testifies to the greatly increased importance Hobbes attached to public

[25] *Elements* II.9.

[26] *Elements* II.9.8.

[27] *Leviathan*, ch. 30, p. 377 [175].

opinion as a factor in the maintenance—or dissolution—of public power.

Hobbes's increased sensitivity to the importance of public opinion as an element of sovereign power is also manifested by his introduction of the concept of authorization, which was not included in earlier versions of his political philosophy, into the argument of *Leviathan*.[28] In *The Elements of Law* Hobbes had argued that two requirements must be met for men to conclude a covenant that will allow them to escape the state of nature. First, each man must agree to divest himself of the right to all things he has by nature. As we have seen, the exact extent of this divestiture is not completely clear in that work, but the basic principle is plain enough. Second, they must appoint some man or council to adjudicate in any disputes that may arise, and they must also agree, of course, to abide by the decisions in such cases. This man or council is called their sovereign. Hobbes recognized that the sovereign must have not only the right, but also the power, to enforce his decisions. Yet the theory worked out in his manuscript does not really explain how the sovereign can acquire this power. Power can be based upon right to the extent to which that right is recognized by others. But the sovereign depicted in Hobbes's manuscript acquires no new rights through the fact of his appointment. His subjects renounce or divest themselves of most of their rights, and so agree generally not to place obstructions in their sovereign's way. They do not actually give the sovereign any rights he did not have before. This formula for a covenant provides for a sovereign whose power is curiously negative in quality. It is difficult to convince oneself that this rather hollow conception of power is really adequate to do the work Hobbes's theory requires it to do.[29]

[28] The following paragraphs draw upon Gauthier's excellent work on this topic in *The Logic of Leviathan*.

[29] See Wolin, *Politics and Vision*, pp. 283-285, for one formulation of this criticism. Wolin applies it to *Leviathan* as well as Hobbes's earlier work.

The theory of authorization in *Leviathan* is an attempt to remedy this difficulty. Hobbes introduces the concept of authorization in chapter 16, immediately before his revised account of the creation of a commonwealth by covenant. Authorization is the act of appointing someone to bear one's person and be one's representative. It makes that representative into an "*Artificial person*" entitled to act on behalf of those by whom he has been authorized. The most important thing about this concept for Hobbes is that authorization involves an actual transfer of right from one person to another, not merely a renunciation of right. It enables the representative created by it to act with the right, or authority, of all those persons who have created that representative.

Authorization is essential to the revised account of the covenant Hobbes gives in chapter 17 of *Leviathan.* In that covenant, in effect, every man says to every other man: "*I Authorise and give up my Right of Governing my selfe, to this Man, or to this Assembly of men, on this condition, that thou give up thy Right to him, and Authorise all his Actions in like manner*."[30] According to this revised account, then, the sovereign has new rights that he did not have before he was made a sovereign by the authorization of his subjects. It is true that his right of nature was already unlimited in scope before he was authorized to be a sovereign and that he continues to enjoy this unlimited natural right afterward. But it is the right of one person only. After his authorization a sovereign adds all of the rights his subjects have transferred to him to that natural right he already possessed. He acts upon the authority, and with the combined rights, of all his subjects.

The adequacy of this theoretical maneuver is a matter of some controversy, but for the present purpose it is less important to weigh in on this question than to notice the direction in

[30] *Leviathan*, ch. 17, p. 227 [87].

which Hobbes was attempting to move.[31] Hobbes's increased sensitivity to the importance of public opinion as an element of sovereign power had led him to be more concerned than ever before that the rights of sovereignty should be recognized, in a widespread and public manner, as legitimate. The concept of authorization helped meet this concern. By depicting sovereignty as the product of a positive act of authorization founded upon the united strength of all subjects, rather than an essentially negative act of renunciation, it implicated those subjects in the acts of their sovereign more fully than the earlier versions of his theory had done. As David Gauthier puts it, "Every man is thus evidently involved in society in a positive manner, for the acts of the sovereign may be considered his own acts."[32] Subjects who have authorized a sovereign as their own representative will be much less likely to regard his actions as those of an alien, and thus illegitimate, power than those who have simply agreed with one another to renounce their natural rights, allowing their sovereign to take up the effective exercise of those rights by default.

Hobbes did not always pursue the implications of this innovation in his political theory as thoroughly as he might have done. His failure to do so sometimes gives rise to ambiguities. One example occurs in his theory of punishment. Hobbes's basic explanation of the right to punish involves no departure from the assumptions of his initial political theory in *The Elements of Law*. The sovereign's right to punish is founded upon his natural right to all things rather than upon any new rights he acquires as a sovereign.[33] Hobbes insisted upon this explanation because he wanted to avoid the suggestion that subjects authorize their own punishment. He apparently considered this

[31] Contrast Hanna F. Pitkin's account in *The Concept of Representation* (Berkeley: University of California Press, 1967), ch. 2, with that of Gauthier in *The Logic of Leviathan*.

[32] *The Logic of Leviathan*, p. 127.

[33] *Leviathan*, ch. 28, pp. 353-354 [161-162].

suggestion inconsistent with his basic premise that the cause and basis of a commonwealth is the legitimate desire of its members to avoid death and all physical harm.[34] For this reason Hobbes refused to make use of his new concept of authorization in his basic theory of punishment.

Even so, Hobbes's heightened concern about the need for widespread and public recognition of the legitimacy of sovereign rights left a significant impression upon his elaboration of this theory. After asserting his basic explanation of the right to punish, he goes on to argue that "the evill inflicted by publique Authority, without precedent publique condemnation, is not to be stiled by the name of Punishment; but of an hostile act."[35] This distinction between punishments and hostilities would have been unintelligible within the framework of Hobbes's initial political theory. No subject could be expected to think of punishments as anything other than intrusions upon his natural right to preserve himself from harm. But in *Leviathan* this distinction is absolutely crucial. In fact, the need to make this distinction clear to all subjects is the reason he cites for saddling the sovereign with such burdensome instructional responsibilities. The people must be "diligently, and truly taught" the grounds of sovereign authority because without that knowledge

> they cannot know the Right of any Law the Soveraign maketh. And for the Punishment, they take it but for an act of Hostility; which when they think they have

[34] Gauthier has correctly observed that Hobbes might easily have reconciled his view of punishment with his theory of authorization by arguing that the right to punish derives from each man's authorization of the sovereign to punish every other man. No man authorizes his own punishment, so consistency with Hobbes's basic premise is maintained; yet the sovereign's right to punish is derived by a grant from his subjects, so the theory remains consistent with his new concept of authorization as well. See *The Logic of Leviathan*, pp. 146-149.

[35] *Leviathan*, ch. 28, p. 354 [162].

> strength enough, they will endeavour by acts of Hostility, to avoyd.[36]

Perhaps as clearly as any others, these passages in *Leviathan* are indicative of the increased importance Hobbes now attached to the ideological or cultural foundations of political power. No sovereign could maintain the power and rights of his office without achieving general recognition of the grounds, legitimacy, and proper scope of those rights. This recognition is in effect the product of an interpretation men impose upon their circumstances, a set of lenses through which they read and understand their relationships with others. Hobbes had already recognized the importance of such recognition in *The Elements of Law*, but in *Leviathan* he demonstrates a much keener awareness of the difficulties involved in procuring this awareness, and of the consequences of failing to do so, than he had ever done before.

Philosophy as a Speaking Picture

By the late 1640's, then, Hobbes had come a very long way indeed from the curtly dismissive stance he had adopted toward the opinions of ordinary people in his first political writing of 1628. For he now regarded these opinions as a vital constituent element of sovereign power in two distinct senses. In the first place, opinions are a crucial determinant of the extent to which men will act rationally to preserve their own lives. If they stray far enough from the pathway of sound ratiocination or "right reason," they are capable of destroying the rational foresight upon which self-preservation depends, and might even destroy the desire for self-preservation itself. But the ultimate basis of a sovereign's power, for Hobbes, lies in his coercive control over the lives of his subjects. If those subjects were to cease acting

[36] *Leviathan*, ch. 30, p. 377 [176].

rationally to avoid death, then this foundation of sovereign power would collapse. Yet in the second place, while Hobbes regarded fear of death as a necessary foundation for sovereign power, he did not consider it a sufficient foundation. For an understanding of the grounds of sovereign rights, he points out, "cannot be maintained by any Civill Law, or terrour of legal punishment."[37] A commonwealth cannot be based solely upon the prudential calculations of self-interested men, for such men would be likely to perceive their sovereign as nothing more than an alien power to be feared, and would have no reservations about rebelling against him at the first reasonable opportunity. Misguided popular opinions are capable of destroying the foundations of a commonwealth in either of two ways: by preventing its subjects from extending to their sovereign genuine recognition of the legitimacy and scope of his rights; or, even more radically, by undermining their fear of death, or their ability to act upon that fear rationally. In *Leviathan* Hobbes was just as inclined as he had ever been to regard popular opinions with disdain. But he could not dismiss their importance, nor that of those who held them, since the opinions of ordinary people were now, in his estimation, a vital element of sovereign power.

For Hobbes this increasingly keen awareness of the dependence of sovereign power upon popular opinions was no cause for celebration. Popular opinions are volatile and, as he had already noted in *The Elements of Law*, extremely susceptible to the manipulations of clever orators.[38] In emphasizing their importance more strongly than ever before, Hobbes was acknowledging what he took to be an unwelcome fact. In *De Cive* (in a new preface composed about the beginning of 1646 and added to the second edition) he reflects upon the importance of this fact and upon the problems it poses for political philosophy. "[T]he

[37] *Leviathan*, ch. 30, p. 377 [175].

[38] *Elements* II.8.12, 14

most antient *Sages*," he argues, judged it prudent to record their doctrine of moral and political philosophy in writing "either curiously adorned with Verse, or clouded with Allegories, as a most beautifull and hallowed mystery of Royall authority; lest by the disputations of private men, it might be defiled." Long before the time of Socrates, political philosophers had the wisdom to withhold all knowledge of their science from ordinary subjects, choosing rather "to have the Science of Justice wrapt up in fables, [than] openly exposed to disputations." The result of this jealous guarding of the secrets of political philosophy was salutary:

> for before such questions began to be moved, Princes did not sue for, but already exercised the supreme power. They kept their Empire entire, not by arguments, but by punishing the wicked, and protecting the good; likewise Subjects did not measure what was just by the sayings and judgements of private men, but by the Lawes of the Realme; nor were they kept in peace by disputations, but by power and authority: yea they reverenced the supreme power, whether residing in one man or in a councell, as a certain visible divinity; . . . Wherefore it was peace, and a golden age, which ended not before that *Saturn* being expelled, it was taught lawfull to take up arms against Kings.[39]

This argument, like his much earlier comments upon esoteric methods of writing, reflects the influence of those cabalistic and Hermetic philosophies which had been so popular among intellectuals during the sixteenth century, and which were very far from being moribund in the seventeenth. Unlike some adherents to these ways of thinking, however, Hobbes did not think the days of these ancient sages could be recaptured. The popular dissemination of political philosophy was like the opening of Pandora's box: once the act was accomplished it

[39] *De Cive*, Preface 2, 6.

could never be reversed. The consequences of this act were catastrophic, both for political philosophy and for the cause of peace:

> And now at length all men of all Nations, not only Philosophers, but even the vulgar, have, and doe still deale with this as a matter of ease, exposed and prostitute to every Mother-wit, and to be attained without any great care or study. . . . they have begotten those hermaphrodite opinions of morall Philosophers, partly right and comely, partly brutall and wilde, the causes of all contentions, and blood-sheds.[40]

These observations are a lamentation for the present condition of mankind, and they have the ring of an elegy for ancient times as well. But Hobbes's conclusion was a forward-looking one. The crucial difference between Hobbes and genuine believers in the Hermetic tradition was that he did not truly believe, as they had, that the ancients had discovered the secrets of the universe or the truths of political philosophy. These truths were his own discovery. Far from wishing to lock them up in fables, he insisted that they would have to be demonstrated publicly and disseminated widely to achieve their desired effect. As he had already argued in *The Elements of Law*, the full benefits of a true political philosophy could not be realized unless *every man* could be brought to hold the opinions to which it points.

Neither *The Elements of Law* nor *De Cive*, the first two versions of Hobbes's political philosophy, was as well-designed as it might have been to achieve this end. The former was still an unpublished manuscript, and its logical form of demonstration was ill-designed to win the assent of any but the most attentive and patient readers. The latter was written in the learned language of Latin, and although it secured a fine reputation for Hobbes among scholars on the continent, it could hardly be expected to shape the political opinions of ordinary men and

[40] *De Cive*, Preface 3, 7.

women. Either of these works might have shaped popular opinion indirectly by being adopted as part of the university curriculum, as he had already suggested should be done in *The Elements of Law.* But this route to popular influence must have seemed highly improbable, since it hinged entirely upon the willingness of a sovereign to force the teaching of Hobbes's doctrine onto independent-minded university faculties.

In *Leviathan* Hobbes repeats, at several points and in increasingly blunt terms, the suggestion that his doctrine should be taught in the universities. At one point he goes so far as to say that "[i]t is therefore manifest, that the Instruction of the people, dependeth wholly, on the right teaching of Youth in the Universities."[41] There was a sense in which he continued to believe in the truth of this statement. Yet he was no longer willing to pin his hopes entirely upon the possibility that his doctrine might be adopted for such teaching. This route left too much to chance. Hobbes ruminates upon the probabilities in the closing sentence of part II:

> I recover some hope, that one time or other, this writing of mine, may fall into the hands of a Soveraign, who will consider it himselfe, (for it is short, and I think clear,) without the help of any interested, or envious Interpreter; and by the exercise of entire Soveraignty, in protecting the Publique teaching of it, convert this Truth of Speculation, into the Utility of Practice.[42]

Hobbes would have been delighted if a sovereign had adopted his doctrine wholeheartedly and prescribed his books for the instruction of young students. But to him, the dissemination of his true political philosophy was too important a matter to be left to chance.

[41] *Leviathan*, ch. 30, p. 384 [180]; cf. Review and Conclusion, p. 728 [395].

[42] *Leviathan*, ch. 31, p. 408 [194].

The aims of *Leviathan* were different, at least in regard to the audience to whom the work is addressed, from those of any previous version of Hobbes's political philosophy. The net he casts is meant to extend beyond "noblemen, and such as may come to have the managing of great and weighty actions"; it is intended, too, to capture more than intellectuals familiar with Latin, and to bring in many more fish than are contained in the halls of the universities. It is noteworthy that the "white paper" metaphor Hobbes had used to describe the minds of university students in *The Elements of Law* is applied in *Leviathan* to ordinary people instead:

> the Common-peoples minds, unlesse they be tainted with dependance on the Potent, or scribbled over with the opinions of their Doctors, are like clean paper, fit to receive whatsoever by Publique Authority shall be imprinted in them.[43]

There are times, however, when public authorities do not prescribe the doctrines that are to be imprinted in the minds of ordinary people, or at least allow a variety of doctrines to compete for their attention. *Leviathan* was published at such a time. It was intended to be read not by this or that special audience, but by the public at large, or at least by as large a segment of that public as could be persuaded to read any work of political philosophy. It was offered, as Hobbes puts it, "to the consideration of those that are yet in deliberation," whomever and however ordinary they may be.[44] It was a book of philosophy, but it was intended for a large, public audience and aimed to shape popular opinion directly, rather than through intermediaries alone as *The Elements of Law* and *De Cive* had been meant. It was perhaps the first work in the history of political philosophy to be designed entirely with this aim in mind.

[43] *Leviathan*, ch. 30, p. 379 [176]; cf. above, p. 76.

[44] *Leviathan*, Review and Conclusion, p. 726 [394].

The differences of literary form that distinguish *Leviathan* from the previous versions of Hobbes's political philosophy must be approached with this difference of aims in mind. For in that work it was less important to demonstrate the truth of his political doctrines than to drive those doctrines into the minds of his readers, to express them in language that would leave a deep and lasting impression upon them. A passage from a short essay Hobbes composed at about the time *Leviathan* was completed can be read as an emblem of his aims for the book:

> But so farre forth as the Fancy of man, has traced the wayes of true Philosophy, so farre it hath produced very marvellous effects to the benefit of mankind. . . . whatsoever distinguisheth the civility of *Europe*, from the Barbarity of the *American* sauvages, is the workemanship of Fancy, but guided by the Precepts of true Philosophy. But where these precepts fayle, as they have hetherto fayled in the doctrine of Morall vertue, there the Architect (*Fancy*) must take the Philosophers part upon herselfe. He therefore that undertakes an Heroique Poeme . . . must not onely be the Poet, to place and connect, but also the Philosopher, to furnish and square his matter, that is, to make both body and soule, coulor and shaddow of his Poeme out of his owne store. . . .[45]

In arguing that the "doctrine of Morall vertue" has failed, Hobbes clearly does not mean that philosophers have failed to *discover* the truths of moral philosophy, since he believed that he had discovered these truths himself. What he does mean is that they—including himself—have failed to *communicate* those truths adequately, that they have failed to imprint them in the minds of those people who must be taught to act in accordance with the dictates of moral virtue. His statement is an indictment of the limitations of his own previous efforts of political

[45] *Answer*, pp. 49-50.

philosophy. And with only a little imagination the places of philosopher and poet in his final observation can be reversed to produce the suggestion that he who undertakes to be an heroic political philosopher should also take upon himself, in some measure, the part of the poet.

From a literary point of view, then, *Leviathan* can be seen as the closing point of a circle that begins with a contrast between the power of the visual image and the powerlessness of the merely conceptual proposition for creating mental impressions, moves through the "dry discourse" of strict philosophical demonstration, and returns once again to the "speaking picture" of poetry—now, to be sure, in the service of philosophy rather than history, and of communication to a large audience rather than an elite one. In this sense there is no real irony or paradox to be discovered in the intensely vivid and figurative language of this book.[46] It is true that Hobbes condemns metaphors, ambiguous words, and other figures of speech as obstacles to strict ratiocination and the discovery of scientific truth—often invoking a metaphor himself to do so.[47] But if the aim of *Leviathan* is less to demonstrate the truth of his political doctrines than to imprint them upon the minds of his readers, then metaphors, along with many other literary devices that have no place in a strict scientific demonstration, are entirely in place. *Leviathan* was designed less as a scientific treatise than as a work of rhetoric. If in the original version of his political philosophy Hobbes had allowed his scientific aims to predominate over his political intentions, in *Leviathan* this order of predominance or priority was reversed. In writing this work Hobbes was, above all else, performing a political act, not a scientific one. My remaining chapters will attempt to complete an explanation of the reasoning and ruminations that led him to do so.

[46] Frederick G. Whelan, "Language and Its Abuses in Hobbes' Political Philosophy," *American Political Science Review* 75 (1981), pp. 59-75.

[47] *Leviathan*, ch. 4, p. 105 [15]; ch. 5, pp. 116-117 [22].

CHAPTER FOUR ✡

The Portrait of Man

REASON VERSUS SUPERSTITION

THE ESSENTIAL foundation of Hobbes's political argument is the proposition that fear of death, guided by rational knowledge of its causes, is so powerful a motive that it is capable of causing men to curb their natural appetites, vanity, and other passions sufficiently to ensure their obedience to the laws and commands of a common sovereign. The behavior of subjects who act rationally to avoid death is thus the ultimate basis of sovereign power, and hence also of the commonwealth itself. This proposition is as important to the theory developed in *Leviathan* as it had been to the earlier version of his political philosophy adumbrated in *The Elements of Law.* In *Leviathan* Hobbes does emphasize more strongly than he had in his earlier works that the coercion made possible by fear of death is not a sufficient foundation of sovereign power, arguing that it must be supplemented by popular recognition of the grounds and rights of sovereignty. But he also repeats as emphatically as ever his argument that coercive power over life and death is the necessary root of all the powers of any sovereign, who must ultimately rely upon "feare of punishment" to tie his subjects to "the performance of their Covenants."[1] The power of a sovereign rests upon his subjects' fear of punishment, especially the ultimate punishment of death, as well as their ability to act upon that fear in a rational way.

Hobbes's claim that fear of death is a sufficiently widespread and powerful motive to form the basis of sovereign power is based, in *Leviathan* as in the earlier *Elements of Law*, upon two rigorous theoretical propositions. The first is that men are by nature egoistic beings, whose actions are all designed to procure good and avoid evil to themselves.[2] The second is that death is the greatest of all evils. These propositions were not mere statements of fact based upon empirical observation. They were universal statements, theoretical postulates that could not be disproved by the mere citation of one or more counter-examples. As such these propositions could not be expected to mirror the

[1] *Leviathan*, ch. 17, p. 223 [85]; cf. ch. 15, p. 202 [71-72], and ch. 17, pp. 227-228 [87-88].

[2] In *The Anatomy of Leviathan* (pp. 115-121) McNeilly argues that in *Leviathan* Hobbes moved away from the egoistic view of human nature he had held earlier. McNeilly argues that pleasure no longer plays any part in Hobbes's analysis of desire in *Leviathan*, as it had before; that egoistic assumptions are no longer embodied in his definitions of such passions as pity and charity; and that his account of the terms "good" and "evil" is relativistic, but not egoistic, in *Leviathan*, unlike the egoistic account given in *The Elements of Law*. Yet McNeilly himself later admits that "[t]here are passages in *Leviathan* in which an egoistic view is quite clearly expressed" (p. 127). These passages are in fact as common and as strongly worded as any in Hobbes's earlier work. Thus Hobbes says that "of the voluntary acts of every man, the object is some *Good to himselfe*"; "all the voluntary actions of men tend to the benefit of themselves"; and "the proper object of every mans Will, is some Good to himselfe" (*Leviathan*, ch. 14, pp. 192 [66], 204 [72]; ch. 25, p. 303 [132]). For some additional arguments on this issue, cf. Gert, Introduction to *Man and Citizen*; David D. Raphael, *Hobbes* (London: Allen and Unwin, 1977), p. 54; John Kemp, "Hobbes on Pity and Charity," in J. G. van der Bend, ed., *Thomas Hobbes: His View of Man* (Amsterdam: Rodopi, 1982), pp. 57-62.

behavior of actual human beings perfectly. The model of human behavior out of which Hobbes constructs his political argument as a whole did not coincide in every detail with the realities of actual behavior, nor did he have any reason to be dismayed at its failure to do so. Some discrepancies between the realities of behavior and the stipulations of Hobbes's model were probably inevitable. Given his idea of science, Hobbes had no reason to regard such discrepancies as blemishes upon the truth of his theory, and as long as they remained relatively small they posed no obstacle to its usefulness, either.

The Artificiality of Reason

There were two ways in which the behavior of actual human beings might diverge from the stipulations of Hobbes's model. First, some people might simply fail to regard death as the greatest of all evils. As we have seen, Hobbes admitted in *The Elements of Law* that there are at least two motives—the desire to escape humiliation, and fear of eternal damnation—that can under some circumstances induce men to accept death voluntarily. These admissions, however, were isolated observations, which played no role in his political argument as a whole. The possibility that men *in general* might *not* fear death as the greatest of evils is neither raised explicitly nor hinted at in this work. Presumably Hobbes did not regard it as a sufficiently likely possibility to merit serious discussion. Second, even people who do regard death as the greatest of all evils might fail to act with sufficient foresight and rationality to avoid it. Hobbes was extremely concerned about this kind of failure in *The Elements of Law.* Its central cause, as elaborated there, is abuse of language, which clouds men's thinking and causes them to misreckon in extraordinary and even, at times, absurd ways. The political consequences of this failure were extremely disturbing to Hobbes, who regarded the capacity of subjects to respond predictably to threats of punishment, and especially to the threat of death, as the ultimate basis of sovereign power and civil order. The opposition between reason and rhetoric, which forms the central theme of that work, is an expression of his deep concern about the ways in which abuse of language can destroy the ability of human beings to act with the degree of foresight and rationality they must have for a commonwealth to sustain itself.

Yet there is also, as we have seen, an optimistic note in Hobbes's account of this problem. For in *The Elements of Law* he regarded reason as an integral and universal attribute of human nature: "Reason is no less of the nature of man than passion, *and is the same in all men*."[3] This optimistic note is completely absent from Hobbes's argument in *Leviathan*.

The conception of reason in *Leviathan* is unchanged from what it had been in his earlier works: "REASON, in this sense, is nothing but *Reckoning* (that is, Adding and Substracting) of the Consequences of generall names agreed upon, for the *marking* and *signifying* of our thoughts."[4] As before, Hobbes defines reason as a faculty of computation or calculation, in sharp contrast with the Platonic conception of reason as a transcendent faculty that allows men to see into the nature of things. But Hobbes no longer argues that reason is a natural attribute shared by all men. Instead he argues that reason, far from being a natural gift, is in fact an acquired skill. Ordinary prudence, the intellectual capacity shared by humans and animals alike, is natural insofar as it requires "no other thing, to the exercise of it, but to be born a man, and live with the use of his five Senses." But reason, like all of the other intellectual faculties, must be "acquired, and encreased by study and industry."[5]

Hobbes places considerable emphasis upon the acquired character of reason in *Leviathan*. When he opens his discussion

[3] *Elements* I.15.1, emphasis added.

[4] *Leviathan*, ch. 5, p. 111 [18].

[5] *Leviathan*, ch. 3, p. 98 [11].

of speech, the basis of reason, he does not plunge into an atemporal analysis of the types and functions of names, as he had done in *The Elements of Law*. Instead, his account begins historically and stresses the artificial character of speech, which he calls "the most noble and profitable invention of all other."[6] He shows an interest in the historical origins of speech and discusses the Biblical story of the Tower of Babel, the one incident in history in which men lost the ability to speak to one another. He introduces his concept of science, which is built by reason, with the same emphasis:

> Reason is not as Sense, and Memory, borne with us; nor gotten by Experience onely; as Prudence is; but attayned by Industry; first in apt imposing of Names; and secondly by getting a good and orderly Method . . . till we come to a knowledge of all the Consequences of names appertaining to the subject in hand; and that is it, men call SCIENCE.[7]

Hobbes had distinguished science from prudence in *The Elements of Law*. His distinction there, however, had been based purely upon the different epistemological capacities of these two faculties. His argument that reason is an acquired skill by contrast with prudence, which is natural, sharpens and adds a new dimension to this distinction.

It is possible that Hobbes had already thought of reason as an acquired skill in 1640, when he wrote *The Elements of Law*. To say that his emphasis upon the acquired or artificial character of reason is new in *Leviathan* is not to assume that he had not. The important point is that Hobbes did not consider the acquired or artificial character of reason to be a feature of sufficient significance to his political theory to merit notice in *The Elements of Law*. Yet in *Leviathan* the acquired character of reason is

[6] *Leviathan*, ch. 4, p. 100 [12].

[7] *Leviathan*, ch. 5, p. 115 [21].

given special emphasis.[8] Something had occurred to suggest to Hobbes that the acquired character of reason was a feature of enough importance to his political theory to deserve a good deal of emphasis.

There is no way to know with certainty what had caused this change in Hobbes's outlook. It is plausible to speculate that the political turmoil of the early 1640's, the civil war, and the chaotic period of parliamentary rule that followed the King's defeat had led him to re-examine his earlier and rather complacent views on human reason. It may well be that he was simply incapable of interpreting some of the actions taken during that period as rational actions in any sense.

Whether these events were responsible for Hobbes's re-examination of his views on reason or not is of no great consequence for an understanding of his theory. What is of consequence is to recognize the effect his new view had upon the basis of his political theory. That effect was clearly subversive. While Hobbes had considered rhetoric to be a great obstacle to the perfection of reason in *The Elements of Law*, he still believed that reason was a natural capacity and that rationality was a natural state of mind. Rhetoric distorts men's reason. To eliminate this distortion one simply has to eliminate the misuse of language that causes it. Natural reason will then assert itself. This line of thinking was no longer possible in *Leviathan.* Reason, in *Leviathan*, is not natural; it is acquired and artificial. Hobbes takes some care to point out the causes that determine whether men will acquire it or not, and in doing so points toward a systematic distinction between those who have cultivated their reason

[8] It might be objected that Hobbes frequently uses the phrase "natural reason" in *Leviathan.* But these instances present no difficulty for the present argument. On the occasions when he uses this phrase, Hobbes is generally opposing "natural" to "supernatural," rather than to "artificial" or "acquired." Thus he argues that men may learn a good deal "from revelation supernaturall: which revelation a man may indeed have of many things above, but of nothing against naturall reason." *Leviathan*, ch. 12, p. 180 [58].

and those who have not.[9] The subversive effect upon his political theory arises from the implication that many people in fact have very little capacity to reason. The notion that some people are incapable of reasoning constituted a challenge to one of the essential premises of Hobbes's political argument. For such men will be incapable of pursuing their own self-interest in a rational manner, as Hobbes's political theory requires them to do. A new skepticism about men's abilities to perceive and pursue their own interests in a rational manner pervades *Leviathan*, as his wry comment that "[k]nowledge of what is good for their conservation . . . is more than man has"[10] suggests.

Fear of Death?

If the argument of *Leviathan* betrays a new skepticism about the ability of men to shape their actions in accordance with the dictates of reason, it also reveals a shift in Hobbes's treatment of the postulate that fear of death is a motive of such overwhelming power that it can be relied upon to subdue men's other passions and lead them to accept the yoke of political authority. This postulate is just as vital to Hobbes's theory in *Leviathan* as it had been before. He sums up its importance pithily in his statement that "[t]he Passion to be reckoned upon, is Fear."[11] Fear, and particularly fear of death, is the motive Hobbes believes must be relied upon to induce men to accept political authority. It is also the ultimate source of a sovereign's control over the behavior of his subjects, since it enables him to threaten them effectively with the ultimate punishment at his disposal, namely death.

Yet Hobbes's discussion of fear and its relation to his political argument is far more complicated in *Leviathan* than it had

[9] *Leviathan*, ch. 8, esp. pp. 134-135 [32-33], 138-139 [35].

[10] *Leviathan*, ch. 2, p. 87 [4].

[11] *Leviathan*, ch. 14, p. 200 [70].

been in the earlier versions of his theory. Hobbes does talk a great deal about fear of death. But much of what he has to say is about other fears. In particular, he devotes a great deal of attention to fear of spirits and of "things invisible." This fear is barely mentioned in *The Elements of Law*. Its importance to the theory of *Leviathan* is so fundamental that it cannot easily be overstated.

Hobbes makes it clear that he believes fear of spirits to be founded upon nothing greater than plain ignorance and superstition. Thus he argues that

> even they that be perfectly awake, if they be timorous, and supperstitious, possessed with fearfull tales, and alone in the dark, are subject to the like fancies, and believe they see spirits and dead mens Ghosts walking in Churchyards; whereas it is either their Fancy onely, or els the knavery of such persons, as make use of such superstitious feare, to passe disguised in the night, to places they would not be known to haunt.

The basis of "the opinion that rude people have of Fayries, Ghosts, and Goblins; and of the power of Witches" is "ignorance of how to distinguish Dreams, and other strong Fancies, from Vision and Sense." All of these spirits are in reality the fantastic products of men's vivid, uncontrolled imaginations. The basis of "this superstitious fear of Spirits" is entirely imaginary.[12]

Yet the fact that the basis of this fear is imaginary does not diminish the fear itself. The reality and power of this fear are manifest in the social institutions that have arisen out of it. It formed the foundation of "the greatest part of the Religion of the Gentiles in time past" and is "the naturall Seed of that, which every one in himself calleth Religion; and in them that worship, or feare that Power otherwise than they do, Supersti-

[12] *Leviathan*, ch. 2, pp. 92-93 [7].

tion."[13] Hobbes also notes that ancient political leaders took advantage of this kind of fear to maintain control over the actions of their subjects.[14] Though the basis of men's fear of spirits is imaginary, the effects of that fear are very real and palpable.

Indeed, these effects are so powerful that Hobbes places them on an equal footing with those which flow from fear of death. He hints at their significance in the continuation of the passage in which he summarizes the importance of fear to his political theory: "The Passion to be reckoned upon, is Fear; whereof there be two very generall Objects: one, The Power of Spirits Invisible; the other, The Power of those men they shall therein Offend."[15] Hobbes continues this passage by saying that "commonly" fear of other men is greater than fear of spirits. But he is keenly aware that the reverse can also be true. There are times when "fear of Darknesse, and Ghosts, is greater than other fears."[16]

Hobbes considered fear of death perfectly rational. This assumption lies at the foundation of his political theory. The desire to avoid death and quell this fear is what causes men to subject themselves to political authority. The reasonableness or legitimacy of this desire is the basis of his view that all men retain the core of their right of nature to preserve themselves even after they become members of a commonwealth. Hobbes considers the desire to avoid death to be so reasonable that he regards it as a justifiable excuse for a subject to refuse his sovereign's command to engage in combat.[17] He also argues that fear of death is a sufficient ground to excuse any man completely from breaking the law: "If a man by the terrour of present death, be compelled to doe a fact against the Law, he is totally

[13] *Leviathan*, ch. 11, p. 168 [51].

[14] *Leviathan*, ch. 12, pp. 177-178 [57].

[15] *Leviathan*, ch. 14, p. 200 [70].

[16] *Leviathan*, ch. 29, p. 371 [172].

[17] *Leviathan*, ch. 21, pp. 269-270 [112].

Excused; because no Law can oblige a man to abandon his own preservation."[18] Fear of death is more than a merely reasonable or admissible ground of argument within Hobbes's political theory. It is the basis of his justification of the scope of sovereign authority and of his view of the irreducible liberty of subjects.

By contrast, fear of spirits is a product of ignorance and superstition. It might therefore be called an essentially irrational fear. The systematic opposition between fear of death and fear of spirits that runs through the entire political theory of *Leviathan* is likewise an opposition between subjects who are rational and those who are irrational. Rational subjects will be amenable to Hobbes's design for a commonwealth based upon fear of corporal punishments, especially death. Irrational subjects will not.

Superstition and Magic

Part I of *Leviathan*, "Of Man," is a short treatise on human nature or psychology. Hobbes claims to have shown "the similitude of the thoughts, and Passions of one man, to the thoughts, and Passions of another."[19] To do so he touches upon the nature of sense, imagination, speech, reason, science, and the intellectual virtues in general as well as that of the will and the most fundamental human passions. But this account of human nature is essentially different from the one he had given in *The Elements of Law.* For throughout it runs a central theme that had hardly made an appearance in that earlier work. This is the contrast between ignorance, superstition, and magic on the one hand and knowledge, reason, and science on the other.

Chapters 1 and 2 of *Leviathan* are ostensibly an exposition on

[18] *Leviathan*, ch. 27, p. 345 [157].

[19] *Leviathan*, Introduction, p. 82 [2].

sense and imagination, which Hobbes defines as "*decaying sense*."[20] Yet at their outset he says that this subject is "not very necessary to the business now in hand."[21] His real purpose is not so much to expose the nature of sense, but to explore the illusions to which sense perception can give rise. Much of the space in these short chapters is devoted to a discussion of dreams, visions, and all those products of the imagination which tend to deceive men, compound their ignorance of things, and lead them into superstition. Chapters 4 and 5 deal with speech, reason, and science. Chapter 4 gives as much attention to the abuses of speech as it does to its uses. The first paragraph ends with a jibe against the "insignificant words of the School."[22] A few paragraphs later, Hobbes issues a lengthy warning about the absurd consequences that can flow from speech when the rules of its proper use are not carefully observed. The last several paragraphs deliver yet another thrust against the scholastic philosophers, one of Hobbes's favorite objects of ridicule, for substituting "insignificant sounds" in place of meaningful speech.[23] Chapter 5, on reason and science, continues this pattern. It exhibits as much interest in error, absurdity, and the derangement of reason as it does in reason itself.

This same pattern recurs in chapter 8, "*Of the* VERTUES *commonly called* INTELLECTUAL; *and their contrary* DEFECTS." The first few pages of the chapter deal with the differences between natural and acquired "Wit" and discuss the causes that lead some men to be so much more adept at reasoning than others. This discussion is only a preliminary, however, to a discourse on madness, which occupies the bulk of the chapter. Throughout the first chapters of *Leviathan* on human nature, Hobbes is fascinated—almost obsessed—with all of the ways in which hu-

[20] *Leviathan*, ch. 2, p. 88 [5].

[21] *Leviathan*, ch. 1, p. 85 [3].

[22] *Leviathan*, ch. 4, p. 101 [12].

[23] *Leviathan*, ch. 4, p. 108 [16].

man imagination, speech, and reason can go wrong. The misdirection of these human faculties results in ignorance, superstition, and belief in magic.

Hobbes's treatment of the failures of imagination and reason is not the mere by-product of a dispassionate examination of human nature. It is evidence of his deep concern for the political consequences of ignorance, superstition, and magic. Superstition and magic constitute an entire world of thought for Hobbes, one that contrasts in a sharp and dismaying way with the rational world of knowledge and science. Every natural phenomenon, he now saw, can be seen from either of two essentially different perspectives. It can be looked at scientifically, and understood with reference to its real or probable causes; or it can be looked at magically, and be made the object of a fantastic pseudo-explanation.

No phenomenon is immune from being looked at in a magical way. Hobbes regarded the Aristotelian views on perception and motion taught by the scholastic philosophers as magical pseudo-explanations. To explain the cause of vision, the scholastics have dreamed up a "*visible species*," which, when transmitted to the eye, causes what we call seeing. To explain hearing, they invented an "*Audible species*" or "*Audible being seen*." For understanding, they imagine something they call an "*intelligible species*" or "*intelligible being seen*" to exist. Hobbes thought that translating the mysterious Latin term "species" into its English equivalent, "being seen," was sufficient to show the absurd and senseless nature of these purported "explanations."[24]

Hobbes was equally scornful of the scholastic views on motion, which he considered hopelessly anthropomorphic. When men are in motion they grow weary after a time. They consider this weariness a natural response to motion; hence they ascribe it to bodies other than themselves. This reasoning leads them to "explain" the fall of heavy bodies by ascribing to them "an

[24] *Leviathan*, ch. 1, pp. 86-87 [4].

appetite to rest, and to conserve their nature in that place which is most proper for them."[25] But to believe that inanimate bodies have appetites and understanding of what is required to preserve their nature is, Hobbes thinks, absurd. In opposing this scholastic view to the Galilean theory of inertia and motion, Hobbes considered that he was opposing a fantastic, magical pseudo-explanation to real science. His attacks upon scholasticism in *Leviathan* constitute merely one variation upon a consistent and much larger theme. That theme is the contrast between ignorance, superstition, and magic on the one hand and knowledge, reason, and science on the other.

Nowhere does this contrast come through more clearly than in Hobbes's discourse on madness:

> The opinions of the world, both in antient and later ages, concerning the cause of madnesse, have been two. Some, deriving them from the Passions; some, from Daemons, or Spirits, either good, or bad, which they thought might enter into a man, possesse him, and move his organs in such strange, and uncouth manner, as mad-men use to do.[26]

Each of these opinions has been elaborated in its own way to a point at which two diametrically opposing visions of the problem of madness have come into being. In the first of these points of view, madmen are simply madmen, who suffer from some disorder or excess of one of the passions. In the second, they are demoniacs, people possessed by demons; or *Spiritati*, possessed by spirits; or even prophets possessed by the spirit of God. The Greeks often considered madness to be the work of the Eumenides or Furies, and sometimes to be the work of other gods. The Romans held a similar opinion. These views do not seem surprising, since the pagan imaginations of both these peoples

[25] *Leviathan*, ch. 2, p. 87 [4].

[26] *Leviathan*, ch. 8, p. 142 [37].

were littered with gods and demons of all kinds and shapes. Hobbes considers it more surprising that the ancient Jews held the similar opinion that madmen must be either demoniacs or prophets, men possessed either by evil spirits or by good ones. For the Jews believed in a single God, and, he argues, none of their great leaders ever pretended to be possessed by a spirit. Hobbes can offer only one explanation for their gullible acceptance of this fantastic view of madness. It must be traced to "the want of curiosity to search naturall causes,"[27] in other words, to the Jews' complete failure to be animated by any interest in science or any form of knowledge other than that which they needed to procure the satisfaction of their immediate desires.

Hobbes considers the magical account of madness, absurd as it is, to be itself a form of madness.[28] It paralyzes those who believe it by convincing them that the phenomenon of madness is entirely beyond human control. Anyone capable of seeing into the true nature of madness can break through this paralysis and effect a cure if he is in a position to apply his diagnosis, as Hobbes suggests by recounting an ancient story:

> Likewise there raigned a fit of madnesse in another Graecian City, which seized onely the young Maidens; and caused many of them to hang themselves. This was by most then thought an act of the Divel. But one that suspected, that contempt of life in them, might proceed from some Passion of the mind, and supposing they did not contemne also their honour, gave counsell to the Magistrates, to strip such as so hang'd themselves, and let them hang out naked. This the story sayes cured that madnesse.[29]

Yet some men have an interest in perpetuating the igno-

[27] *Leviathan*, ch. 8, p. 144 [38].

[28] *Leviathan*, ch. 8, p. 146 [39].

[29] *Leviathan*, ch. 8, pp. 142-143 [37].

rance, superstition, and indeed madness of others. Hobbes suggests that ultimately such an interest lies behind the numerous absurdities of scholastic philosophy. Many people have undoubtedly fallen into these absurdities "through misunderstanding of the words they have received, and repeat by rote." But there are others who adopt them quite deliberately "from intention to deceive by obscurity."[30] These people are not necessarily mad themselves. The apparent madness of their voluminous writings and sayings may in fact be the product of a cunning design to confuse, deceive, and hence achieve control over others, as Hobbes suggests by asking: "When men write whole volumes of such stuffe, are they not Mad, *or intend to make others so*?"[31]

Two Models of Man

Hobbes's frequent restatements of his egoistic premise make it clear that he continued to believe that the final cause of all the voluntary actions of every man is always "some Good to himself." But he also argued that the efficient cause of men's actions is always some belief or opinion:

> For it is evident to the meanest capacity, that mens actions are derived from the *opinions* they have of the Good, or Evill, which from those actions redound unto themselves.
>
> . . . by necessity of Nature they choose that which *appeareth* best for themselves. . . .[32]

What accounts for men's actions is not what is truly good for them so much as what appears to them to be so. This appear-

[30] *Leviathan*, ch. 8, p. 146 [39].

[31] *Leviathan*, ch. 8, p. 147 [39], emphasis added.

[32] *Leviathan*, ch. 42, p. 567 [295]; ch. 27, p. 339 [153], emphasis added.

ance is a product of the beliefs or opinions they have about the world.

This caveat to Hobbes's egoistic theory of human nature was the basis of his fundamental theme in *The Elements of Law*: the sharp contrast between logic and rhetoric, and the attack upon the latter for its systematic abuse of language. Rhetoric misinforms and thus leads men to act in ways that are contrary to their own best interests. Hobbes's diagnosis of the causes of irrationality and confusion is much more complex in *Leviathan* than in this earlier work. The designs of cunning rhetoricians who seek to manipulate others for their own ends play a part in that diagnosis. But the essential problem of irrationality stems from the powerful hold superstitious and magical beliefs exercise over the popular imagination. These beliefs are not simply the fabrications of cunning rhetoricians. They arise spontaneously out of fear of the unknown:

> Ignorance of naturall causes disposeth a man to Credulity, so as to believe many times impossibilities . . . so that Ignorance it selfe without Malice, is able to make a man both to believe lyes, and tell them; and sometimes also to invent them. . . . And they that make little, or no enquiry into the naturall causes of things, yet from the feare that proceeds from the ignorance it selfe, of what it is that hath the power to do them much good or harm, are enclined to suppose, and feign unto themselves, severall kinds of Powers Invisible; and to stand in awe of their own imaginations.[33]

The seeds of irrationality, as conceived by Hobbes in *Leviathan*, lie much more deeply imbedded in human nature than he had apparently believed when he wrote *The Elements of Law*. In the earlier work, linguistic abuses are the only source of irrationality to which he devotes any close attention. In *Leviathan*, how-

[33] *Leviathan*, ch. 11, pp. 166-168 [51].

ever, such abuses are only a secondary cause of irrationality, which is ultimately rooted in a dark side of human nature that, as Hobbes pointedly remarks, can never be completely "abolished out of humane nature."[34]

Nor is confusion about the means to an end on which all people agree—namely, their own preservation—the only consequence of irrationality depicted in *Leviathan*. In *The Elements of Law* Hobbes gives no indication that he considers failure to regard death as the greatest of all evils a serious problem for his political theory. In *Leviathan*, however, he is absolutely clear that the consequences of irrationality can run so deeply as to divert men from pursuing the ends prescribed to them by nature, including self-preservation—just as a fit of madness had once caused a suicide epidemic among the young women of one ancient Greek city.

In *The Elements of Law*, Hobbes had sketched a model of human behavior as essentially egoistic, rational action. He did not assume that the realities of human behavior would always coincide with the stipulations of his model. But he does give every appearance of having assumed that the only important cause of discrepancies between model and reality was the failure of men to foresee, accurately and dispassionately, the way to their own preservation and good, the end prescribed to them by nature. When men fail to pursue this end, it is generally, he seems to have thought, because they do not know the entire way to it. In *Leviathan* Hobbes replicates this model of human behavior as egoistic, rational action. Beside it, however, he places another portrait of man as he really is, at least under some circumstances: an ignorant, superstitious being who has little understanding of the world or of the way to, and even the nature of, his own good within it.

The opposition between logic and rhetoric, between the rational use of language and its abuse, which had formed the cen-

[34] *Leviathan*, ch. 12, p. 179 [58].

tral theme of *The Elements of Law*, gives way in *Leviathan* to a new and broader opposition between knowledge, reason, and science on the one hand and ignorance, superstition, and magic on the other. The crucial difference between these two works is evident from the diverse ways in which Hobbes's account of human nature ends in each of them. In *The Elements of Law* Hobbes closes that account with a chapter concerning "How by language men work upon each other's minds." The subject of this chapter is rhetoric and the contrast between logic and rhetoric, genuine teaching and mere persuasion. In *Leviathan* he closes with two chapters: "OF *the difference of* MANNERS" and "OF RELIGION." In the former of these, Hobbes speaks over and over again of ignorance and its effects upon human behavior. In the latter, he discusses Christianity and paganism, making it exceedingly clear that ignorance, superstition, and magic are the very stuff of the pagan religions, and intimating strongly that Christianity is not entirely free of these defects either:

> In like manner they attribute their fortune to a stander by, to a lucky or unlucky place, to words spoken, especially if the name of God be amongst them; as Charming, and Conjuring (the Leiturgy of Witches;) insomuch as to believe, they have power to turn a stone into bread, bread into a man, or any thing, into any thing.[35]

The picture Hobbes places into the immediate background of his account of the state of nature in *Leviathan* is one of ignorant, superstitious, gullible men who have so little sense that they stand in fear of their own imaginations.

What is the significance of this new and broader opposition between the rational and the irrational, science and superstition, fear of men and fear of imaginary spirits, for Hobbes's po-

[35] *Leviathan*, ch. 12, p. 172 [54]. The allusion to the Catholic doctrine of transubstantiation in this passage is typical of Hobbes's references to Christianity throughout the chapter.

litical theory in *Leviathan*? In recent years some critics have begun to argue that Hobbes's recognition of the pervasiveness of ignorance and the power of superstitious beliefs led him to abandon the original project of his political philosophy: the depiction of a commonwealth founded upon the rational actions of subjects who are guided by the egoistic pursuit of good and avoidance of evil to themselves, especially that greatest of evils, death. Thus it is claimed that in opposing the essentially rational fear of death, the greatest evil any man can impose upon another, to the superstitious fear of spirits, Hobbes was implicitly acknowledging that the former and more rational kind of fear can never be an adequate motivational foundation for any commonwealth in the real world. For men in the real world are typically too ignorant, superstitious, and gullible to bear any recognizable resemblance to his abstract model of man as an essentially rational, egoistic, self-possessed being. The coercive power of sovereigns over the lives of their subjects is not enough to keep those subjects in awe. They must believe that their sovereign has supernatural powers as well, powers that enable him to offer punishments greater than death and rewards greater than life. The ultimate basis of sovereign power as described in *Leviathan*, according to this view, is therefore not rational fear of death, guided by a knowledge of the actions required to avoid it. Instead, sovereign power rests ultimately upon supernatural belief, myth, and illusion. The difference between a secure commonwealth and a fragile, unstable one is the difference between a commonwealth in which the supernatural beliefs that arise spontaneously among the people as a result of ignorance are cleverly and effectively exploited by the sovereign power and one in which these beliefs are allowed to become rampant—or, even worse, to be captured and controlled by some person or power other than the sovereign.[36]

[36] Charles D. Tarlton, "The Creation and Maintenance of Government: A Neglected Dimension of Hobbes's *Leviathan*," *Political Studies* 26 (1978), pp.

This is an intriguing and novel interpretation, but it ignores completely the implication Hobbes himself draws, in plain and unambiguous terms, from his contrast between science and superstition, between the rational fear of death and the irrational fear of imaginary spirits. Hobbes does suggest that some ancient sovereigns played upon the superstitious fears of their subjects to "keep the people in obedience, and peace."[37] In *De Cive*, as we have seen, he looks back upon the era in which they did so as a kind of golden age. But he did not believe that the conditions which had made this golden age possible—most important, the monopolistic control by a high priesthood over the doctrines and teaching of moral and political philosophy, which had been carefully preserved from the scrutiny of ordinary subjects by being "wrapt up in fables"—could or even should be recaptured. What Hobbes argues in *Leviathan* is that superstitious fear of spirits, if allowed to become sufficiently powerful, can pose a real and mortal danger to any commonwealth. It can, as he puts it, "induce simple men into an obstinacy against the Laws and Commands of their Civill Soveraigns even to death. . . ."[38] It destroys the ultimate basis of sovereign power, the control a sovereign exercises over men by virtue of his right to determine whether they will live or die.

This is why superstition is a matter of such grave concern to Hobbes in *Leviathan*, and why it poses such a potent threat to his political system. Hobbes did not argue that the real power of a sovereign over the lives (and deaths) of his subjects should be supplemented by the kind of awe that derives from belief in the supernatural. Such beliefs could only be subversive of the

307-327; Eldon J. Eisenach, *Two Worlds of Liberalism: Religion and Politics in Hobbes, Locke, and Mill* (Chicago and London: University of Chicago Press, 1981), pp. 13-71, esp. pp. 15, 47, 70; Eisenach, "Hobbes on Church, State, and Religion," *History of Political Thought* 3 (1982), pp. 215-243, esp. pp. 216, 224-225.

[37] *Leviathan*, ch. 12, p. 177 [57].

[38] *Leviathan*, ch. 47, pp. 707-708 [383].

kind of commonwealth he envisaged, which was based upon the rational actions of subjects who both are driven by the desire to pursue ends that will result in good for themselves and understand clearly the importance of avoiding death. Hobbes frames this conclusion in clear, unequivocal terms in the early pages of his book:

> If this superstitious fear of Spirits were taken away, and with it, Prognostiques from Dreams, false Prophecies, and many other things depending thereon, by which, crafty ambitious persons abuse the simple people, men would be much more fitted than they are for civill Obedience.[39]

Superstition and magic are fundamentally inimical to the obedience of subjects and the power of sovereigns. In *Leviathan*, Hobbes considered them the most destructive of all the forces opposed to civil peace.

The implication of Hobbes's contrast between the rational fear of death (and those men capable of inflicting it), on the one hand, and the irrational fear of imaginary spirits, on the other, is that the ignorant, superstitious state of mind which provides such a fertile breeding ground for this latter kind of fear must, as far as is humanly possible, be eradicated for the kind of commonwealth he envisaged to be made secure. It would be foolish to suppose that Hobbes believed, in writing *Leviathan*, that ignorance and superstition could be eradicated from human nature entirely, just as it would be implausible to suggest that he considered it possible to eliminate all abuses of speech from a natural language. But the direction of his thought in *Leviathan* is essentially the same as it had been in his earlier *Elements of Law*. In that earlier work he had opposed reason to rhetoric, suggesting that the abuses of speech encouraged by rhetoric tended to distort men's thinking and prevent them from acting

[39] *Leviathan*, ch. 2, p. 93 [7-8].

in their own interests with the degree of foresight of which they were capable by nature. The prescription implied by this diagnosis was that those abuses should be stamped out, or at the very least severely discouraged. In *Leviathan* Hobbes opposes reason to ignorance and superstition, which he regards as fundamentally inimical to the interests of peace. The prescription suggested by this opposition was the obvious one: that everything possible should be done to eradicate these scars from the face of human culture, and hence to make the foundations of all rationally constructed commonwealths more secure.

Notwithstanding this similarity of direction, however, there were two major differences between the diagnoses of irrationality offered in these different works. First, the consequences of irrationality depicted in *Leviathan* were more severe and fundamental than those described in *The Elements of Law.* In the earlier work, Hobbes argues that misreckoning leads men to mistake the way to their ends; in the later one, he suggests that irrationality induces them to misunderstand the very nature of those ends. Second, his account of the causes or roots of irrationality is deeper and in a sense more pessimistic in his later work than it had been in the initial version of his political theory. In *The Elements of Law*, Hobbes had pointed to linguistic abuses as the principal source of misreckoning. In *Leviathan* he continues to criticize these abuses, but also suggests that a propensity toward irrational belief in supernatural things is rooted in human nature itself. The direction of the prescription offered in *Leviathan* was very similar to that proposed in *The Elements of Law*, but Hobbes's sense of the magnitude of the task, and of the obstacles that would have to be overcome in pursuing it, was much greater than it had been when he first set out to compose a political philosophy.

CHAPTER FIVE ✲

Theory and Transformation

THE POLITICS OF ENLIGHTENMENT

APART from the vigor and vividness of its language, the feature of *Leviathan* that distinguishes it most clearly from Hobbes's earlier political works is the great extent and detail of the attention it devotes to Scriptural exegesis and theological argumentation. In *The Elements of Law*, a work of twenty-nine chapters, Hobbes had devoted two chapters to a discussion of potential conflicts between religious and political authority. In *De Cive* he expanded this discussion considerably, creating a new division of four chapters on religious subjects, which he placed at the end of his book. Even with this expansion of their role, however, Scriptural and religious questions remained a distinctly subordinate subject in Hobbes's work. Their status in *Leviathan* is very different from that which they had held in these earlier compositions. *Leviathan* includes a new chapter on religion in general, placed in a pivotal position at the end of Hobbes's account of human nature and immediately before the portrait of the state of nature with which his theory of the generation of a commonwealth begins. Of four parts into which he now divided his treatise, the third and longest is devoted almost entirely to Scriptural interpretation, while the fourth is concerned mainly with the diagnosis of spiritual errors. In short, Scriptural and religious questions occupy more space in *Leviathan* than any other topic discussed in the work, including Hobbes's theory of the commonwealth itself.

What is the significance of Hobbes's introduction of these new arguments into the body of his work? What bearing do they have upon the political argument detailed in parts I and II of his book? Until very recently these questions received scant attention in the critical literature. The traditional interpretation has been that the theological views developed in parts III and IV of *Leviathan*, however interesting they may be in themselves, are of no real significance for his political philosophy. The foundation of that philosophy, according to this interpretation, is entirely naturalistic. Hobbes develops his political argument out of an analysis of human nature, especially the passions, and its consequences for social interaction. He does not derive it from a set of theological presuppositions, as political philosophers had customarily done since early medieval times. From this viewpoint, then, the theological arguments adumbrated in *Leviathan* appear to be mere appendages to the true work. They are addressed to concerns that are local and transitory, by contrast with the more enduring concerns of Hobbes's political philosophy in the proper sense.[1] While many adherents to this interpretation regard these theological arguments as mere trappings, designed to make Hobbes's doctrines palatable to a nation of Christian believers, it has also been maintained by critics who have taken them to be an elaboration of his sincere religious beliefs.[2] Raymond Polin has expressed the essence

[1] Polin, *Politique et Philosophie chez Hobbes*; Strauss, *Political Philosophy of Hobbes*; Oakeshott, *Hobbes on Civil Association*, p. 48. Strauss adopts a somewhat different view in his later essay, "On the Basis of Hobbes's Political Philosophy," in *What Is Political Philosophy?* (Glencoe, Ill.: The Free Press, 1959), pp. 170-196.

[2] Paul J. Johnson, "Hobbes's Anglican Doctrine of Salvation," in Ralph Ross, Herbert W. Schneider, and Theodore Waldman, eds., *Thomas Hobbes in His Time* (Minneapolis: University of Minnesota Press, 1974), pp. 102-125.

of this interpretation clearly and forcefully by arguing that Hobbes's theology is "superimposed" upon his political philosophy, and should in no sense be regarded as an integral part of that philosophy.[3]

This interpretation was strongly challenged some years ago, mainly as a result of Howard Warrender's thorough and carefully argued study of Hobbes's theory of obligation. Warrender argued that the pivotal concept in Hobbes's theory of obligation was that of natural law. The laws of nature are the basis upon which men acquire all their obligations, including those toward their civil sovereign. In this sense they provide the foundation for all commonwealths and all civil laws. But these laws of nature, he suggested, are intelligible only as expressions of divine will. Furthermore, the obligation to obey them, which must exist prior to and independently of all acquired obligations, cannot be understood without reference to divine sanctions. No obligation can be operative or valid unless those obliged by it have a sufficient motive to obey. The only motive sufficient to validate men's obligation to obey the laws of nature is provided by the divine sanction of salvation. Hence the theological concepts of divine will and divine sanctions are basic to Hobbes's entire political philosophy, the foundations of which are in this sense essentially theological rather than naturalistic.[4]

Warrender and others who have advocated this revisionist interpretation have provided many new insights into the structure of Hobbes's political argument, and some of these have proven themselves to be valuable correctives to the traditional view of Hobbes. But their thesis that the foundation of that argument is religious or theological rather than naturalistic is unconvincing. The general source of the confusion is not difficult to identify. Advocates of this revisionist interpretation have fo-

[3] *Hobbes, Dieu, et les hommes* (Paris: Presses Universitaires de France, 1981), p. 61.

[4] *The Political Philosophy of Hobbes: His Theory of Obligation* (Oxford: Clarendon Press, 1957), esp. pp. 99-100, 272-277.

cused their attention sharply upon the juridical concepts and language of Hobbes's political philosophy. By so doing they have forced defenders of the traditional, naturalistic view to take this language much more seriously than they have sometimes done in the past. At the same time, however, the revisionists have tended to neglect the behavioral and causal language that is also an integral component of Hobbes's political argument, and have thus underestimated the importance of this entire dimension of his political philosophy, which is encapsulated, among many other places, in his characterization of the laws of nature as "dictates of Reason, . . . or Theoremes *concerning what conduceth to the conservation and defence of themselves*."[5]

The most curious thing about this revisionist interpretation, however, is that its advocates have made almost no effort to draw upon the voluminous evidence of Hobbes's own theological argumentation in parts III and IV of *Leviathan.* In spite of their claims about the importance of Hobbes's theological concepts or religious beliefs to his political philosophy, these revisionists seem to have accepted, either tacitly or expressly, the traditional view that those portions of *Leviathan* are of no very great or enduring interest.[6] While postulating that his theological views are integral to, or indeed the very foundation of, his political philosophy as a whole, these revisionist critics have actually had little more to say about Hobbes's own theological argumentation than their traditionalist adversaries.

Only very recently has a new cohort of scholars, more interested in and sensitive to the historical context and concreteness of Hobbes's political philosophy than earlier generations of critics, begun to rectify this omission. The seminal work on this point was an essay on Hobbes's religious and historical views by J.G.A. Pocock. Analyzing Hobbes's argument in the latter half

[5] *Leviathan*, ch. 15, pp. 216-217 [80], emphasis added.

[6] In addition to Warrender, cf. on this point F. C. Hood, *The Divine Politics of Thomas Hobbes* (Oxford: Clarendon Press, 1964), esp. p. 252.

of *Leviathan* more closely than any previous critic in recent times, Pocock was led to conclude that this second half of the work is neither strictly subordinate to the political argument of its first half, as most defenders of the traditional interpretation have asserted, nor an elaboration of views that form the theoretical foundation of that political argument, as advocates of the revisionist view have claimed. Instead, he argues, Hobbes simply "embarks on a new course" at the midpoint of *Leviathan.* The first half of that work deals with the domain of nature and reason, while its second half deals with the historical domain of prophecy and faith; and this latter domain is not, in spite of the usual opinion to the contrary, "reabsorbed" into the former. For Pocock, then, *Leviathan* is in effect two separate works, composed in two distinct languages, which stand side by side, neither being subordinate to the other.[7]

Perhaps the greatest virtue of Pocock's work is that it demonstrates emphatically the importance of taking Hobbes's words in the latter half of *Leviathan* seriously. But taking his words seriously is not the same thing as taking him at his word, as Pocock also tends to do. Thus, for example, he argues that Hobbes would never have written "chapter after chapter of exegesis with the proclaimed intention of arriving at the truth about it" had he not believed that the Christian Scriptures constitute the true prophetic word of God.[8] This argument from bulk is unconvincing, if only because it underestimates Hobbes's capacity for political wile. Pocock is absolutely right to chastise most previous scholars for ignoring what Hobbes actually wrote about the Scriptures and sacred history,[9] but his own methodological dictum that critics should concern themselves less with Hobbes's sincerity of conviction than with the

[7] "Time, History, and Eschatology in the Thought of Thomas Hobbes," in J.G.A. Pocock, *Politics, Language, and Time* (New York: Atheneum, 1973), pp. 148-201, esp. pp. 159, 167, 191.

[8] "Time, History, and Eschatology," pp. 167-168.

[9] "Time, History, and Eschatology," pp. 160-162.

effects his words seem designed to produce does not lead to the conclusions he reaches in his essay.

From a strictly logical point of view, the traditional interpretation, according to which parts III and IV of *Leviathan* are a mere appendage to the "real" political argument of that work, is substantially correct. The theological argumentation of Hobbes's work is neither the foundation nor in any other sense an integral part of his political philosophy, if we understand that philosophy to be an abstract, timeless scheme for the organization of political society. That scheme is constructed by interweaving a set of observations about human behavior and interaction, formulated as theoretical propositions, with a set of legalistic or juridical propositions about the grounds, origins, and distribution of rights and obligations. In no essential way does it involve or rest upon theological concepts or religious beliefs. From this point of view, then, the second half of the book is indeed a superimposition, which can be explained only by going outside the bounds of its central argument.

But this conclusion flows from the adoption of assumptions about the nature of Hobbes's work that are different from those held by Hobbes himself. For him, as I have sought to suggest, *Leviathan* was not simply and exclusively a work of "science" or abstract speculation about the causes and organization of political society. It was above all else a work of political persuasion and engagement, which sought to shape popular opinion in ways designed to benefit the cause of peace.

Considered as a political act, the metaphysical, theological, and historical argumentation of parts III and IV of *Leviathan* are integral to the design of Hobbes's book as a whole. Indeed, from this practical point of view it can be argued that they constitute the core of, and lay the foundation for, his project in *Leviathan.* If, in other words, we focus upon the effects Hobbes's words seem designed to produce, we find that (Pocock's investigations notwithstanding) there is a close, even intimate, relationship between the argumentation of the second half of the book and that of its first half. The second half of *Leviathan* is designed to shape the thoughts and opinions of its readers in ways that will make the argumentation of the first half persuasive and compelling. In this sense, parts III and IV lay the groundwork upon which the practical effects envisaged in parts I and II of the work are to arise.[10] The balance of this chapter will sketch the reasoning behind my interpretation, while the chapters that follow will attempt to demonstrate its validity by examining the content and implications of Hobbes's metaphysical, theological, and historical argumentation.

The Struggle for Enlightenment

The discrepancy between the theoretical model of man upon which Hobbes had drawn to build the initial version of his political theory and the descriptive portrait of man developed in *Leviathan* opened up a problem of fundamental importance for Hobbes's political philosophy. If men are ignorant, superstitious, and irrational, none of the basic mechanisms upon which his political argument relies will be likely to work. Men who do not fear death, or at least do not allow their fear of death to override all conflicting passions, cannot be relied upon to live together in peace under the authority of an acknowledged sov-

[10] The nearest approach to this interpretation in the existing literature is that offered by Eisenach in *Two Worlds of Liberalism*. Like Pocock, however, Eisenach greatly exaggerates the disjunction between the two halves of *Leviathan*, going so far as to argue that the work "contains two separate languages, logics, psychologies, and politics" (p. 70). This claim arises out of his acceptance of Pocock's assumption that faith and prophecy constitute a form and realm of knowledge for Hobbes, whereas in fact Hobbes treats faith as a form of mere opinion, not as knowledge, and seeks to undermine the entire concept of prophecy, as the argument of Chapters 6 and 7, below, attempts to show. For another attempt to revise Pocock's interpretation in a similar direction, see Patricia Springborg, "*Leviathan* and the Problem of Ecclesiastical Authority," *Political Theory* 3 (1975), pp. 289-303.

ereign. Fear of death is the ultimate basis of sovereign power and the ultimate inducement for men to remain at peace with one another. If men allow their imaginations to subordinate their fear of death to any other passion or end, the whole basis of sovereign power and civil peace is destroyed.

One possible response to this discrepancy would have been for Hobbes to throw out the theoretical model of man that had underpinned his initial political philosophy. If man had shown himself to be a different creature from the one depicted in his model, Hobbes might have reacted by scrapping that model and making a new beginning. Yet he did not. Instead, as we have seen, he formulated a portrait of man characterized by a systematic opposition between two models. One of these was the model of man as an egoistic, rational being that had underlain his political philosophy from the beginning. The other was a descriptive model of man as an ignorant, superstitious, irrational being. The first model had been an integral component of Hobbes's political philosophy from the outset. The second, descriptive model was subversive of that philosophy in the sense that it depicted man as a creature who could not be tamed by the arguments, threats, and punishments Hobbes had originally envisaged. Perhaps as a consequence of the years of civil war and violent sectarianism, Hobbes was more acutely conscious than he had initially been of how far from his original model of man human behavior could stray. Yet he continued to cling to his initial model of man as an egoistic, rational actor. Why, in the face of all the evidence that had accumulated against it, did he do so? Why, in other words, did he think that the basis of his political philosophy could be saved?

The answer is that Hobbes believed actual human behavior might, in time, come to resemble the pattern described by his model. In the present, men were ignorant, superstitious, and irrational. Their behavior was poles apart from the pattern described by his model and required by his political theory. But Hobbes did not think that men were essentially and permanently irrational beings. They remained for him potentially rational actors of the kind described by his model of human nature. The discrepancy between that model and Hobbes's description of actual men as irrational beings might have led him to abandon both the model and the theory of political society that rested upon it. In fact his reaction was the reverse. Instead of treating observed reality as a given datum and adjusting his political theory accordingly, Hobbes held fast to his theory of human nature and politics. The inconsistency between that theory and observed behavior called for a change in the behavior, not an alteration of the theory. If actual men were ignorant and irrational, they remained rational beings in potential. The validity of Hobbes's theory rested upon the assumption that the irrationality which seemed to characterize human behavior in the present was neither an essential nor a permanent feature of human nature.

This response was, of course, entirely consistent with Hobbes's idea of science. Like that of a geometrical theorem, the truth of a scientific proposition about human nature was not dependent, for him, upon its accuracy as a representation of empirical reality. As long as there was a chance that reality could be reshaped in accordance with the dictates of theory, there was reason for Hobbes to hope that his science of politics could prove its validity through practical use.

Hobbes had strong reasons for supposing that such a chance existed. He believed himself to be living in the opening stages of a new age of discovery and science. He was extremely conscious of the impact that the discoveries and inventions of modern times had left upon the practical arts and the societies that supported them. Already in his manuscript of 1640 he had cited the achievements of these practical arts as the features that distinguish a civilized society from a savage one:

> For from the studies of these men hath proceeded, whatsoever cometh to us for ornament by navigation; and

> whatsoever we have beneficial to human society by the division, distinction, and portraying of the face of the earth; whatsoever also we have by the account of times, and foresight of the course of heaven; whatsoever by measuring distances, planes, and solids of all sorts; and whatsoever either elegant or defensible in building: all which supposed away, what do we differ from the wildest of the Indians?[11]

The shape of a society, for Hobbes, was dependent upon the state of its practical arts; and the achievements of these arts flowed from advances in learning. In the recent experience of European society these advances had been dramatic. The techniques of navigation that had led to the great voyages of discovery would not have been possible without a relatively modern European invention, the compass. Mapmaking had advanced in great strides during the age, and even during Hobbes's own lifetime, aided both by the discoveries of navigators and by the invention of new mathematical techniques for portraying the earth's geography on a flat surface.[12] The new, Gregorian calendar began to come into general use during the first half of the seventeenth century, and the science of astronomy was revolutionized by acceptance of the Copernican view of the universe during the same period.[13] Hobbes's life was a time of discovery and rare excitement, and no one was more affected by the spirit of intellectual ferment than he.

This spirit is captured by the letter of dedication Hobbes af-

[11] *Elements* I.13.3.

[12] In his autobiography Hobbes reports that as a young student in Oxford he took great interest in maps and the voyages of discovery. See J. E. Parsons, Jr. and Whitney Blair, trans., "The Life of Thomas Hobbes of Malmesbury," *Interpretation* 10 (1982), pp. 1-7. Hobbes also drew up a map of his own to accompany his translation of Thucydides, and makes a special point of its accuracy and reliability in *Thucydides*, p. x.

[13] For a general account of many of these discoveries, see Marie Boas, *The Scientific Renaissance, 1450-1630* (New York: Harper and Row, 1962).

fixed to *De Corpore*, the lengthy study of natural philosophy he began working on in the late 1630's or early 1640's and completed four years after finishing *Leviathan.* Geometry, logic, and astronomy, he argues, had all been developed to very advanced stages of learning by scientists in ancient times. Later on, however, many of these ancient achievements had been "strangled with the snares of words" by ignorant, meddling scholastic philosophers. The chain of learning they had broken had begun to mend only in recent times. Copernicus, Galileo, and William Harvey were the great heroes of its revival; indeed, Harvey was the only one of these who, "conquering envy, hath established a new doctrine in his life-time." Before these men, Hobbes argues, there was "nothing certain" in natural philosophy; but since their time "astronomy and natural philosophy in general have, for so little time, been extraordinarily advanced by Joannes Keplerus, Petrus Gassendus, and Marinus Mersennus," all of whom were contemporaries of Hobbes. "Natural philosophy is therefore but young; but Civil Philosophy yet much younger, as being no older . . . than my own book *De Cive*."[14]

Hobbes had some reason, then, to imagine that great things might flow from the recent revival of learning. That revival was new and fresh; who could say what achievements it might produce? Already it had led to numerous improvements in many specific practical arts. To have an impact upon the prospects of his political philosophy, however, the new wave of learning would have to achieve an even broader effect: the forging of a new and more rational cast of mind, not only within scientific and intellectual circles, but among ordinary people as well.

Formidable obstacles to the achievement of such a vast effect existed, as Hobbes very plainly understood. For in the first

[14] *De Corpore*, Epistle Dedicatory, pp. viii-ix. Hobbes cites *De Cive* rather than *The Elements of Law* presumably because the former work was published in 1642, eight years before the latter, even though *The Elements of Law* was written first.

place, the seeds of superstition and irrationality, he suggests in *Leviathan*, lie deeply imbedded in human nature. Reason, after all, is an acquired skill, not a natural gift. It is far easier to remain ignorant than to become informed and enlightened. Superstitions arise naturally, without any conscious effort on the part of those who hold them. The imagination is naturally lively and uncontrolled. Magical pseudo-explanations appeal to it, since their falsity cannot be revealed without deliberate and careful scrutiny. The human mind is ripe ground for the "Weeds, and common Plants of Errour and Conjecture."[15] It is not enough merely to implant the seed of reason into the minds of men and expect it to flourish without further cultivation. The weeds of error will crowd and eventually extinguish the life of that seed unless they are forcibly uprooted and destroyed.

Yet, in the second place, there are many men who inadvertently propagate these weeds, and some who deliberately cultivate them. The minds of ordinary people are like clean paper, but only if they have not been "tainted with dependance on the Potent, or scribbled over with the opinions of their Doctors."[16] In practice few people enjoy the clarity of thought and openness of mind needed to make them receptive to the rational teachings of science. Most have been subjected to delusive, confusing doctrines propagated by people who have an interest in maintaining the ignorance of others. "The Enemy has been here in the Night of our naturall Ignorance," sowing and cultivating the weeds of superstition and darkness.[17] That darkness cannot be dispelled unless its authors can be identified and routed.[18]

The magnitude of these obstacles to reason and enlightenment, and the strength with which he emphasizes them, have contributed to the view that in *Leviathan*, at least, Hobbes must have regarded supernatural beliefs—understood either in

[15] *Leviathan*, ch. 46, p. 683 [368].

[16] *Leviathan*, ch. 30, p. 379 [176].

[17] *Leviathan*, ch. 44, p. 628 [334].

[18] *Leviathan*, ch. 47, esp. pp. 704-706 [381-382].

a Machiavellian way as myths and illusions or in a pious manner as truths of Christian faith—as an appropriate source for the ideological foundations that must underpin any political society.[19] But this conclusion is neither stated by Hobbes himself nor implied necessarily by what he does say. Those seeds of superstition which cannot be "abolished out of humane nature" are only, when reduced to their most primitive core, "an opinion of a Deity, and Powers invisible."[20] The shape these opinions assume when they have matured into a fully grown plant is very much dependent upon the precise way in which they have been cultivated. Belief in God, in itself, is in no way inimical to science or truth, since reason, too, leads us to the conclusion that a deity must exist.[21] And with sufficient cultivation and care even a belief in invisible powers could probably be refined into a form entirely consistent with the truths of science. After all, Hobbes himself habitually attempted to explain physical phenomena by invoking the idea that space is filled with an enormous number of tiny, invisible particles.[22] Properly cultivated, even the seeds of superstition can be transformed into ideas consistent with reason and science.

The real obstacle to any such transformation lay in the entrenched positions of those who opposed it. Yet there was some reason for hope here, too. The forces of darkness had not always held such a tight stranglehold over the minds of ordinary people, and there were grounds for believing that their grip was beginning to loosen. Throughout *Leviathan* there are signs that Hobbes believed he was living in a time of virtually unprecedented ferment and cultural transition—a view that is hardly surprising, given the extraordinarily millenarian atmosphere that had enveloped the English imagination by the time of his

[19] Tarlton, "The Creation and Maintenance of Government"; Eisenach, *Two Worlds of Liberalism* and "Hobbes on Church, State, and Religion."

[20] *Leviathan*, ch. 12, p. 179 [58].

[21] *Leviathan*, ch. 11, p. 167 [51].

[22] Brandt, *Thomas Hobbes' Mechanical Conception, passim.*

writing.[23] Philosophy and the sciences had begun to break loose of their theological shackles, as the achievements of Copernicus, Galileo, Harvey, and others showed. Their revival was still a fragile one, as Hobbes suggests in the opening paragraph of *De Corpore*:

> Philosophy seems to me to be amongst men now, in the same manner as corn and wine are said to have been in the world in ancient time. For from the beginning there were vines and ears of corn growing here and there in the fields; but no care was taken for the planting and sowing of them.

Yet a foothold had been gained, and it opened up a greater opportunity both for the advancement of scientific learning—or, as Francis Bacon had called it, the true "natural magic"[24]—and for the broader enlightenment of ordinary people than any that had occurred for centuries.

The benefits of such a general enlightenment, if it could be achieved, would be very great. By drawing men away from the superstitious habits of thinking to which they had long been accustomed, a movement toward enlightenment would be helping to lay the foundations for a new kind of commonwealth, stronger and more lasting than any that had ever existed before. Instead of resorting to myths and fables, as the founders of past commonwealths had done, the architects of a modern state could rest it upon the firmer, more permanent basis of enlightened, rational self-interest.

Hobbes did not imagine, therefore, that he would have to fall back upon myth to provide the ideological underpinnings of the commonwealth he envisaged. He was acutely aware of the power of myth, but he also believed that rational self-interest, once established as the principal motive of an enlightened

[23] This view is elaborated in Chapter 8, below.

[24] *Advancement of Learning*, p. 97.

people, would prove itself a more enduring foundation for political society than any fable or superstitious fabrication could ever be. He emphasized the magnitude of the obstacles to enlightenment because, unlike Bacon, he was convinced that it would never be achieved without an immense and bitter struggle. A victory would clear the way for philosophy and enlightenment to flourish together, and for commonwealths to be laid upon new, more rational foundations; a defeat would strangle these achievements before they had had a chance to establish strong roots. The struggle for enlightenment, Hobbes believed, was coming to a head in his own lifetime. Its outcome would be of historic importance; but at mid-century, when he was completing *Leviathan*, that outcome was not secure.

The Politics of Cultural Transformation

By becoming linked with the historic struggle for "enlightenment," as he conceived it—a struggle he might easily have traced back to Erasmus and other representatives of earlier Renaissance humanism—Hobbes's political philosophy acquired a temporal dimension that had not been present in its initial formulation. In *The Elements of Law*, he had analyzed the commonwealth and the distribution of rights and obligations within it in essentially ahistorical and abstract terms. He had based a timeless theory of government and politics upon an equally timeless model of human nature. In *Leviathan* he clung to all the essential features of that theory. But the discrepancy between that model of human nature and his portrait of man as an irrational being gives *Leviathan* an historical dimension that had been lacking from Hobbes's earlier works. His theory of the commonwealth still had an abstract, timeless quality about it, but the model of man upon which it rested was now linked to a specific historical moment. Hobbes's theory would not achieve practical realization until men became the rational actors they had always had the potential to be. This would not occur until knowledge had triumphed over ignorance, reason had driven out superstition, and enlightenment had vanquished the forces of darkness. The practical realization of Hobbes's political philosophy had become linked to a possible event in future time: the transformation of human beings into the relatively enlightened, rational creatures that had always been the inhabitants of his vision of political society.

This possible future transformation of man became, for Hobbes, the crucial event in human history. The prospects for a commonwealth as he envisaged it were vitally dependent upon the outcome of the struggle between superstition and enlightenment. His theory of the state could not fully be put into practice before the movement toward enlightenment had triumphed. Yet there was no certainty that this triumph would take place. Hence Hobbes was led by what seemed to be inexorable necessity to a basic reformulation of the design of his political theory. His original aim had been to demonstrate the proper distribution of rights and obligations in a commonwealth. This demonstration, he hoped, would help convince men of the need for absolute sovereignty. Now, however, Hobbes saw that he would have to take on aims much broader than these original ones. To promote enlightenment itself, an entire outlook and approach to life, became an integral part of Hobbes's political purpose. His original theory was now encapsulated within a project of even grander design. The cultivation of rational modes of thought and action was an essential step toward the realization of his political aims. It became an aim in itself, distinct from, but inseparably wedded to, the original purposes of Hobbes's political theory.

This new aim generated a stratum of argument that was new in *Leviathan.* Hobbes had touched upon certain religious themes and used Scriptural arguments in both of the earlier versions of his political theory. But in each of these previous works the religious and Scriptural argumentation had been strictly subordinated to his central political aims. Its purpose had been to show that there could be little or no conflict between a man's duties to God and his obligations to his earthly sovereign, and thereby to remove one important potential obstacle to civil obedience. Though Hobbes reproduces many of the arguments of these earlier works in *Leviathan*, the theological argumentation in that work as a whole has a very different character from that which it had before. The doctrines of Christianity, as he portrays them, have been infiltrated over the centuries by many superstitious and magical traditions. As taught by some of the established churches, Christianity has become a carrier of superstition and spiritual darkness. The struggle for enlightenment is, in very large measure, a struggle against these tendencies within established Christian doctrine. The theological argumentation of *Leviathan* is essentially different from that of Hobbes's earlier works because the central aim of that argumentation is new. That new aim was to expose the superstitious and magical elements in Christianity so that these could be expelled from Christian doctrine. Ultimately, it was to lay the groundwork for a fundamental change in the habits of thought and action that had prevailed throughout most of the Christian era—amounting almost to a transformation of the human psyche that would prepare men and women to be assembled, for the first time in history, into a truly lasting political society.

The formulation of this new aim was the pivotal event in the development of Hobbes's political philosophy. It stands behind all the alterations that distinguish *Leviathan* from his earlier works. The new ambition to appeal to a large, public audience and thus shape popular opinion directly; the vividness of language, designed to leave a deep and lasting impression upon his readers; the new stratum of theological argumentation, so vastly more developed than it had been in his previous works—all these changes were linked to this one great shift in Hobbes's aims. The philosophical treatise that was designed to show the need for absolute sovereignty by means of logical demonstration, and that had constituted the main content of *The Elements of Law*, is contained in *Leviathan* as well. But in *Leviathan* that treatise is merely one part of a work of much larger extent and scope. The opposition between reason and rhetoric had been Hobbes's basic theme in *The Elements of Law*. In *Leviathan*, it was replaced by a new theme, that of the struggle between enlightenment and superstition, between the forces of light and the forces of darkness. And the form in which he presents this theme is less that of a philosophical argument in the ordinary sense than that of an epic, with all the grandeur of conception that term implies.[25]

The fact that Hobbes presents this theme in a new form is intimately related to the reorientation of his aims. "The Sciences," he points out, "are small Power. . . . For Science is of that nature, as none can understand it to be, but such as in a good measure have attayned it."[26] This observation is especially applicable when the aim is not so much to demonstrate the truth of a scientific conclusion from principles that are already accepted as to establish the validity of those principles themselves. For the principles of science, as Hobbes often remarks, cannot be demonstrated by scientific methods. They are self-evident truths, and must simply be presented to the reader in the hope that he or she will recognize them as such: "For this kind of Doctrine, admitteth no other Demonstration."[27] Science cannot prove that the principles upon which it rests are true. But this limitation inherent in the nature of science need not prevent its advocates from using other means to persuade their readers to accept those principles as truths. The vigor and vividness of Hobbes's language in *Leviathan*, as well as the extremely polemical cast of his theological argumentation, are de-

[25] Cf. Sheldon Wolin, *Hobbes and the Epic Tradition of Political Theory* (Los Angeles: Clark Memorial Library, 1970), which argues a thesis similar to that of this and the following paragraph.

[26] *Leviathan*, ch. 10, p. 151 [42].

[27] *Leviathan*, Introduction, p. 83 [2]; cf. *De Corpore* I.6.5, 13, 15.

signed to accomplish just this aim. The language of *Leviathan* was necessarily rhetorical, in a deeper sense than the language of his earlier works of political philosophy had been, because the aim of that work was not merely to demonstrate the truth of Hobbes's political argument. That aim, rather, was to establish the authority of science, and through it to promote rational modes of thought and action, with a superstitious people. The form in which Hobbes presents his argument was a consequence of his adoption of this new and extra-scientific aim. In this sense *Leviathan* is at least as much a polemic *for* science and enlightenment as it is an instance of scientific or philosophical argument.

By recasting his argument into this new form, Hobbes effected a synthesis between some of the possibilities inherent in his own idea of science, on the one hand, and the rhetorical lessons he had imbibed during the years before he had conceived that idea, on the other. From the beginning, his idea of science had left open the question of what was to be done to reconcile discrepancies between scientific theory and empirical reality. In fact, the geometrical archetype implied that such discrepancies should be interpreted as signs of the imperfection of reality, not evidence of defective theory. The analogy with geometry did not immunize the theorems of science from empirical criticism entirely, of course, since for Hobbes any science should be capable of proving its mettle through its usefulness in changing and controlling reality. Until an opportunity to apply its theorems had been seized, however, empirical criticism of science would remain meaningless. Recasting the argument of *Leviathan* was a way of helping to create such an opportunity for his political theory. By drawing upon the lessons of the rhetorical tradition, which emphasized the power of the visual image or "speaking picture" in contrast to the weakness of merely conceptual discourse for creating mental impressions, Hobbes was attempting to create conditions under which the validity of his own theory of government and politics could be confirmed through its practical realization.

Hence the change in form and methods that distinguishes the argumentation of *Leviathan* from that of his earlier works of political philosophy represents neither an abandonment nor in any essential sense a modification of his original purposes. The truth is that this change is a sign and consequence of Hobbes's increased determination to achieve those purposes. The final aim—to bring into being a commonwealth based upon firmer, more rational foundations than any that had ever existed before—remained unchanged. But attainment of this aim now seemed to be contingent upon a prior cultural transformation. The polemical defense of science and enlightenment against magic and superstition was designed to help bring about this transformation, to implant those (in Hobbes's view, rational) habits of thought and action which were required if his scheme for the organization of political society was to work. This defense led Hobbes to offer interpretations of the metaphysical, prophetic, and historical dimensions of human existence as well as the assessment of man's political situation already expressed in earlier versions of his political philosophy. The next three chapters will explore these interpretations and their implications for his political philosophy.

CHAPTER SIX ✲

The Disenchanted World

THE MECHANICAL MATERIALIST

HOBBES DRAWS attention to the novelty of his Scriptural interpretations both at the beginning and toward the close of *Leviathan.* Four paragraphs from the end, he candidly acknowledges that his book contains "some new Doctrines"[1] in part III, which deals with a Christian commonwealth. At the opposite end of the book, in his brief letter of dedication, he issues a warning about these reinterpretations:

> That which perhaps may most offend, are certain Texts of Holy Scripture, alledged by me to other purpose than ordinarily they use to be by others. But I have done it with due submission, and also (in order to my Subject) necessarily; for they are the Outworks of the Enemy, from whence they impugne the Civill Power.[2]

The reinterpretation of Scripture contained in his book was, in Hobbes's own estimation, its most controversial part. Yet he did nothing to soften the harsh edges of this reinterpretation, and insisted that it was essential to the design of his work. The principal reason for this insistence was that the Bible was the

[1] *Leviathan*, Review and Conclusion, p. 726 [394].

[2] *Leviathan*, Epistle Dedicatory, p. 76.

single most important source of those beliefs and traditions which had shaped the thoughts and actions of his readers.

It is difficult to recapture a sense of the central place the Bible occupied in the lives of seventeenth-century Englishmen. For many readers today religion occupies a segment of life that is strictly demarcated from most of its other dimensions. For most Englishmen three hundred years ago, however, the religious life was all-encompassing. Every aspect of life was capable of containing religious meaning. The Scriptures were the indispensable guide to the interpretation of this meaning. The Bible was not just a book of religious history and doctrine, but a guide to all conduct and understanding. It was a prism through which Hobbes's contemporaries viewed their world.

For Christians, the Biblical word was absolutely authoritative. This assumption had lain behind the struggle for a vernacular Bible at the outset of the English Reformation. William Tyndale, Miles Coverdale, and the other famous leaders of that movement were above all else translators, whose historic mission was to bring God's word directly to their people. The numerous new translations that appeared after the Reformation gained official recognition in the 1530's testify to the authoritative status of this text. A precise rendition was vitally important because the Scriptures were deemed to be the sole essential guide to life. This assumption grew increasingly pervasive as the Puritan movement spread throughout England in the late sixteenth and early seventeenth centuries, and it had not yet begun to wane at mid-century.[3] Even skeptics and atheists, who rejected the authoritative status of the Bible, could not escape its influence. It shaped men's perceptions and provided the categories through which the world was made comprehensible to them. This is one reason why it is often nearly impossible to

[3] Two old but still valuable surveys of the history of this movement are M. M. Knappen, *Tudor Puritanism* (Chicago: University of Chicago Press, 1939), and William Haller, *The Rise of Puritanism* (New York: Columbia University Press, 1938).

distinguish atheists from believers in seventeenth-century England.

If Hobbes wanted to reshape men's thinking, then, there was no better place for him to begin than with the Bible. Yet their influence alone is not sufficient to explain the kind of attention he bestows upon the Christian Scriptures. The fact is that Hobbes considered the Bible, or at least certain interpretations of it, to be the chief agent and carrier of superstitious beliefs in his time. Men do not perceive this "spirituall darknesse" in their own beliefs because they have never known a greater degree of light than that which they have already beheld. But if we contemplate our own actions, we can tell that they are guided no more surely than gropings in the dark:

> Whence comes it, that in Christendome there has been, almost from the time of the Apostles, such justling of one another out of their places, both by forraign, and Civill war? such stumbling at every little asperity of their own fortune, and every little eminence of that of other men? and such diversity of ways in running to the same mark, *Felicity*, if it be not Night amongst us, or at least a Mist?[4]

Men's failure to understand in clear and simple terms how to conduct themselves is not fortuitous. There is a "Kingdome of Darknesse" in this world, a

> *Confederacy of Deceivers, that to obtain dominion over men in this present world, endeavour by dark, and erroneous Doctrines, to extinguish in them the Light, both of Nature, and of the Gospell; and so to dis-prepare them for the Kingdome of God to come.*[5]

The Scriptures have been deliberately corrupted to prevent our seeing their full light, which can be revealed only through a radical reinterpretation of their contents.

Hobbes's insistence upon the radicalism of his reinterpreta-

[4] *Leviathan*, ch. 44, p. 628 [334].

[5] *Leviathan*, ch. 44, pp. 627-628 [333].

tion cannot easily be reconciled with the common view that the theology of *Leviathan* was designed to make his political doctrine more palatable to Christian readers than it would have been without that theology.[6] The theological claims of his work caused greater outrage than his strictly political arguments, as he anticipated they would.[7] The provocative character of his interpretation was evidently intentional, and the furor it raised was probably not entirely unwelcome. For Hobbes's aim was not simply to accommodate his political doctrine to the existing prejudices of his readers. Such an aim, if accomplished, would have left them in the same ignorant, essentially irrational condition in which he had found them. And in Hobbes's view, as we have seen, this condition made the establishment of a genuinely well-constructed, lasting commonwealth impossible. The aim of his political argument, in the narrow sense, was to demonstrate how such a commonwealth could be established. The aim of his theological argument was to help prepare the way for such a commonwealth. To accomplish this aim Hobbes had to jolt his readers out of their old ways of thinking, to provoke them into reconstructing their own interpretations of the world and their place within it. The radicalism of his reinterpretation of Scriptures was simply one element in a larger design: to transform his readers into more rational and predictable beings, and by doing so to make them better suited for membership in a new kind of political society.

The Rules of Scriptural Interpretation

Hobbes's claim that the Scriptures have been widely misunderstood implies that there is an urgent need for a correct interpretation to be formulated. Such an interpretation, he points out, cannot flow from a naive reading of the texts. A naive, undis-

[6] Polin, *Hobbes, Dieu, et les hommes*, pp. 46-48.

[7] Cf. Samuel I. Mintz, *The Hunting of Leviathan* (Cambridge: Cambridge University Press, 1962).

ciplined reading would only reinforce misunderstandings and prejudices that have already been acquired. The true light of the Scriptures can be revealed only by a disciplined reading governed by careful adherence to sound principles of interpretation.

Hobbes formulates two main principles to govern his reading of the Scriptures. The first of these is laid down at the outset of *Leviathan* part III, which contains the bulk of his Scriptural argumentation. Hobbes points out that the basis of his argument in part III differs from that underlying the foregoing two parts of his book. The theory of human nature in part I and the theory of the state in part II were based upon a reading of God's "Naturall Word"—that is, upon the application of reason to the evidence of the natural senses. Part III, on the other hand, is based upon God's "Propheticall Word," by which Hobbes means the Bible. "Neverthelesse," he argues,

> we are not to renounce our Senses, and Experience; nor (that which is the undoubted Word of God) our naturall Reason. For they are the talents which he hath put into our hands to negotiate, till the coming again of our blessed Saviour; and therefore not to be folded up in the Napkin of an Implicate Faith, but employed in the purchase of Justice, Peace, and true Religion. For though there be many things in Gods Word above Reason; that is to say, which cannot by naturall reason be either demonstrated, or confuted; yet there is nothing contrary to it; but when it seemeth so, the fault is either in our unskilfull Interpretation, or erroneous Ratiocination.[8]

This was not, in itself, a radical thesis. Hobbes does not deny that the Bible contains mysteries that are beyond our comprehension. And his claim that these mysteries cannot contain

[8] *Leviathan*, ch. 32, pp. 409-410 [195].

anything that is, in principle, contrary to reason, while certainly controversial, was not unprecedented.[9]

Nevertheless, some of the interpretative consequences that flowed from Hobbes's application of this principle were extremely unorthodox. Hobbes drew two corollaries from this general rule. The first was that the teachings of Scripture cannot be understood to contravene the rules of logic, "[f]or both parts of a contradiction cannot possibly be true: and therefore to enjoyne the beleife of them, is an argument of ignorance."[10] Anyone who appeals to supernatural revelation to justify a belief in contradictories is discredited by the fact of that appeal. Supernatural revelation is no more capable of contravening reason than is the written word of God itself.

The second corollary was that no interpretation which appears to bring the Scriptures into conflict with our knowledge of the natural world should be accepted without extremely close, careful scrutiny. Every effort should be made to reconcile the evidence of the texts with that of our experience, since experience and reason are the voice of God's natural word, just as the texts are that of his prophetic word.

Hobbes admits that there are many things in God's word "above Reason." When we encounter anything of this kind, which is genuinely beyond our power to comprehend, we ought

> to captivate our understanding to the Words; and not to labour in sifting out a Philosophicall truth by Logick, of such mysteries as are not comprehensible, nor fall under any rule of naturall science.[11]

[9] Richard Sherlock's argument that Hobbes's principle of "the priority of natural reason to faith" is alien to the Augustinian-Calvinist tradition is correct, but he mistakenly implies, in an otherwise fine article, that this principle was contrary to the entire tradition of Christian theology, whereas in fact it was well within the range of medieval Catholic orthodoxy. "The Theology of *Leviathan*: Hobbes on Religion," *Interpretation* 10 (1982), pp. 43-60.

[10] *Leviathan*, ch. 12, p. 179 [58].

[11] *Leviathan*, ch. 32, p. 410 [195].

But to captivate the understanding in this sense, Hobbes insists, is not to abdicate our power of reasoning. It is to be willing to obey God's commands even when the reason for those commands is beyond our understanding. In no event should we allow the words of Scripture to confute the knowledge we derive from experience and reason, or to be interpreted as a source of knowledge of the natural world.

This last conclusion is also implied by the second main principle Hobbes adopts in his reading of the Scriptures. Although it governs his entire reading, this principle is not actually formulated until the end of part III, after the presentation of most of his argument. Hobbes presents it, in fact, as a general rule for the interpretation of any work:

> For it is not the bare Words, but the Scope of the writer that giveth the true light, by which any writing is to bee interpreted; and they that insist upon single Texts, without considering the main Designe, can derive no thing from them cleerly; but rather by casting atomes of Scripture, as dust before mens eyes, make every thing more obscure than it is; an ordinary artifice of those that seek not the truth, but their own advantage.[12]

The Scriptures, Hobbes argues, have two very simple purposes: to prepare men to become God's obedient subjects and to show them the way to salvation. "The Scripture was written to shew unto men the kingdome of God; and to prepare their mindes to become his obedient subjects."[13] It is no part of their purpose to deliver knowledge of the natural world, which God has left "to the disputation of men, for the exercising of their naturall Reason."[14] Indeed, the attempt to discover such knowledge in Scriptures is bound to go astray, since they are written in the

[12] *Leviathan*, ch. 43, p. 626 [332].

[13] *Leviathan*, ch. 8, p. 145 [38-39]; cf. ch. 45, p. 663 [355].

[14] *Leviathan*, ch. 8, p. 145 [39].

inexact language of ordinary life.[15] The Bible is not a guide to the understanding of nature, and any attempt to treat it as such a guide is likely to result in the suppression of truth.[16]

This "minimum theology," the origins of which can be traced back to the immensely popular writings of Erasmus, who spent most of his life campaigning for reform of the Catholic church from within, implies that those who insist on interpreting the Bible according to its literal sense are fundamentally mistaken about the nature of their text. The Bible is not a key to all knowledge of the universe. It was written for a specific purpose, to guide men toward obedience and salvation. It was written for ordinary people in their own language, a language that is ill-designed to convey any information about the world other than that which is necessary for obedience and salvation. In many places this language has become archaic. If taken literally it sometimes seems to conflict with the truths of science. For Hobbes the occurrence of such a conflict is sufficient reason to discard the literal meaning of the text.[17] Yet when literalism seems to support a naturalistic interpretation of Scriptural teachings, Hobbes insists upon it.[18]

Although Hobbes implies repeatedly throughout *Leviathan* that he accepts the Scriptures as absolutely authoritative, the combined effect of his two main principles of interpretation is to diminish that authority severely. His first principle subjects the Bible to the controls of reason and experience. It thus inverts the Augustinian view that man's imperfect reason is subordinate as a form of knowledge to the prophetic word of God revealed in the Scriptures. When combined with Hobbes's mechanical materialism, this inversion prepared the way for a ra-

[15] "As for that our Saviour speaketh to the disease, as to a person; it is the usuall phrase of all that cure by words onely, as Christ did . . ." (*Leviathan*, ch. 8, p. 145 [39]; see also ch. 45, pp. 660-664 [353-356]).

[16] *Leviathan*, ch. 46, p. 703 [380].

[17] See the discussions of inspiration, *Leviathan*, ch. 34, pp. 440-442 [214-215], and incorporeal spirits, ch. 45, pp. 661-664 [354-356].

[18] *Leviathan*, ch. 35, p. 442 [216].

tionalization of the Biblical teaching that left very little room for the mysteries that had played such a large part in traditional Christian teachings. His second principle delivered another telling blow to Scriptural authority. By arguing that the Bible must be interpreted in the light of its main design, Hobbes diminished its scope dramatically. The Bible is not, he argued, a lense through which men can interpret the whole of their experience, as most of his contemporaries were accustomed to assume. It points the way toward obedience and salvation, the most important of all human concerns, but it is not an infallible guide to knowledge of the entire world. The Bible whose authority Hobbes accepted had been severely diminished in its range of application and bridled by the rule of reason, interpreted through the filter of Hobbes's own mechanical conception of the natural world.

The Corporeal Soul

Hobbes applies these interpretative principles to the Scriptures with relentless virtuosity. Since all sound reasoning rests upon a foundation of consistent linguistic usage, he argues, the first task is to settle the meanings of certain ambiguous terms. These meanings cannot be determined by arbitrary definition, as is the case in natural science, or by common usage, as they are in ordinary conversation. Their usage in the Bible itself is the sole reliable guide to their Biblical meaning.[19] Hobbes examines this usage in great detail. Underlying his examination at every point, however, are these two principles of interpretation, which guide his argument surely toward metaphysical and historical conclusions designed to underpin his views of politics and man.

Hobbes himself groups his analysis of Scriptural "errors" and "abuses" under three main headings. One consists of those er-

[19] *Leviathan*, ch. 34, p. 428 [207].

rors which have to do with the nature and fate of the soul. These errors arise principally "from the Misinterpretation of the words *Eternall Life, Everlasting Death*, and the *Second Death*. . . . All which Doctrine is founded onely on some of the obscurer places of the New Testament." Another "generall abuse of Scripture" has to do with "the turning of Consecration into Conjuration, or Enchantment," and more generally with the character of prophecy, miracles, and magic. Hobbes's final category of Scriptural misinterpretations, which he calls the "greatest, and main abuse of Scripture" has to do with the attempt "to prove that the Kingdome of God . . . is the present Church, or multitude of Christian men now living, or that being dead, are to rise again at the last day."[20]

Hobbes had already developed the rudiments of his minimum theology in *The Elements of Law* by drawing a strong distinction between those points of faith which are necessary to salvation and those which are mere "SUPERSTRUCTION," as well as by distinguishing between "matter[s] of faith" and those "of philosophy."[21] Yet of the three topics into which he groups his analysis of Scriptural misinterpretations, only the third, which has to do with misunderstanding of the nature of the kingdom of God, was developed in that work. And in *De Cive*, where he elaborates his analysis of the kingdom of God in detail, Hobbes remains silent on the nature of the soul, and nearly so on the subject of "Conjuration, or Enchantment." Both works contain passages in which he might easily have commented on these topics. In *The Elements of Law*, for example, he notes that the belief that Jesus is the Messiah necessarily implies a belief in "the immortality of the soul, without which we cannot believe he is a Saviour."[22] But he comments neither upon the nature of the soul nor upon the meaning of its immortality.

Hence of the three main topics into which Hobbes divides

[20] *Leviathan*, ch. 44, pp. 636-637, 633, 629 [339, 337, 334].

[21] *Elements* II.6.5, 9.

[22] *Elements* II.6.6.

his analysis, only one had received serious treatment in his previous works. This observation is significant because the first two topics, the soul and magic, play a different role in his argument from that played by his analysis of the kingdom of God. Misunderstanding of the concept of God's kingdom was important to Hobbes because that kingdom was sometimes identified with an existing authority, such as the Catholic or Presbyterian church. This kind of identification was dangerous because it meant that men would consider themselves subject to two distinct powers, one temporal and one spiritual, with all the potential for conflicts of loyalty implied by that dual subjection. In *The Elements of Law* and *De Cive* his arguments are designed to minimize this potential for conflict; in *Leviathan* they are designed to eliminate it.[23] But erroneous beliefs about the soul and magic, in Hobbes's view, raised different sorts of problems. Mistaken opinions on these topics could induce men into disobedience of all established authority of any kind whatsoever. For such opinions could lead men to believe, falsely, that there are rewards greater than life and punishments greater than death. Men who believe in such rewards and punishments will not respond to real, mundane sanctions in rational ways. In short, Hobbes's discussion of misinterpretations of Scripture concerning the soul and magic is an attempt to get at the roots of a fundamental derangement of the psyche, of the way in which men and women think of themselves and of their relationships and connections with the world. It is an attempt, not conceived before *Leviathan*, to combat that irrationality which he saw as a threat to all forms of political authority. The remainder of this chapter will examine that attempt, while Hobbes's arguments concerning the kingdom of God will be discussed in the next.

[23] In *De Cive* XVII. 14, for example, Hobbes accepts as legitimate the distinction between spiritual and temporal things without hinting at the wholesale attack upon the distinction between spiritual and temporal powers he was to mount later, in *Leviathan*. Cf. below, p. 170.

Hobbes begins his interpretation by defining the meaning of the term *spirit* in its Biblical usage.[24] Body and spirit are commonly juxtaposed to one another as opposites by scholastic philosophers. They consider body to be a corporeal substance, while spirit is an incorporeal substance. Properly speaking, however, the words body and substance signify exactly the same thing. We call things *body* because they occupy some space or place in the universe. We call them *substance* because they are subject to change. All real parts of the universe, Hobbes argues, possess both of these attributes: all occupy some place, and all are subject to change. The only reason for the existence of these two different words is that everything in the universe has both of these distinct attributes, and can therefore be described in two different ways. In the strictest sense of these terms, then, the phrase "Substance incorporeall" is self-contradictory and nonsensical. Substance and body are the same thing; no real part of the universe can ever genuinely be incorporeal.

This opening argument belies Hobbes's claim that his interpretation is based upon Scriptural usage alone. The basis of his definitions is a strict, materialist metaphysics. In the pages that follow, he reconciles these definitions with Scriptural evidence, but at no point does he actually base them upon such evidence.

The significance of the term *body* in common usage differs from its proper meaning. In general, things are called bodies only when they are perceptible to the external senses of vision and touch. Fine or subtle substances like air are called by other names, such as wind, breath, or spirits, from the Latin term *Spiritus*. The term *spirit* is also applied to figments of the imagination, which are

> Nothing at all, I say, there where they seem to bee; and in the brain it self, nothing but tumult, proceeding either

[24] *Leviathan*, ch. 34, pp. 428-434 [207-211].

> from the action of the objects, or from the disorderly agitation of the Organs of our Sense.[25]

There are also several metaphorical meanings of *spirit* in common usage, as when the term is used to describe a disposition of the mind, an exceptional ability, or a passion of extraordinary strength.

These common usages give rise to considerable confusion. If the term *corporeal* is applied only to substances that are perceptible to the external senses, then it makes some sense to say that incorporeal substances exist. These subtle and invisible substances might be called spirits without giving rise to confusion if that term were used in a clear and consistent way. In fact, however, its meaning in common usage is riddled with ambiguities. Because *spirit* is used metaphorically and applied to figments of the imagination as well as realities, its meaning in any given instance is often very obscure. The net result of these overlapping usages has been to foster the opinion that genuinely incorporeal substances—substances that have no bodily nature at all—exist. In Hobbes's eyes this opinion is a manifest absurdity. A clear understanding of the meanings of the terms that make up this phrase is all that is required for its self-contradictory character to become evident. Such an understanding is obstructed by common or "vulgar" usage, and it is made nearly impossible by the nonsensical philosophy of the scholastics.[26]

Since the Bible was written in ordinary language to lead men toward obedience and salvation, the significations of *spirit* in it are as various as they are in everyday speech. Sometimes the term refers to a fine substance, such as wind or some "Aeriall *Body*."[27] At other times it is used metaphorically, in a variety of different senses. But at no time, Hobbes argues, is it used to

[25] *Leviathan*, ch. 34, p. 429 [208].

[26] Cf. *Leviathan*, ch. 4, p. 108 [17], and ch. 5, p. 113 [19].

[27] *Leviathan*, ch. 34, pp. 433-434 [210].

denote a substance that has no bodily nature at all. Such a usage would be utterly meaningless. The Bible was not designed to deliver knowledge of nature, but it must be assumed that nothing in it actually contradicts a true understanding of the natural world. *Spirit*, therefore, means a number of different things in Scripture, but it never refers to that natural impossibility, a genuinely incorporeal substance.

The significance of this argument is not merely metaphysical. Hobbes draws a variety of inferences from it. One of these is that angels, when they are real and permanent beings at all, must be corporeal, bodily beings. As such beings, their movements must obey the natural laws of motion that govern all material things. Another is that all Scriptural usages of the term *inspiration*, which literally means the blowing into a man of "some thin and subtile aire,"[28] are metaphorical.

But the most important inference Hobbes draws from this argument is that the soul is a corporeal, material substance. As such a substance the soul cannot be independent of the body, since it is itself a body. Nor can it be intrinsically eternal, since all substances are subject to change. According to this unorthodox, though not wholly unprecedented interpretation, the soul, like any spirit, is an ordinary, corporeal substance.[29]

This interpretation has great political significance. The notion of an immaterial, eternal soul is a "window" which "gives entrance to the Dark Doctrine" that the souls of sinners are consigned to a place of "Eternall Torments" after their death.[30] Alongside this imaginary hell, there arose a second—and for the church of Rome even more profitable—fiction: that of purgatory. The doctrine of purgatory gave rise to belief in ghosts,

[28] *Leviathan*, ch. 34, p. 440 [214].

[29] Hobbes cites the fourteenth chapter of Job, a complaint about human mortality, in support of this interpretation in *Leviathan*, ch. 38, pp. 483-484 [241]. In ch. 44, pp. 644-649 [343-346], he defends his view against a set of Scriptural passages that seem to imply the soul is immortal by nature.

[30] *Leviathan*, ch. 44, pp. 638-639 [340].

which in turn provided a foundation for the fantastic practices of exorcism, conjuration, and invocation of the dead; and to the doctrine of indulgences, which has proved to be so profitable to the Catholic Church over the centuries. Although their object is purely a figment of the imagination, the fears raised by the notion of an immaterial, eternal soul have proved themselves to be powerful weapons in the struggle between spiritual and temporal leaders for control of men's actions. Hobbes's refutation of this concept of the soul, which he regards as a "contagion" in Christianity originating in the "Daemonology" of the Greeks,[31] is a major element in his struggle to purge the Christian religion of the superstitious, magical strands of thought with which it has been infected since its earliest days.

Hobbes's conclusion that the soul must be an ordinary material thing is a straightforward inference from his own metaphysical materialism, a view he considered to be justified by science and therefore necessarily consistent with Scripture. Perhaps his boldest statement of this materialism occurs in chapter 46 of *Leviathan*:

> The World, (I mean not the Earth onely, that denominates the Lovers of it *Worldly men*, but the *Universe*, that is, the whole masse of all things that are) is Corporeall, that is to say, Body; . . . And because the Universe is All, that which is no part of it, is *Nothing*; and consequently *no where*. Nor does it follow from hence, that Spirits are *nothing*: for they have dimensions, and are therefore really *Bodies*.[32]

Yet Hobbes's materialist views, which were already completely formed when he composed *The Elements of Law* and *De Cive*, did not lead him to draw this inference about the nature of the soul in these earlier works. The evident reason for this

[31] *Leviathan*, ch. 45, p. 659 [353].
[32] P. 689 [371].

omission was that in neither earlier work had he fully grasped the political significance of the way in which men conceived their souls. In *Leviathan*, however, his grasp of that significance is absolutely clear and direct. Answering his own rhetorical question about what place such seemingly arcane metaphysical speculations can have in a work of political philosophy, he argues:

> It is to this purpose, that men may no longer suffer themselves to be abused, by them, that . . . would fright them from Obeying the Laws of their Countrey, with empty names; . . . For it is upon this ground, that when a Man is dead and buried, they say his Soule (that is his Life) can walk separated from his Body, and is seen by night amongst the graves . . . that the Figure, and Colour, and Tast of a peece of Bread, has a being, there, where they say there is no Bread . . . that Faith, and Wisdome, and other Vertues are sometimes *powred* into a man, sometimes *blown* into him from Heaven; . . . and a great many other things that serve to lessen the dependance of Subjects on the Soveraign Power of their Countrey.[33]

The ultimate root of Hobbes's argument lies in his recognition that men can be moved by imaginary rewards and punishments, and that these imaginary sanctions can exercise even greater power over men's actions than the real benefits of life or the real evil of death. The Christian mythology of the immortal soul is like a dagger aimed at the heart of every commonwealth that must endure its presence. Men who believe in eternal life will not hesitate to disobey their sovereign if they think that obedience will prevent them from attaining it. Those who believe in eternal torment will not be deterred by the threat of an earthly death if they consider that death a step on the way to their salvation. The concept of the soul that has contaminated

[33] *Leviathan*, ch. 46, pp. 691-692 [372-373].

Christianity since its inception is, Hobbes believes, a metaphysical absurdity. More important to him, however, is the fact that this concept is inimical to all sovereign power and civil peace. For, as he points out, "[i]t is impossible a Commonwealth should stand, where any other than the Soveraign, hath a power of giving greater rewards than Life; and of inflicting greater punishments, than Death."[34]

In reality Hobbes does not believe that there is any greater punishment than death. But those who have accepted the Christian mythology of the immortal soul believe in such punishments. Though these punishments are imaginary, the imagination of them is real, and has very palpable effects upon the actions of believers. If these effects lie under the control of the sovereign, then the myth of the soul poses no great threat to secular power. If they are subject to the manipulations of a separate clergy, however, that myth could prove to be the undoing of all civil peace. Hobbes's attempt to destroy the Christian mythology of the immortal soul with the weapon of metaphysical materialism is the first prong of a strategy designed to lead men toward that enlightened, rational understanding of their own interests which he believes will form the firmest foundation possible for a truly lasting commonwealth.[35]

Prophecy, Miracles, and Magic

The mythology of the immortal soul was not the only superstition Hobbes considered dangerous to commonwealths. He was

[34] *Leviathan*, ch. 38, p. 478 [238].

[35] Hence Warrender's argument, in his *Political Philosophy of Hobbes*, that divine sanctions underpin and support Hobbes's entire political theory, is virtually the opposite of the truth, which is that Hobbes viewed those sanctions as inimical to all rational political authority. The significance of this point is also misconstrued in a rather obscurely argued passage in Eisenach's *Two Worlds of Liberalism*, pp. 47-50.

equally concerned about the impact that belief in prophecy, miracles, and magic had upon the behavior of Christian subjects. The thread uniting these beliefs was the idea of a supernatural event. At the creation God had laid down certain laws to govern the ordinary operations of natural phenomena. A supernatural event was a suspension or interruption of these laws. Such an event was usually called a miracle. Among their other purported uses, miracles were thought to be God's way of validating the testimony of his prophets. Some people believed that only God could perform miracles, but others thought human beings or spirits could possess supernatural powers, too. The exercise of such powers by beings other than God was called magic.

These beliefs were dangerous because they led men to attribute powers to others who were not necessarily their civil sovereigns. This attribution traveled by two distinct routes. Prophets were powerful because it was believed that they possessed special knowledge of God's will. Their sayings were thought to be divine in origin. Those who believed in them considered obedience to their words to be obedience to God. Since God was superior to all civil sovereigns, it was unthinkable that his prophetic words should be disregarded even if those words should clash with a sovereign's commands. Those men who were believed to have the gift of prophecy were in a position to override the commands of their sovereign. Anyone who disobeyed his sovereign could be punished by him; but one who disobeyed a prophet would be punished by God. Magicians, on the other hand, were thought to exercise supernatural powers directly. The powers available to them were not as great as those of God himself, but they were more than enough to terrify those who believed in magic. It was no uncommon thing for men and women to be so mesmerized by their imagination of these powers that their very lives came to seem unimportant to them.[36]

36 For a general account of magical beliefs in seventeenth-century England,

Nothing prevented sovereigns from taking advantage of these beliefs to supplement their powers. Ancient kings had done so with great regularity and success.[37] They presented themselves as prophets or agents of God and made their laws appear to be prescribed by his divine commands. They set up ceremonies and festivals to cultivate and regulate their subjects' beliefs. They established an entire pantheon of gods to promote peace and obedience among their subjects and installed their poets as high priests of the heathen religions they had formed. In these many ways they made the superstitions of their subjects into a tool of their own policies. Modern sovereigns claimed to exercise supernatural powers, too. Throughout most of the seventeenth century, subjects flocked to the royal court, sometimes at a rate of thousands each year, in the hope that their diseases could be cured by the King's touch. James I appears to have considered this practice a superstitious relic, but prudently decided to continue it anyway. Magical healing powers were also attributed to coins the King would hang around the necks of the sick. Belief in the King's magical powers continued to flourish until after Hobbes's death in the late years of the century.[38]

The problem was that modern sovereigns did not possess a monopoly over these powers, and that there was no evident way for them to acquire such a monopoly.[39] Others claimed them, too, and often managed to have these claims believed. Neither magicians nor prophets were in short supply in England during Hobbes's lifetime. They were especially active and visible during the 1640's, when the social controls which had been main-

---

see Keith Thomas, *Religion and the Decline of Magic* (Harmondsworth, Middlesex: Penguin, 1973).

[37] *Leviathan*, ch. 12, pp. 177-178 [57], and ch. 45, pp. 658-659 [352-353].

[38] Thomas, *Religion and Magic*, pp. 227-242.

[39] Contrast Tarlton's argument on this point in "The Creation and Maintenance of Government," p. 315.

tained by the monarchy had broken down and those which were later put in place by the parliamentary regime had not yet been established. In Hobbes's eyes, magicians and prophets were the mortal enemies of sovereign power and civil peace. The root of their claims to supernatural power was a desire to exercise real power over other men and women. To thwart this desire was an aim of paramount importance to the argument of *Leviathan.* The beliefs in prophecy, miracles, and magic would have to be tamed before sovereign authority could be established upon firm foundations.

Hobbes might have swept aside the ideas of prophecy and magic in the same uncompromising manner with which he rejected the concept of the immortal soul. Miracles and magic, he might have argued, are impossibilities because the entire universe is governed by strict, inescapable, mechanical laws of nature. Hobbes must have been tempted to frame his argument in this simple way. Many of his arguments seem to presuppose the view that the universe is governed by such a mechanical determinism. This view was a basic premise of his natural philosophy.[40] It was also fundamental to his attack on the concept of free will, which developed into the most celebrated of several controversies in which he was a principal.[41] At times he portrays mechanical determinism, along with materialism, as a view that cannot be denied without absurdity.[42]

In spite of his apparent commitment to mechanical determinism, Hobbes did not argue that supernatural events are impossible in principle. In *Leviathan*, at least, he accepts their metaphysical possibility. Having done so, he then subjects the idea of a supernatural event or miracle to very detailed critical

[40] See Brandt, *Thomas Hobbes' Mechanical Conception.*

[41] See Hobbes's comments on liberty and necessity in *Leviathan*, ch. 21, p. 263 [108], and Mintz's summary account of this controversy in *Hunting of Leviathan*, pp. 110-133.

[42] Hobbes ridicules the ideas of "*A free Subject*" and "*free-Will*" along with that of "*Immateriall Substances*" in *Leviathan*, ch. 5, p. 113 [19].

scrutiny by logical, textual, and historical means. The net result of his arguments is almost as negative as—and, given the presuppositions of his readers, immensely more effective than—a metaphysical rejection would have been. The concept of magic is dismissed entirely. The ideas of miracles and prophecy are surrounded by hedges. As metaphysical ideas they linger on in his account, but only in a form that drains them of all political potency.

Throughout its history, the chief beneficiary of the belief in magic had been the Church of Rome. Its leaders had tapped this belief brilliantly. They had turned the eucharist, baptism, and many other rites that had originally been designed as acts of commemoration into magical ceremonies intended to inspire men with awe.[43] They encouraged people to believe that their bodies could be entered and their souls possessed by evil spirits, and claimed to have the magical powers needed to exorcise these spirits.[44] They invented the fiction of purgatory and used it as the basis of an elaborate doctrine of indulgences, asserting an ability to affect God's dispensation of individual souls.[45]

By claiming the ability to influence the fate of men's souls, the Church of Rome managed to acquire an enormous reservoir of power over its members. This power made it into a "Kingdome of Fayries,"[46] a center of control over human beings based entirely upon the fantasies of superstitious Christians. The ultimate results of this control were disastrous. In every area except that limited territory over which it exercised civil sovereignty, the papacy became a kingdom within a kingdom, a center of power which often clashed with that of the sovereign. Subjects were asked to obey two masters, both of whom insisted that their commands be observed as law, "which," Hobbes ob-

[43] *Leviathan*, ch. 35, pp. 450-451 [221]; ch. 44, pp. 633-636 [337-339].

[44] *Leviathan*, ch. 45, pp. 664-665 [356].

[45] *Leviathan*, ch. 44, pp. 638-639 [340].

[46] *Leviathan*, ch. 29, p. 370 [171].

serves, "is impossible."[47] The final consequence of this clerical power was to sap the strength of all the commonwealths it invaded and to afflict them with the permanent threat of dissolution and civil war.

Hobbes opens his attack on magic by pointing out that all powers in the universe proceed from God. Just as God is the cause of all events that occur in the ordinary course of nature, so too is he the cause of all extraordinary or supernatural events. No mere man, nor any "Devil, Angel, or other created Spirit," can be such a cause.[48] To claim that an enchanter can perform a miracle by his own independent power is to deny this universally accepted premise and, in effect, to commit the sin of idolatry. If, on the other hand, an enchanter does anything by a power given him by God, then it must be a natural effect, not a supernatural or magical one.

This argument has little logical merit. There is no reason why God could not have granted extraordinary, supernatural power to agents subordinate to himself. Such power would both proceed from God and be supernatural. But Hobbes's argument does not really rest upon this logic. The main points in his argument are Scriptural and circumstantial, not philosophical.

Hobbes admits that there are certain texts of Scripture which seem to attribute magical powers to created beings. Thus, for example, the Bible speaks of magicians in Egypt who, following the miracles performed by God to call his people to the prophet Moses, turned their rods into serpents, changed water into blood, and brought pestilences onto the land "*with their Enchantments*." And yet, he points out, the Scriptures do not tell us what they mean by an enchantment:

> If therefore Enchantment be not, as many think it, a working of strange effects by spells, and words; but Imposture, and delusion, wrought by ordinary means, and so

[47] *Leviathan*, ch. 29, p. 371 [171].

[48] *Leviathan*, ch. 37, p. 474 [235].

> far from supernaturall, as the Imposters need not the study so much as of naturall causes, but the ordinary ignorance, stupidity, and superstition of mankind, to doe them; those texts that seem to countenance the power of Magick, Witchcraft, and Enchantment, must needs have another sense, than at first sight they seem to bear.[49]

When any apparently miraculous act has been done for any purpose other than the edification of God's people, Hobbes argues, no genuine act of magic has taken place. Instead, the spectator has been enchanted by deception: "For such is the ignorance, and aptitude to error generally of all men, but especially of them that have not much knowledge of naturall causes, and of the nature, and interests of men; as by innumerable and easie tricks to be abused."[50] This is exactly what the Egyptian conjurers mentioned in the book of Exodus did, deluding their spectators by a "false shew of things."[51]

There is no difference in kind, Hobbes argues, between this deception and that which takes place every day in the rituals of Catholic worship. By "turning the holy words into the manner of a Charme," the priests "face us down, that it hath turned the Bread into a Man; nay more, into a God." Nothing could be more absurd. When Christ says in the Bible, "*This is my Body*," he means that the bread signifies or represents his body. The priestly attempt to twist this ordinary figure of speech into a literal statement is a transparent effort to shore up their own claims to magical power in order to solidify their control over men. The same kind of distortion occurs in their interpretation of the sacraments of baptism, marriage, extreme unction, and the rest; and always with the same motive, to increase the power of the Catholic church.[52]

[49] *Leviathan*, ch. 37, pp. 474-475 [235-236].

[50] *Leviathan*, ch. 37, p. 475 [236].

[51] *Leviathan*, ch. 44, p. 634 [337].

[52] *Leviathan*, ch. 44, pp. 634-636 [337-339].

None of these arguments proves that genuinely magical events cannot take place. Yet it is important to remember that rigorous proof was not Hobbes's aim. What mattered to him was to destroy the credibility of those who used claims of magical power to gain control over their fellow men. For this purpose, the arguments he did produce were probably more effective than any rigorous proof would have been, even if such a proof had been available to him. And the fact is that no such proof was possible. Like the principles of science itself, those which underlie a magical interpretation of the world can neither be proved nor disproved. Hobbes probably considered the principles behind all magic absurd; but if he did so, he must have regarded their absurdity as a self-evident truth that cannot be demonstrated by logical or scientific means. He did not, in fact, deny the metaphysical possibility of supernatural events. What he did deny was that any human being—or for that matter any created being at all—possesses magical power, the power to cause supernatural events at his own discretion. His arguments were essentially circumstantial and *ad hominem.* They were not designed to disprove the possibility of magic so much as to cast doubt upon the genuineness and sincerity of those who claimed magical powers. The central issue for Hobbes was not whether magic is possible, though he almost certainly believed that it is not. The issue was whether some men had taken advantage of a widespread belief in magic to build bases of power for themselves to the detriment of their commonwealths and sovereigns.

Belief in magic posed a serious threat to the centralization of power Hobbes considered necessary to peace and security in any commonwealth. The argument of *Leviathan* is designed to undermine and ultimately destroy that belief. Hobbes did not think this destruction could best be accomplished by a direct philosophical attack. Such an attack might leave its victim logically crippled, but this would not ensure its destruction as a popular belief. The more important instruments of his attack were the suggestions of deception and insinuations of dishonest intentions that run through his comments on magic from the first mention of the subject in *Leviathan* until the end. Once implanted in men's minds, he hoped, these suggestions would lead them to see their world in a new light, gnawing away slowly at the superstitious beliefs and fears that had held men in their clutches for so long. The destruction of these beliefs and fears would clear the way for that new, rational approach to life upon which Hobbes hoped a commonwealth of perfected design and greatly enhanced security would arise.

The central object of Hobbes's attack, then, was neither the Catholic church as such—in spite of the blasting criticisms he throws in its direction—nor Christianity itself. His real target lies deeper than the institutions and traditions of Christianity; it consists of a state of mind, a set of underlying beliefs about the self and the world that underpins those institutions and makes those traditions possible. Hobbes's polemic was directed not simply at the church itself, but at the entire mental outlook upon which it rested; and its aim was to transform that outlook so thoroughly that neither those institutions and traditions nor any others prejudicial to sovereign power would be able to arise again.

Although Hobbes's arguments were designed to destroy the credibility of magic in all of its forms, he did not reject the ideas of prophecy and miracles in the same sweeping way. Along with natural reason and supernatural revelation, prophecy is one of the ways in which God makes his will known to man. He performs miracles to make his prophets known to others.[53] A great deal of the Bible itself is a record of his prophetic word and of the miracles by which it has been validated. Hobbes was not prepared to challenge the very ideas of prophecy and miracles, which were central to the entire corpus of Christian Scripture.

[53] *Leviathan*, ch. 31, p. 396 [187].

Yet the important role played by prophecy in Christian life is fraught with difficulties. It is extremely hard, he argues, to distinguish a true prophet from the many false pretenders to this title: "For he that pretends to teach men the way of so great felicity, pretends to govern them; that is to say, to rule, and reign over them; which is a thing, that all men naturally desire."[54] Some men may become genuinely convinced that they are prophets by confusing their dreams and fantasies with supernatural visions.[55] Others simply set out to deceive their fellow men in order to gratify their own ambitions. Whatever their motives, the bulk of all those who claim to be prophets are false ones.[56]

The only way to ensure against being misled by a false prophet, Hobbes argues, is constantly to bear in mind the two marks for discerning a true prophet laid down in Holy Scripture. These are, first, that a true prophet must perform miracles; and second, that his teaching must not conflict with the religion already established in his country.[57] Neither of these marks alone is sufficient. The Bible warns repeatedly that false prophets can sometimes perform miracles as genuine as those evoked by true prophets. Nor is preaching the established doctrine enough to mark any man a prophet. Miracles are necessary, but not sufficient, for the identification of prophets.

Even so, it is obvious that an ability to distinguish genuine miracles from mere deceptions would do much to prevent men from being misled by false prophets. Hobbes defines a miracle as "*a work of God, (besides his operation by the way of Nature, ordained in the Creation,) done for the making manifest to his elect, the mission of an extraordinary Minister for their salvation.*"[58] The simplicity of this definition is deceptive. In the first place, Hobbes

[54] *Leviathan*, ch. 36, p. 466 [230].

[55] *Leviathan*, ch. 32, p. 411 [196].

[56] *Leviathan*, ch. 32, p. 412 [196-197].

[57] *Leviathan*, ch. 32, pp. 412-414 [197-198]; ch. 36, p. 467 [231].

[58] *Leviathan*, ch. 37, p. 473 [235].

had already argued that God performs many miracles in order to test men's faith, and not to confirm his prophets. The example with which he illustrates this point is curious. It is that of the Egyptian sorcerers whom, as we have seen, he later brands as deceiving impostors. Here, however, he says that their works, "though not so great as those of *Moses*, yet were great miracles."[59] In the second place, immediately before formulating his definition, Hobbes makes it clear that many miracles only *seem* to lie outside the ordinary operations of nature. One of his examples is that of the first rainbow to be seen in the world.[60] This rainbow was, he says, a miracle simply because it was the first. Its appearance caused admiration and wonder in those who saw it, making it a suitable means for God to convey his intentions to his people. Since that time, though, rainbows have been commonplace, their natural causes have been discovered, and they are therefore no longer miraculous.

Indeed, the criteria by which Hobbes proposes we should recognize miracles appear to be inherently vague. The first of these is strangeness. An event that is unique, or nearly so, is likely to produce wonder in those who see it, and may very well be a miracle. The difficulty with this criterion is that an event which seems strange to some people will not necessarily seem so to others. The strangeness of an event is at least partly dependent upon the eyes of its beholders, as the example of the first rainbow testifies. The second criterion for recognizing a miracle is even more peculiar: inexplicability; that is, "if when it is produced, we cannot imagine it to have been done by naturall means, but onely by the immediate hand of God."[61] This formula contains a serious ambiguity. If Hobbes means that an event is miraculous when no natural explanation of it is in principle imaginable, then this criterion is a reasonably strict one.

[59] *Leviathan*, ch. 32, p. 412 [197].

[60] *Leviathan*, ch. 37, pp. 470-471 [233].

[61] *Leviathan*, ch. 37, p. 470 [233].

But an alternative reading is that he means to call an event a miracle simply because those actually present cannot imagine a natural explanation for it. The consequences of this reading are very different from those of the first.

There are strong signs that the second reading is the one Hobbes really intends. His examples are one such sign. When he first mentions them, he calls the works of the Egyptian sorcerers genuine miracles; twelve chapters later, he brands them flagrant but extremely clever deceptions. Similarly, he calls the first rainbow a miracle; yet, in the same paragraph, he points out that rainbows are no longer miraculous because their natural causes are now understood. Hobbes draws the obvious inference himself:

> Furthermore, seeing Admiration and Wonder, is consequent to the knowledge and experience, wherewith men are endued, some more, some lesse; it followeth, that the same thing, may be a Miracle to one, and not to another.[62]

An event is miraculous because it is *perceived* to be strange and inexplicable, not because it really is inexplicable. In this sense miracles are products of their social setting. And as Hobbes immediately goes on to point out, "ignorant, and superstitious men make great Wonders of those works, which other men, knowing to proceed from Nature, (which is not the immediate, but the ordinary work of God,) admire not at all."[63] In short, the implication of his analysis is that the distinction between genuine miracles and mere deceptions is spurious. "Miracles" are actually, despite appearances, the concoctions of ignorant, superstitious minds.

This result may seem strange at first glance. Hobbes makes a great show of the importance of an ability to distinguish gen-

[62] *Leviathan*, ch. 37, p. 471 [234]. Cf. ch. 26, p. 332 [148]: "Miracles are Marvellous workes: but that which is marvellous to one, may not be so to another."

[63] *Leviathan*, ch. 37, p. 471 [234].

uine miracles from deceptions. Why should he propose criteria that cannot possibly be used to make this distinction? The answer lies in an historical corollary of his conclusion. Miracles occur among the ignorant much more often than among the educated. If man's power to fathom the causes of natural phenomena grows, his capacity to experience miracles will diminish proportionally. Ultimately the growth of knowledge may cause it to disappear. Miracles will become a thing of the past, an historical relic, like dinosaurs. Indeed, Hobbes suggests that this event has already come to pass:

> For in these times, I do not know one man, that ever saw any such wondrous work, done by the charm, or at the word, or prayer of a man, that a man endued but with a mediocrity of reason, would think supernaturall: and the question is no more, whether what wee see done, be a Miracle; whether the Miracle we hear, or read of, were a reall work, and not the Act of a tongue, or pen; but in plain terms, whether the report be true, or a lye.[64]

By supplying a naturalistic explanation of the commonplace Reformation doctrine that miracles have ceased,[65] Hobbes casts grave doubt upon the validity of the concept of a miracle as such. And if, as his analysis implies, all miracles are spurious, then the concept of prophecy is called into question as well, since one of the essential credentials of any prophet must be an ability to perform miracles.

The searing implications of this argument for those who claimed miraculous or prophetic powers in his own time are obvious, and its political significance is explicit:

> he that presumes to break the Law upon his own, or anothers Dream, or pretended Vision, or upon other Fancy of the power of Invisible Spirits, than is permitted by the

[64] *Leviathan*, ch. 37, p. 477 [237].

[65] *Leviathan*, ch. 32, p. 414 [198].

> Commonwealth, leaveth the Law of Nature, which is a certain offence, and followeth the imagery of his own, or another private mans brain, which he can never know whether it signifieth any thing, or nothing, nor whether he that tells his Dream, say true, or lye; which if every private man should have leave to do, (as they must by the Law of Nature, if any one have it) there could be no Law be made to hold, and so all Common-wealth would be dissolved.[66]

A rational commonwealth is possible at all only because miracles have ceased and prophecy has become a thing of the past—if, indeed, either ever really existed. And if "miracles" have ceased, it is because mankind has finally become sufficiently enlightened to see through them. Now all that remained to be done was for that process of enlightenment to be brought to completion, an achievement that would lay the groundwork for the kind of commonwealth Hobbes envisaged as a possibility actually to come into being.

[66] *Leviathan*, ch. 27, p. 344 [156].

CHAPTER SEVEN ✡

Scriptures and Sovereigns

THE SUBORDINATION OF PROPHECY

The Kingdom of God

HOBBES IDENTIFIES the Christian mythology of the immortal soul and the belief in conjuration, enchantment, and magic as two of the most widespread and dangerous of all misinterpretations of Christian doctrine. But the "greatest, and main abuse of Scripture," he argues, flows from a misinterpretation of its frequent references to the kingdom of God.[1] The kingdom of God is commonly thought to consist of an existing church, or of the body of all Christians living in the present, or of all Christians, living and dead. All these views, according to Hobbes, derive from a basic misunderstanding of the text. Like the mythology of the soul and beliefs in magic and contemporary prophecy, they also have extremely dangerous political implications.

In chapter 31 of *Leviathan*, "*Of the* KINGDOME OF GOD BY NATURE," Hobbes discusses three distinct meanings of this phrase.[2] The omnipotence of God makes him ruler of the entire universe. In this sense the whole world is sometimes called

[1] *Leviathan*, ch. 44, p. 629 [334], and pp. 630-639 [335-340].

[2] Pp. 395-397 [186-187].

God's kingdom. But this first use of the phrase is merely metaphorical. To reign in the proper sense, Hobbes argues, is to govern men by commands backed by the promise of rewards and the threat of punishments. Neither inanimate bodies nor animals can be God's subjects in this sense; nor, indeed, can atheists, since they take no heed of God's words. In this proper sense, God has two different kingdoms on earth. One of these is his kingdom by nature, which God rules through those natural laws by which he makes his will known to all those who will take the trouble to discern them. The other is his prophetic kingdom, in which he rules his chosen people by positive laws as well as the natural dictates of reason.

This last meaning is the one ordinarily carried by this phrase in Scripture.[3] The kingdom of God was a real, worldly kingdom constituted by a covenant between God and his chosen people. On some rare occasions in the New Testament the phrase is used metaphorically to denote God's dominion over sin. This usage, however, is exceptional and secondary; the primary sense is the most literal one.

This sense, Hobbes points out, is quite different from that which is commonly adopted in the writings and sermons of divines. They routinely identify the kingdom of God with a condition of eternal felicity in heaven. But this meaning is never reflected in Scriptural usage. The original kingdom of God was established by a covenant between God and Abraham, and was intended to apply to all of Abraham's descendants.[4] In it Abraham promised that he and his posterity would always obey God, and God promised Abraham everlasting possession of the land of Canaan. God did not at this time call himself a king, nor his dominion over Abraham a kingdom; but the effect was to establish God as sovereign over Abraham and all his descendants.

This original covenant was renewed by Moses at Mount

[3] *Leviathan*, ch. 35, p. 442 [216].

[4] *Leviathan*, ch. 35, pp. 443-448 [216-220].

Sinai. By mutual consent the Jews instituted a civil government to regulate their relations toward one another, toward other nations, and toward God. The commonwealth they created in doing so was a kingdom, with God as its sovereign and with Moses, and after him the high priests, as his lieutenants. When the Jews later rejected God, it was their desire for an earthly sovereign that led them to do so.

Still later Jesus was sent to re-establish this earthly kingdom over God's chosen people. That his mission was an earthly as well as spiritual one is proved, Hobbes argues, by several passages in Scripture. The angel Gabriel said of Jesus that he would sit upon "*the throne of his Father David*." His cross carried the inscription, "*King of the Jews*." His persecution and death flowed from his claim to be their king, which the Roman rulers took to be a threat to their own power; and according to one text, his disciples refused to recognize Roman decrees, "*saying there was another King, one Jesus*." All these places in Scripture prove that Jesus was sent to renew the sovereignty of God over his chosen people, first established by his covenant with Abraham and later revived by Moses.[5]

Thus, Hobbes concludes, the kingdom of God, as this phrase is used in both the Old and New Testament, is to be understood as a real, earthly kingdom. It is not merely a metaphorical assertion of God's omnipotence. Otherwise, he asks, what sense would it make to pray "*Thy Kingdome come*," as we do in the Lord's Prayer? We could not pray for the coming of God's kingdom if by that phrase we meant nothing more than the rule he always exercises over the entire world by virtue of his omnipotence. It is plain, then, that the kingdom referred to in that prayer is God's earthly kingdom over his chosen people. That kingdom was overthrown when the Jews revolted against the commonwealth instituted by their ancestors through Abraham

[5] *Leviathan*, ch. 35, p. 447 [218-219].

and Moses; it will return when they accept God's sovereignty, with Christ as his lieutenant, once again.

Hobbes's textual evidence for this literal interpretation is actually far from decisive. It is true that the texts he presents show that the kingdom of God referred to in the Bible cannot simply be a metaphorical expression for God's omnipotence. But this metaphorical interpretation was not the one about which he was most concerned. Perhaps his central point is that the kingdom of God is an earthly commonwealth rather than a spiritual unity. This latter view was prevalent in Christian thought, and had been a basic tenet of Catholic orthodoxy for centuries. None of the texts Hobbes cites, taken on their own, disprove it. Behind his argument lies a tacit premise: that the Old Testament lays down a pattern or model by which we are to interpret the New. Thus, he argues, one of the Old Testament prophecies concerning Christ was that he would be like Moses.[6] Moses chose twelve princes, one from each of the Hebrew tribes, to rule under him; Christ likewise chose twelve apostles to do the same. Moses chose seventy elders to assist in the spiritual guidance of his people; Christ ordained seventy disciples after the same pattern. Moses instituted the rite of circumcision and the sacrament of Passover; Christ imitated these in the new rite of baptism and the new sacrament of the Lord's Supper. By thus inverting the usual Christian view that the New Testament completes, perfects, and hence is superior in authority to the Old, Hobbes was able to argue that Christ's "office" or function was also dictated by the pattern established by Moses and his successors.

Indeed, Hobbes takes the roles of Abraham and Moses to be paradigmatic in an even wider sense.[7] In principle both were God's viceroys or lieutenants. God was sovereign over his chosen people, and his authority was strictly analogous to that of

[6] *Leviathan*, ch. 41, pp. 517-521 [264-266].

[7] *Leviathan*, ch. 40.

any mortal sovereign. In practice, however, he exercised this sovereignty exclusively through his sole lieutenant. Abraham was sovereign over the Jewish people before his convenant with God, and the covenant through which God's sovereignty over them was established was made with Abraham, as their authorized representative, rather than with the Jewish people directly. Moses, likewise, was sovereign of the Jews when they renewed their covenant with God. His authority derived originally from their consent, not from God's appointment. For the Jewish people, obedience to him was obedience to God. Both Abraham and Moses were sovereigns in their own right before becoming God's lieutenants, and for all practical purposes they remained sovereigns afterward.

Hobbes draws three general lessons from the examples of Abraham and Moses. The first is that all subjects to whom God has not spoken directly must receive his commands through the intermediary of their sovereign, whoever he may be. God did not speak to the Jewish people as a whole, Hobbes claims, but to Abraham alone in his time, and to Moses alone in his. Likewise, he does not often speak to private subjects in other commonwealths. In the absence of any supernatural revelation to the contrary, such subjects must take the word of their sovereign to be that of God. Second, no subject can be exempted from punishment for disobedience by claiming a private revelation or vision from God. Neither Abraham nor Moses granted such exemptions, and other sovereigns are not bound to do so either. Third, no member of a Christian commonwealth is entitled to interpret God's word against his sovereign. God spoke only to Abraham, who alone had the right to interpret God's word; other sovereigns have the same exclusive rights that Abraham enjoyed.

Thus Hobbes presents the pattern laid down by Abraham and Moses as a model for all sovereigns as well as for the rule of Christ over the Jews. There is no textual evidence to support his view that their rule should be adopted as such a model. But the purpose of this adoption, as a part of the argument of *Leviathan*, was the same as that which lay behind his interpretation of the kingdom of God. Hobbes's insistence that the kingdom of God was a real, earthly kingdom was designed to buttress a general conclusion of his political theory: that in any commonwealth, or at the very least any Christian commonwealth, supreme authority in religious matters must reside in the civil sovereign. By arguing that the kingdom of God described in Scripture was a kingdom in the literal sense, Hobbes could claim that no division between spiritual and civil authority had existed in Biblical times:

> To conclude; from the first institution of Gods Kingdome, to the Captivity, the Supremacy of Religion, was in the same hand with that of the Civill Soveraignty; and the Priests office after the election of Saul, was not Magisteriall, but Ministeriall.[8]

By tacitly assuming that the forms of government instituted by Abraham and Moses provided a model for all subsequent commonwealths to imitate,[9] Hobbes implied that no such division should ever be made.

One principal target of these arguments was, of course, the Catholic church. The distinction between spiritual or ecclesiastical power on the one hand and civil power on the other had served that church admirably. It provided the leverage by means of which successive popes had gradually established their ascendancy over civil sovereigns throughout Christendom. This ascendancy was the product of a number of doctrines and practices that had become institutionalized over the course of time. The distinction between clergy and laity, which had been ab-

[8] *Leviathan*, ch. 40, p. 509 [254-255].

[9] Joel Schwartz argues, by contrast, that the ancient Hebrew "kingdom of God" was *not* a model for Hobbes, while the "kingdom of God to come" is a "Hobbesian utopia." For this interesting if far-fetched view, see "Hobbes and the Two Kingdoms of God," *Polity* 18 (1985), pp. 7-24.

sent from the primitive Christian churches, was one of the first of these doctrines to achieve general recognition. The practice of coronation by bishops, which could be interpreted as implying clerical superiority over civil rulers and was therefore resisted by Charlemagne, was a later addition. The establishment of canon law as a vital framework for dispensing justice as distinct from the civil law, completed in the twelfth century with the general acceptance of Gratian's *Decreta*, was another. Finally, benefit of clergy, which exempted clerics from the jurisdiction of civil courts even for such extreme crimes as murder, completed the immunization of church personnel, at least in theory, from control by their civil sovereigns.[10] But all these doctrines and practices were rooted ultimately in two fundamental arguments: that spiritual power is essentially distinct from the temporal power exercised by civil sovereigns, and that the Roman popes are the legitimate holders of spiritual power throughout the Christian world. The Catholic church, according to this argument, is the existing kingdom of God, a body constituted by the spiritual union of all believers.

Hobbes's rejection of these arguments was absolute. Power, he asserted, is power, whatever men may choose to call it:

> For this distinction of Temporall, and Spirituall Power is but words. Power is as really divided, and as dangerously to all purposes, by sharing with another *Indirect* Power, as with a *Direct* one.[11]

The Catholic distinction between temporal and spiritual powers is mere verbiage. Its purpose has always been to camouflage the church's strenuous efforts to subject the civil sovereigns of Christendom to its control. This consideration alone can explain the fact that Hobbes's interpretation of this doctrine has not hitherto achieved universal acceptance:

[10] *Leviathan*, ch. 44, pp. 630-633 [335-337].

[11] *Leviathan*, ch. 42, p. 600 [315].

> There be so many other places that confirm this interpretation, that it were a wonder there is no greater notice taken of it, but that it gives too much light to Christian Kings to see their right of Ecclesiasticall Government.[12]

The view that the kingdom of God referred to in Scripture was a merely spiritual kingdom is so obviously false that no other explanation for it is possible. It is a deliberately contrived misinterpretation, one designed to conceal from Christian kings the true extent of their sovereign rights.

The second target of these arguments was the Calvinist view that the kingdom of God had begun again with Christ's resurrection. Hobbes agreed with the Calvinists that the kingdom of God is a real, earthly kingdom, in which spiritual and temporal powers are combined in one authority. Unlike him, however, they insisted that that authority was not the civil sovereign, but the presbytery.

This interpretation was far more difficult for Hobbes to rebut than the Catholic view. The key text had been identified by Theodore Beza, Calvin's successor at Geneva. This text is a statement by Jesus to his apostles: "*Verily I say unto you, that there be some of them that stand here, which shall not tast of death, till they have seene the Kingdome of God come with power.*"[13] Hobbes admits that, understood literally, this text implies either that the kingdom of God exists in the present or that some of those men to whom Christ was speaking remain alive, still awaiting the coming of that kingdom. The latter possibility is absurd; hence the former seems inescapable. But, he points out, there are other places in Scripture that contradict this conclusion. Immediately before his ascension, Christ speaks of the restoration

[12] *Leviathan*, ch. 35, p. 447 [219]. Hobbes develops his argument against the papal claim to supreme ecclesiastical power even further in a lengthy and ingenious polemic against Cardinal Bellarmine in *Leviathan*, ch. 42, pp. 576-609 [300-320].

[13] *Leviathan*, ch. 44, p. 640 [341]; the passage is from Mark 9:1.

of the kingdom of God as an event that will occur in the future; the speech is inconsistent with the view that this event had already taken place at the resurrection. St. Paul speaks of waiting for Christ to come to restore his kingdom. And that famous phrase in the Lord's Prayer, one of Hobbes's favorite Scriptural texts, in which worshippers supplicate God to let *"Thy Kingdome come,"* implies that the coming of God's kingdom remains an event of the future. With all this evidence against it, the most obvious interpretation of Jesus' words, Hobbes argues, cannot possibly be correct.

The conjecture Hobbes offers to explain these words is that they are to be explicated by reference to the event that follows immediately after them, both in the gospel of St. Mark and in that of St. Luke. This event was the transfiguration, in which Christ appeared in a radiant, physically altered state and spoke in person with the prophet Elias and with Moses. Three of his disciples witnessed this event. Hobbes conjectures that it was by way of this vision that Christ's promise was fulfilled. Some of the apostles saw the kingdom of God come with power; but they saw this in a vision rather than in its actual appearance on earth.

Whatever may be the true interpretation of this text, Hobbes argues, the weight of Scriptural evidence shows that the kingdom of God did not begin at the resurrection. It begins with Christ's second coming, an event that will occur at some time in the indefinite future. There is no kingdom of God presently existent in this world. Hence the claims of Presbyterians to represent the real, earthly kingdom of God are ill-founded. Their attempts to assert directly the power of their own church government over that of civil sovereigns by claiming jurisdiction as the keepers of God's earthly kingdom are ultimately no more plausible, and no less destructive, than the Catholic efforts to gain political control over sovereigns through a specious distinction between temporal and spiritual powers.

Both Catholics and Presbyterians, then, are fundamentally

mistaken about the nature and locus of ecclesiastical power. Catholics argue that ecclesiastical power is essentially distinct from temporal power: that the kingdom of God is an existing, spiritual unity of all Christians regulated by ecclesiastical power; and that the Roman pope is the legitimate successor to this power. Presbyterians argue that ecclesiastical power is not so much distinct from, as superior to, all temporal power; that the kingdom of God is a real, earthly kingdom, not merely a spiritual unity of all Christians; and that the presbyteries of each independent city or country are the rightful holders of this power. The Presbyterians are right to reject the Catholic division between ecclesiastical and temporal power, but wrong to consider the former superior to the latter. They are also right to reject the Catholic notion that the kingdom of God is a merely spiritual entity, but absolutely wrong to claim that it began with the resurrection and exists in the present.

These mistakes and misinterpretations are not, Hobbes emphasizes, merely the products of honest misunderstanding, and their consequences are far from benign. Both Catholic and Presbyterian doctrines on the kingdom of God are designed to help usurp legitimate sovereign power. Even where they have failed to achieve their ultimate aim, these attempts at usurpation have succeeded in clouding men's understanding and, by so doing, have seriously undercut the authority of sovereigns:

> This power Regal under Christ, being challenged, universally by the Pope, and in particular Common-wealths by Assemblies of the Pastors of the place, (when the Scripture gives it to none but to Civill Soveraigns,) comes to be so passionately disputed, that it putteth out the Light of Nature, and causeth so great a Darknesse in mens understanding, that they see not who it is to whom they have engaged their obedience.[14]

[14] *Leviathan*, ch. 44, p. 630 [335].

For Hobbes a "correct" interpretation of the Scriptures is, almost by definition, one that leads to the conclusion that those who hold civil sovereignty must also hold the supreme power in ecclesiastical matters. Thus he argues that to understand the true location of ecclesiastical power we must distinguish the time since the ascension of Christ into two periods: the first running from the ascension to the time when kings were converted to Christianity, the second extending from that time onward.[15] At the beginning of the first of these periods, ecclesiastical power lay with the apostles, who were personally chosen by Christ to carry on his mission as a teacher. Thereafter, this power was passed on to others ordained by them to continue this work. Their commission to teach Christ's doctrine was sealed by a ceremony called the imposition of hands. Thus, during the first of these periods, ecclesiastical power was passed from Christ to his apostles, and thence to others ordained by them to teach Christ's doctrine.[16]

This power was never in any sense coercive. It was a power to teach, to persuade men to believe in God and follow the example set by Christ.[17] It included no power whatsoever to punish men for their refusal to follow Christ's teaching. Nor did it detract from every person's liberty to interpret the Scriptures in his own way. In these days before the conversion of kings to Christianity, there was no authoritative interpretation of the Bible. Each man was free to approve or reject any interpretation he liked. This was true even after independent churches had collectively decided upon the interpretations they would preach:

> When a difficulty arose, the Apostles and Elders of the Church assembled themselves together, and determined what should bee preached, and taught, and how they

[15] *Leviathan*, ch. 42, p. 521 [267].

[16] *Leviathan*, ch. 42, pp. 521-524 [267-269].

[17] *Leviathan*, ch. 42, pp. 524-545 [269-281].

should Interpret the Scriptures to the People; but took not from the People the liberty to read, and Interpret them to themselves.[18]

At no time before the conversion of civil sovereigns to Christianity did church leaders deprive the people of their basic right to their own private interpretation of the Scriptures.

The conversion of kings to Christianity brought an end to this period of interpretative anarchy and initiated a new hierarchy in ecclesiastical power. The general theory of the commonwealth in part II of *Leviathan* demonstrates that civil sovereigns necessarily have the right to decide what doctrines may be taught in their lands.[19] This principle is all the more applicable to Christian sovereigns in relation to Christian doctrine than it is to heathen monarchs. With their conversion, Christian sovereigns acquired the supreme ecclesiastical power within their own territories. The apostolic succession and laying on of hands were superseded by sovereign appointment of ministers to preach Christian doctrine.[20] The right of Christians to interpret the Scriptures for themselves came to an end. This right became the exclusive possession of the civil sovereign. Thus, with the conversion of sovereigns to Christianity, civil power was united with ecclesiastical power.

The congruence between this result of Hobbes's Scriptural exegesis and one of the central conclusions of his political philosophy is far from "fortuitous," as at least one scholar has recently suggested.[21] Any possibility of conflict is ruled out by

[18] *Leviathan*, ch. 42, pp. 544-545 [281].

[19] *Leviathan*, ch. 42, p. 567 [295].

[20] *Leviathan*, ch. 42, p. 569 [295-296].

[21] Eisenach, *Two Worlds of Liberalism*, p. 68. Eisenach's argument is nevertheless much closer to the truth than that of Pocock, who argues that the historical structure of authority which Hobbes derives from Scripture exists, in a Christian commonwealth, in "direct and potentially competitive coexistence" with that structure which he derives from the political philosophy of the first half of *Leviathan*. See "Time, History, and Eschatology," p. 166.

the principles of interpretation that govern his exegesis. For the conclusions of that political philosophy are based upon a reading of God's "Naturall Word," and are thus to be presupposed in any reading of the Scriptures as surely as are the conclusions of natural philosophy. In this sense there is no more room for the conclusions of sacred history to conflict with the prescriptions of political philosophy than there is for Scriptural usage of terms like "spirit" and "enchantment" to contradict our knowledge of the natural world. We know what the Bible can and cannot have meant by these terms because we know that the world is composed of nothing but matter governed by mechanical laws of motion. In exactly the same way, the conclusions of sacred history are rigidly confined within limits imposed by the political knowledge we derive from "the nature of Men, known to us by Experience, and from Definitions . . . universally agreed on": in other words, from "the Principles of Nature onely."[22] Given Hobbes's first principle of Scriptural interpretation, which rules out any possibility of finding anything in these sacred texts contrary to "naturall reason," the findings of sacred history are bound from the outset to coincide with those of political philosophy.

The central conclusion of Hobbes's reading of Biblical history, then, is that both ecclestiastical and civil power must necessarily be united, throughout the era following the conversion of kings to Christianity, in the hands of a single civil sovereign. Even before this era, "in all Common-wealths of the Heathen, the Soveraigns have had the name of Pastors of the People, because there was no Subject that could lawfully Teach the people, but by their permission and authority." And necessarily so:

> For it is evident to the meanest capacity, that mens actions are derived from the opinions they have of the Good, or Evill, which from those actions redound unto themselves; and consequently, men that are once possessed of an opin-

[22] *Leviathan*, ch. 32, p. 409 [195].

> ion, that their obedience to the Soveraign Power, will bee more hurtfull to them, than their disobedience, will disobey the Laws, and thereby overthrow the Commonwealth, and introduce confusion, and Civill war; for the avoiding whereof, all Civill Government was ordained.[23]

It is utterly impossible for the conclusions of sacred history to be contrary to those of political philosophy, for those latter conclusions are merely the simple principles of sound government, which tell us, among other things, that no rational commonwealth is possible—as Hobbes, evoking Plato, suggests—unless "Kings were Pastors, or Pastors Kings."[24]

The Basis of Scriptural Authority

The transfer of supreme ecclesiastical power into the hands of Christian sovereigns gives them the right to determine the composition as well as the interpretation of the Bible. The true source of Scriptural authority, Hobbes points out, is highly controversial:

> It is a question much disputed between the divers sects of Christian Religion, *From whence the Scriptures derive their Authority*; which question is also propounded sometimes in other terms, as, *How wee know them to be the Word of God*, or, *Why we beleeve them to be so.*[25]

The reason these questions are so difficult to answer is that they are framed inadequately. The ultimate source of Scriptural authority, as all sides agree, is God; hence there is no dispute about this question. No one can know the Scriptures to be God's word except those to whom this knowledge has been

[23] *Leviathan*, ch. 42, pp. 567-568 [295].

[24] *Leviathan*, ch. 42, p. 545 [281].

[25] *Leviathan*, ch. 33, p. 425 [205].

supernaturally revealed; thus this question is also poorly put. As for our belief, Hobbes argues that "because some are moved to beleeve for one, and others for other reasons, there can be rendred no one generall answer for them all."[26] The explanations of belief are so various that no single answer is possible. The real source of contention is captured by another question: by what authority are the Scriptures made law?

The answer to this question is simple. No part of the Scriptures has ever been made law except by the authority of a civil sovereign. This was true even before the New Testament was written. The Ten Commandments were the first part of Scripture ever to have the obligatory force of law.[27] They were laid down by God himself, and in this sense their authority derives from him. But only by the decree of Moses, the civil sovereign of the Jews, did they acquire the full force of law. Later, other laws (contained in the book of Deuteronomy) were added to these, again by the authority of Moses. At no time were the Scriptures made law by any authority other than that of the civil sovereign. This conclusion remains true in modern times. The Bible derives its legal force from its authorization by a civil sovereign.[28]

This conclusion is subtly but effectively supported by a long discussion of the authorship and assembly of the Bible into a complete text.[29] At first glance this discussion seems to have little to do with Hobbes's conclusion. If the Bible, or parts of it, are given legal force by the authority of civil sovereigns alone, why should we need to identify its original authors and assemblers? All we need is to be able to identify the canonical text, and we can do this only by heeding the decrees of our sovereign. The initial impression created by this conclusion is that most of Hobbes's discussion is pointless. Yet the real intention

[26] *Leviathan*, ch. 33, p. 425 [205].

[27] *Leviathan*, ch. 42, pp. 545-552 [281-285].

[28] *Leviathan*, ch. 33, p. 415, 426 [199, 205].

[29] *Leviathan*, ch. 33, pp. 416-425 [200-205].

of this discussion is probably different from its ostensible aim, which is to establish the antiquity and authorship of the various books of the Bible. In the course of doing this, Hobbes repeatedly calls attention to the human origins of the Bible. Though God is its ultimate author, the actual text was written by human hands. Human beings, again, assembled the text as a whole. They had to make many choices to do so, and these were human choices, not necessarily guided by divine inspiration. The Bible, in short, is an artifact of human design. A kind of artificiality, perhaps even arbitrariness, is embodied in the composition and selection of its parts. If the Bible itself is an artifact in this way, it is not surprising that its legal force should be left to the artifice of sovereigns.

Nor is this conclusion, which casts doubt upon the independent authority of the entire corpus of Holy Writ, the most skeptical implication of Hobbes's analysis. Toward the beginning of his Scriptural exegesis in part III of *Leviathan*, as we have seen, Hobbes refuses to say what the cause of our belief in Scriptures might be, arguing that no single answer to this question is possible. In the final chapter of that exegesis, however, Hobbes reverses himself. The cause of our belief is the same as that of all faith: namely, "the Hearing of those that are by the Law allowed and appointed to Teach us, as our Parents in their Houses, and our Pastors in the Churches."[30] The Christian faith and Scriptures are taught to men and women from infancy onward. It is hardly surprising that so many people believe in that faith and accept the Bible as the word of God; they have been told to do so all their lives. Some men may be deprived of this faith, since it is ultimately a gift of God. But its immediate cause, Hobbes emphasizes, is human teaching. The composition of the Scriptures themselves, their legal force in a commonwealth, and our very belief in them as the word of God are in this sense all artificial products of human design.

[30] *Leviathan*, ch. 43, p. 614 [324].

Neither the artificiality of Scripture nor that of faith itself constitutes a sufficient reason to deny the validity of faith as a way to knowledge of God's word. Nevertheless, the implications of Hobbes's analysis cast serious doubt upon the thesis that the exegetical and historical arguments of the latter half of *Leviathan* form his "contribution to the study of faith . . . as a system of revealed truth."[31] Already in *The Elements of Law* he had identified faith as a form of opinion, the propositions of which "we are not said to know," since they "are admitted by trust or error."[32] Faith is specifically opposed in that work to any kind of knowledge, whether scientific or historical. The same sharp opposition between faith and knowledge is also implied in *Leviathan* by the omission of faith and sacred history from the scheme of knowledge set out in chapter 9 of that work.[33] Indeed, in *Leviathan* Hobbes makes a point of observing that "Christian men doe not know, but *onely* beleeve the Scripture to be the Word of God."[34] "Sacred history" for him was, above all, a history of subterfuge and deception. God's "Propheticall Word" was in reality a document of ordinary human origin, and the motives for its composition and assembly were in some instances far less pure than the faithful generally believed them to be.

This deep skepticism about the status of prophecy was in fact a logical if unstated implication of Hobbes's inference about the historicity of miracles. If prophecy must be validated by the performance of miracles, as he claims, and miracles are actually nothing more than artifacts of ignorance, as my analysis of his arguments in the foregoing chapter has sought to suggest, then it seems to follow that prophecy itself is a product of ignorance as well. Thus, insofar as the prophetic word of God contained

[31] Pocock, "Time, History, and Eschatology," p. 163.

[32] *Elements* I.6.6, 7.

[33] Pocock mentions, but offers no explanation of, this omission in "Time, History, and Eschatology," p. 160.

[34] *Leviathan*, ch. 43, p. 614 [324], emphasis added.

in the Scriptures has any authority at all apart from that conferred upon it by civil sovereigns, who alone can give those Scriptures the force of law, it appears that authority is rooted in the same ignorant state of mind that nourishes belief in miracles. And if miracles have ceased because men have finally become sufficiently enlightened to see through them, might not the same fate await the Christian Scriptures as well?[35]

Hobbes did not, of course, raise this question directly. It would have been literally suicidal for him to do so. And in any case, no direct challenge to the authority of Scripture was necessary. As a rhetorical strategy it was far more effective to accept that authority ostensibly and, by raising questions and implanting doubts in the minds of his readers, to turn it toward his own purpose. But that purpose was clear. It was to subvert many of the most central tenets of Christian theology, Protestant as well as Catholic, and to replace them with Hobbes's own rationalized version of Christian doctrine.

The doctrine Hobbes envisaged was almost entirely bereft of the mystical elements that had been associated with Christianity since early times. The established concept of the soul as a mysterious spiritual substance was rejected in favor of the idea that the soul, and indeed the entire universe, is an ordinary material thing. Like other bodies, the soul is mortal by nature. This view had the extremely important consequence of implying that no one is liable to suffer eternal torment in hell at the end of his life on earth. There is no hell and no purgatory; these places are fictions invented by some men to frighten their more

[35] Hood's assumption that Hobbes's acceptance of the authority of Scripture was wholly sincere ignores these implications of his argument, and rests ultimately upon nothing more than his view that it is "historically more credible that he believed what he wrote than that he wrote with his tongue in his cheek" (*Divine Politics*, p. 253). Yet even Hood admits that Hobbes sometimes made "prudent excisions," deliberately concealed his "whole thought" on certain political issues, and was occasionally "somewhat disingenuous" (pp. 1, 248, 126).

ignorant fellows into submission. Enlightened, rational men—those who reject these sophistical mysteries—will not be moved by such superstitious fears.

The traditional mystical interpretation of the Christian sacraments was the second major victim of Hobbes's reinterpretation. The priestly view of the eucharist, baptism, and other Christian rites is nothing more than an attempt to gain power over men by deception. These clerical claims to magical power are, if anything, even less plausible than the pretenses of the ancient Egyptian enchanters. Nor were these claims, which had been asserted primarily by Catholic theologians, the only form of deception by pretense of supernatural power. Though it had helped suppress the magic of Catholicism, the Reformation had also opened the way for many false prophets and miracles. In Hobbes's view all these contemporary claims to prophecy were necessarily false. The age of prophecy and miracles, if these phenomena ever really occurred, is long gone. All that remains is the prophetic word of God recorded in the Bible. And the validity of even this word as a source of truth is extremely dubious. The world operates according to strict, mechanical laws of motion laid down by nature. Anyone who pretends to have performed a miracle is a liar; anyone who believes he has seen one is a fool.

The third and final major point of Hobbes's exegesis was to prove that the kingdom of God spoken of in Scripture could not be identified with any existing church, Catholic or Protestant. The Catholic interpretation of the kingdom of God as a realm of spiritual power is baseless. The kingdom of God in Scripture is always a real, earthly kingdom, utterly unlike the mystical unity of all believers to which the Catholics pretend. The Presbyterian interpretation, though more plausible, is also wrong. A careful reading of the Bible shows that the kingdom of God will not return until Christ's second coming. These attempts to identify the kingdom of God with an existing church are simply one more element in the clerical campaign to wrest power from the civil sovereigns who possess it by right. Power is power, whether it be called spiritual or temporal. When it has been successful, the assertion of clerical power within civil domains has had disastrous results. It has given rise to competing claims for the obedience of subjects and destroyed the foundations of commonwealths.

The cumulative effect of Hobbes's Scriptural argumentation was to point toward what one scholar has aptly described as a "refounding" of Christianity.[36] But what was the ultimate aim of this refounding? Was it to turn Christianity into a civil religion, compatible with sovereign authority as Hobbes conceived it, but leaving man essentially what he had been before, a *homo religiosus*?[37] For *De Cive* this interpretation is probably correct. The principal thrust of his argument in that work is to expose false understandings of the kingdom of God, and by so doing to reconcile the essential spiritual teachings of Christianity with the requirements of absolute sovereignty. The theological argumentation of *Leviathan*, however, goes well beyond that of his earlier work, and has a different center of gravity. The arguments about God's kingdom are developed here, too—in some respects more thoroughly than they had been before. But the greater part of his exposition is designed to puncture those beliefs about the soul and magic which Hobbes regarded as the vivid and powerful, yet essentially irrational, products of men's wayward imaginations. The aim of part III of *Leviathan* is not solely to cleanse Christianity of those doctrines most repugnant to absolute sovereignty. Rather, it is an attempt to get at the roots of superstition, to jolt men and women into recognizing the irrationality of some of their most deeply held beliefs about their own natures, and about the nature of the universe itself. It is not merely a proposal outlining the main tenets of a civil religion that could be instituted by

[36] Sherlock, "Theology of *Leviathan*," p. 47.
[37] Sherlock, "Theology of *Leviathan*," pp. 46, 48.

some future sovereign. It is a direct attempt to stimulate a transformation of the human psyche, to change the ways in which men and women conceive of themselves, by demonstrating to them through graphic and vivid (though not necessarily scientific) means the untenability or absurdity of many of the concepts and categories that make up the larger prism through which they interpret their own experience. Hobbes's refounding of Christianity was an attempt to transform men and women into the rational and predictable beings they would have to be before his vision of political society could ever be realized.

CHAPTER EIGHT ✲

Sovereignty at the Crossroads

THE PRESENT IN HISTORICAL PERSPECTIVE

HOBBES ANTICIPATED that the greatest objections to his political doctrine would be based upon its alleged impracticality. At no time in history, critics would argue, had a commonwealth like that envisaged by him ever existed. "The greatest objection is, that of the Practise; when men ask, where, and when, such Power has by Subjects been acknowledged."[1] There are moments when Hobbes himself seems on the verge of accepting this objection as decisive:

> And now, considering how different this Doctrine is, from the Practise of the greatest part of the world, especially of these Western parts, . . . I am at the point of believing this my labour, as uselesse, as the Common-wealth of *Plato.*[2]

Hobbes's emphasis upon the special repugnance of his doctrine to Western practice is revealing, and recalls to mind the fact

[1] *Leviathan*, ch. 20, pp. 260-261 [107].

[2] *Leviathan*, ch. 31, p. 407 [193].

that he had once attributed absolute powers to ancient sovereigns.[3] Even so, the objection seemed a strong one. How could a doctrine so novel and so utterly opposed to the traditions of those countries in which it would be circulated ever be expected to achieve practical realization? How could men be persuaded of the benefits that would flow from its adoption when the principles of his political philosophy were so alien to those embodied in the political doctrines and practices to which they had been accustomed for so long? And even if they could be persuaded in theory, would not the weight of entrenched habits prove an insuperable barrier to the implementation of those principles?

Hobbes was keenly aware of the gravity of these objections, but ultimately they seemed to him unconvincing. In the first place, he points out, the past can hardly be held up as a guide to good practice in politics and government:

> But one may ask them again, when, or where has there been a Kingdome long free from Sedition and Civill Warre. In those Nations, whose Common-wealths have been long-lived, and not been destroyed, but by forraign warre, the Subjects never did dispute of the Soveraign Power. But howsoever, an argument for the Practise of men, that have not sifted to the bottom, and with exact reason weighed the causes, and nature of Common-wealths, and suffer daily those miseries, that proceed from the ignorance thereof, is invalid. For though in all places of the world, men should lay the foundation of their houses on the sand, it could not thence be inferred, that so it ought to be.[4]

Prevailing practice has failed absolutely to preserve commonwealths from disobedience, sedition, and civil war. Far from

[3] *De Cive*, Preface 6.

[4] *Leviathan*, ch. 20, p. 261 [107].

constituting an objection to his principles, experience tends instead to confirm them, if only by providing a graphic demonstration of the complete futility of established political forms.

Second, Hobbes argues that a realistic alternative to reliance upon past practice for political guidance now exists:

> Time, and Industry, produce every day new knowledge. And as the art of well building, is derived from Principles of Reason, . . . So, long time after men have begun to constitute Common-wealths, imperfect, and apt to relapse into disorder, there may, Principles of Reason be found out, by industrious meditation, to make their constitution (excepting by externall violence) everlasting.[5]

As he suggests elsewhere, "The skill of making, and maintaining Common-wealths, consisteth in certain Rules, as doth Arithmetique and Geometry; not (as Tennis-play) on Practise onely."[6] The nature of firm political foundations is discoverable only by the art of reasoning, not by reliance upon custom or experience alone. The rational principles by which commonwealths could best be constituted are now known, and are embodied as theorems in Hobbes's own civil philosophy. All that remains necessary to validate the overwhelming superiority of those theorems is that they be implemented in practice.

But this implementation is far easier to imagine than to achieve. *Knowledge* of the rules by which commonwealths ought to be constructed is not enough. Some of the benefits derived from our knowledge of geometric theorems were not realized in practice until many years, in some cases centuries, after their original discovery. Applied sciences, such as that of mechanics, had to be developed, and appropriate materials had to be found and shaped to their specifications. The theorems of civil philosophy must travel a similar road before they can be put into prac-

[5] *Leviathan*, ch. 30, p. 378 [176].

[6] *Leviathan*, ch. 20, p. 261 [107].

tice. Like the materials of a building, the human materials out of which a commonwealth is to be constructed must first be shaped to conform to the architect's requirements:

> For men, as they become at last weary of irregular justling, and hewing one another, and desire with all their hearts, to conforme themselves into one firme and lasting edifice; so for want, both of the art of making fit Lawes, to square their actions by, and also of humility, and patience, to suffer the rude and combersome points of their present greatnesse to be taken off, they cannot without the help of a very able Architect, be compiled, into any other than a crasie building, such as hardly lasting out their own time, must assuredly fall upon the heads of their posterity.[7]

A scientifically correct design is vital to the success of a commonwealth, but an adequate design alone cannot guarantee that success. The materials must first be made to conform to specifications. No commonwealth can be made to last if the "rude and combersome points" of those who are to constitute it are not first eliminated from their characters. The men and women of whom a commonwealth is to be constructed must first be transformed if the resulting structure is to be made sound.

The scope of the change in human character required for Hobbes's conception of political society to be put into practice was, as we have seen, very great. Hobbes was in effect proposing nothing less than a transformation of the human psyche, an uprooting of those weeds of error and superstition that had hitherto held the human imagination in their tight, almost hypnotic grip. But was there any real prospect that such a transformation could be effected? What reasons, if any, did Hobbes have to believe that the fundamental changes in outlook demanded by his political philosophy could be brought about?

[7] *Leviathan*, ch. 29, p. 363 [167].

It is a commonplace observation that Hobbes viewed his own time as one of extraordinary ideological ferment as well as political upheaval, and that he consequently considered the mid-seventeenth century a moment of unusually great opportunity for political change. The fact, therefore, that he envisaged the possibility of a cultural transformation on the scale suggested is not a matter of dispute. The aspect of his theory that is generally held to express this outlook, this notion of his own time as one of great political opportunity, most clearly is his concept of the state of nature. For Hobbes the state of nature represents much more than a breakdown of political authority. Rather, it describes a moment of almost primordial chaos, of absolute disorder, or even annihilation, comparable in some ways to the condition of the universe immediately before the creation.[8] In short, the state of nature for Hobbes was synonymous with destruction of the capacity for meaningful social intercourse itself. Interpreted in this way as a condition of absolute privation, Hobbes's state of nature set the stage upon which the radical reconstructive pretensions of his political philosophy could appear as a plausible act of political creation.

In some respects, however, Hobbes's concept of the state of nature obscures almost as much as it illuminates. By appearing to insist that there can be no middle way between absolute order and absolute chaos, his political analysis implies that every breakdown of sovereignty must be equally complete. But this conclusion is certainly not what Hobbes really believed, nor is it consistent with his interpretation of history. If the state of nature is in one sense the most perfect expression of Hobbes's belief in the possibility of political and cultural transformation, the grounds for that belief lie in a reading of history that in

[8] The most penetrating discussions of Hobbes's state of nature in the critical literature occur in Wolin, *Politics and Vision*, ch. 8, and Manfred Riedel, *Metaphysik und Metapolitik* (Frankfurt: Suhrkamp, 1975), pt. 3. Cf. also Ball's essay, "Hobbes' Linguistic Turn," which draws a very illuminating parallel with Thucydides' discussion of the aftermath of the Corcyrean Revolution.

some important ways undercuts the rigidity of his atemporal analysis of political order and political chaos. To understand Hobbes's reasons for believing that a cultural transformation of the kind he envisaged was genuinely possible, then, we must for a moment set aside the timeless, strictly logical analysis of chaos, commonwealth, and the transition from the former to the latter for which he is so famous, and focus instead upon his interpretation of history. The central theme of this interpretation, which has been almost universally neglected by Hobbes's critics, is the genesis, corruption, and decline of Christianity.

The Origin of Christianity

Rational inquiry into the natural causes of things, Hobbes argues, is bound to lead men to conceive of a deity. When any effect is explained through discovery of its causes, those causes become the next object for investigation. To explain them, still earlier causes must be sought. The causal chain thus begun suggests necessarily the idea that there must be a first cause which has no prior cause of its own. This idea of a first cause is what men call God. Anyone who engages in serious inquiry will be led by this chain of reasoning to believe that there is a God. But this concept of God is purely an abstract idea. It is impossible to infer anything about God's characteristics or attributes by rational means. The words we apply to God—infinite, omnipotent, omniscient, and so forth—do not describe his nature. They are all essentially negative terms, through which we honor God by describing our own incapacity to imagine him. Rational inquiry leads men to believe that there is a God, but it also compels them to admit that it is beyond their capacity to comprehend or conceive any concrete idea of him.[9]

[9] *Leviathan*, ch. 11, p. 167 [51]; ch. 3, p. 99 [11]; ch. 31, pp. 401-406 [190-192].

This rational but abstract concept of God, however, is by no means the usual foundation of religious belief. That foundation consists of ignorance and fear. Ignorant men "are enclined to suppose, and feign unto themselves, severall kinds of Powers Invisible; and to stand in awe of their own imaginations." They create their own Gods, invest them with qualities of all sorts, and then make them into objects of their fears. When erected upon this foundation, as historically it always has been, religion is nothing more than a form of superstition: "And this Feare of things invisible, is the naturall Seed of that, which every one in himself calleth Religion; and in them that worship, or feare that Power otherwise than they do, Superstition."[10] The difference between religion and superstition, this passage bluntly suggests, is purely subjective and illusory. While Hobbes appears later to draw a distinction between false religions and the true one, it is important to notice his explicit argument that both kinds of religions grow out of the same seeds, which are "Opinion of Ghosts, Ignorance of second causes, Devotion towards what men fear, and Taking of things Causall for Prognostiques." Even if his distinction between those leaders who have cultivated religion "according to their own invention" and those who have done it "by Gods commandement, and direction" is sincere, it is absolutely plain that Hobbes considered the beliefs of their followers, whether pagan, Jewish, or Christian, to be founded upon pure superstition.[11] In principle a religion founded upon the idea of God conceived in an abstract and rational way might be possible, but in practice all religions, including Christianity, have grown in the soil of ignorance and superstition.

Apart from these rudimentary foundations, there is nothing about religion that is not artificial, and therefore malleable.

[10] *Leviathan*, ch. 11, pp. 167-168 [51].

[11] *Leviathan*, ch. 12, pp. 172-173 [54]. These observations render the meaningfulness of Hobbes's distinction between "humane Politiques" and "Divine Politiques" extremely doubtful.

The diversity of religious practices throughout history proves this point. The natural seed of religion "hath grown up into ceremonies so different, that those which are used by one man, are for the most part ridiculous to another."[12] This growth has not been entirely spontaneous. Religion has been cultivated by men. It is a product of artifice, and has been shaped by human authors.[13] Though its basis may be natural, the trappings or superstructures of any religion are artificial. These superstructures include all the opinions and beliefs incorporated into a religion apart from the basic ideas of a deity and invisible powers on which it is founded.

Most of these authors used religion to make men more obedient, more pliable, and more suited to membership in civil society. The founders of ancient commonwealths propagated myths in pursuit of this aim.[14] Many of them claimed divine status for themselves. Those who did not pretended, at least, to have special access to divine sources. Numa, one of the founders of Rome, made a show of having communicated with a deity before instituting religious ceremonies in that city. The founders also persuaded their subjects that the laws they had prescribed were of divine origin, and they invented a variety of ceremonies and festivals to cultivate and channel their subjects' religious sentiments. In these various ways, Hobbes concludes, "the Religion of the Gentiles was a part of their Policy."[15]

Hobbes suggests strongly that the religion of the ancient Hebrews was manipulated in exactly the same way. Although Moses was operating under God's direction, his purpose, like that of the ancient pagans, was to make his people "more apt to Obedience, Lawes, Peace, Charity, and civill Society."[16] Late in *Leviathan* he calls Moses the "first founder of a Common-

[12] *Leviathan*, ch. 12, pp. 172-173 [54].

[13] *Leviathan*, ch. 12, pp. 172-179 [54-58].

[14] *Leviathan*, ch. 12, p. 177 [57].

[15] *Leviathan*, ch. 12, p. 178 [57].

[16] *Leviathan*, ch. 12, p. 173 [64].

wealth,"[17] plainly evoking his earlier discussion of the political manipulation of religious beliefs by the "first Founders, and Legislators of Common-wealths amongst the Gentiles."[18] And, as we have seen, he repeatedly emphasizes his view that supreme religious authority was always combined with civil sovereignty in the commonwealth of the ancient Jews, both under Moses and his successors. Whether or not Moses' use of religion was actually inspired by political motives makes little difference. The important point is that the sentiments and ceremonies cultivated by the Jewish faith in the time of Moses worked to sustain sovereign authority and the commonwealth.

This relationship of mutual reinforcement began to erode as the Jews came under the influence of Greek ideas. The Greeks, like other ancient people, had extremely primitive ideas about the natural world. They had not yet learned to distinguish between the subjective qualities we impose upon objects in the act of perception and the real, objective qualities of those things. They were also prone to confuse fancies of the imagination and dreams with genuine perceptions. In short, they mistook many purely imaginary objects for material realities. They called these imaginary objects by one general name: demons. Like other superstitious peoples, they fabricated an entire religion, or "Daemonology," around these fantasies.[19]

By their conquests and colonizations, the Greeks spread these ideas into Asia, Egypt, and Italy, where they were picked up by the Jews. From this point onward, Hobbes argues, the Jewish religion began to become "much corrupted."[20] The Jews began to believe in good and evil spirits and to incorporate this belief into their religion. They called the evil spirits demons in imitation of the Greeks. They adapted the idea of good spirits to their own monotheistic religion by calling them all the spirit

[17] *Leviathan*, ch. 40, p. 503 [251].

[18] *Leviathan*, ch. 12, p. 177 [57].

[19] *Leviathan*, ch. 45, pp. 657-659 [352-353].

[20] *Leviathan*, ch. 40, p. 511 [256].

of God. This concoction was the root of their belief in supernatural prophecy. A prophet, to these latter-day Jews, was a man possessed by the spirit of God. Thus their belief in supernatural prophecies and events flowed from the "contagion" of Greek demonology.[21]

The picture of Jewish history that emerges from Hobbes's account is one of slow but unremitting decline. In the beginning, as it were, the Jews were given a monotheistic—and perhaps essentially rational— religion by their sovereign and religious leader, Moses. Moses may have invented rituals and ceremonies that were inessential to rational deism, but the religious doctrines he inculcated were relatively free of superstitious concoctions. All the ceremonies and doctrines of Judaism were designed to foster the qualities of peace and obedience that make men good subjects, and Moses ensured that control of these ceremonies and doctrines would remain in the hands of the civil sovereign.

These good institutions and habits began to break down after Moses had gone.[22] The Jews began to imitate other peoples. They longed for visible images to worship and demanded a human king like those who ruled other nations. The passing of Samuel, the last of the high priests to exercise sovereign authority over the Jews, brought an end to the kingdom of God that had been instituted by Moses. But the decisive event in the decline of Judaism was its corruption by the demonology of the Greeks. The rational religion with which the Jews had begun gave way to a polyglot conglomeration of superstitious beliefs and fears. The Jews came to believe in spirits and supernatural prophecy, magic and idolatry. Their religious doctrines were no longer under the control of sovereigns—nor, for that matter, of anyone else. Their religious ceremonies were now contaminated by innumerable relics of Greek paganism and no longer

[21] *Leviathan*, ch. 45, pp. 659-660 [353].

[22] *Leviathan*, ch. 40, pp. 506-511 [253-260].

worked to sustain sovereign authority. The condition of chaos into which they had fallen was so great that "nothing can be gathered from their confusion, both in State and Religion, concerning the Supremacy in either."[23] Jewish history, both political and religious, had reached its nadir.

It was at this point, a time of extreme corruption, that Christ came into the world. His arrival offered the possibility of a new beginning. He asked men to turn away from idolatry and superstition, to cast aside the false beliefs and rituals into which they had fallen, and to return to their ancient and simpler faith in the one true God. Yet, it is important to notice, Hobbes's account plainly implies that this mission was flawed from its very beginning. The Jews had already been fundamentally corrupted by the pagan superstitions of the Greeks. The gentiles, to whom Jesus and his followers opened their arms as well, were hopeless idolaters.[24] These superstitious beliefs and rituals had been inculcated for many generations. Perhaps in a time of such great confusion they might have been swept away by a single decisive stroke. The historic fact, however, is that they were not. The pagan superstitions of the old, polytheistic Greek and Roman faiths lived on, mingling gradually with the new religion. In time they merged so thoroughly that no one could really distinguish the old from the new. But the merger could never quite be completed. The old elements were still essentially superstitious and corrupting, however well their new guise hid these qualities for a while. These "old empty Bottles of Gentilisme" remained incompatible with the "new Wine of Christianity."[25] In the long run, Hobbes argues, this incompatibility was bound to lead the new, essentially syncretic religion of Christianity to collapse under the weight of its own internal contradictions, as in his own time it finally did.

[23] *Leviathan*, ch. 40, p. 511 [260].

[24] *Leviathan*, ch. 45, pp. 665-678 [356-364].

[25] *Leviathan*, ch. 45, p. 681 [366].

The History of Ecclesiastical Power

In the beginning there was no one Christian church.[26] The faith was maintained by a series of independent congregations. Ecclesiastical power had passed from Christ into the hands of his apostles. But this power was not coercive. It was simply an authority to evangelize, or preach the gospel, and to help prepare men for Christ's second coming. The apostles had no authority, in the proper and coercive sense of the term, over Christian congregations. They did not even have the power to impose their own interpretations of Scripture. The New Testament had not yet been assembled into a single text. Each man retained the liberty to read and interpret the Scriptures for himself. The early churches left each of their members free to understand the Christian faith in his own way.

In practical matters, too, the early churches were marked by a lack of structure. The Christians of every city lived communally, supported entirely by the voluntary contributions of the faithful.[27] Their common stocks of money were raised through the sale of the private lands and possessions of their members. Property was held in common. All important decisions were taken by the community as a whole. The last of the apostles, Paul, Barnabas, and Matthias, were chosen by two of the earliest churches. All churches elected their own leaders, who were commonly called elders, as well as the councils or presbyters that conducted their business.[28] No significance was attached to the different titles of bishop, pastor, elder, doctor, and so forth. All these titles "were but so many divers names of the same Office in the time of the Apostles."[29] In these early times Christianity was held together by nothing more than a common

[26] *Leviathan*, ch. 42, pp. 521-567 [267-294].

[27] *Leviathan*, ch. 42, pp. 555, 565 [287, 293].

[28] *Leviathan*, ch. 42, pp. 556-561 [288-291].

[29] *Leviathan*, ch. 42, p. 557 [289].

faith that Jesus was the Messiah whose coming had been prophesied in the Old Testament. No authority, in the proper sense of the term, was exercised within the churches. Each congregation remained completely self-governing and independent of all other churches. In this first phase of their existence, the Christian churches were the very antithesis of any hierarchical organization.

With the conversion of the Emperor Constantine to Christianity, however, an ecclesiastical hierarchy came into being.[30] In addition to their secular functions, Christian sovereigns became the supreme pastors of their people.[31] They acquired the right, previously nonexistent, of establishing an authoritative interpretation of Christian doctrine. They also acquired the authority to appoint other pastors. These men had formerly been appointed by their own independent congregations; they now became the subordinates of a supreme spiritual leader, and were answerable only to him. Sovereigns also acquired the right to administer sacraments, consecrate temples, and perform all functions related to Christian worship; and, finally, to authorize subordinates to carry out these functions. Thus the conversion of sovereigns transformed the Christian churches in a fundamental way. Hobbes describes the consequence of this conversion as a "consolidation of the Right Politique, and Ecclesiastique in Christian Soveraigns."[32] According to his own account, however, this event also had a prior and equally important consequence. It transformed amorphous collectivities held together by common faith alone into organized hierarchies. It did not just combine ecclesiastical and civil power. It *created* ecclesiastical power by transforming the churches into something very different from what they had been before: namely, structures of authority.

[30] *Leviathan*, ch. 42, pp. 567-576 [295-300].

[31] *Leviathan*, ch. 42, p. 568 [295]; ch. 43, p. 613 [323].

[32] *Leviathan*, ch. 42, p. 575 [299].

This transformation of churches into structures of power led to a subtle, but momentous, change in the spirit with which they were led. All men, according to Hobbes, desire power. Ecclesiastics are no exception. The new character of the churches led them to conceive new ambitions. Ecclesiastical positions had once been offices of pure service and devotion. They now became positions of authority. The transformation of the churches led to a transformation of the clergy. No longer selfless men of service, ecclesiastics acquired a taste for power.

Though formally subordinate to their Christian sovereigns, these ambitious ecclesiastics set out to create a network of power of their own. The corrupt, pagan elements within the new religion provided much of the ammunition they needed to achieve this aim. What could be more useful than to encourage men to adopt the old Greek belief in an immortal soul: an immaterial self, subject to priestly influences but beyond the reach of any civil power? What could be more effective than to convince men that priests are capable of literally making Christ and performing other magical marvels? What, finally, could be more valuable than to make men believe that they, the priesthood, are the magistrates of God's kingdom on earth, with a right to governance that supersedes that of any mere civil sovereign? These ideas, inherited from paganism or concocted by willful misinterpretation of the Scriptures, provided the core of an elaborate doctrinal structure that allowed the clergy to free itself from the yoke of sovereign control. The church had been made into a structure of power by the conversion of sovereigns to Christianity. The scheming of ambitious ecclesiastics gradually detached it from sovereign control. It became a power unto itself, with its own "sovereign," the Bishop of Rome, who claimed spiritual dominion over all Christians.[33]

The skein of power built up by the Catholic church made it

[33] Hobbes describes the "*Synthesis* and *Construction*" of papal power synoptically in *Leviathan*, ch. 47, p. 710 [384-385].

a formidable rival to all Christian sovereigns. The church became a state within a state or, as Hobbes puts it, a "*Kingdome of Fairies*" existing alongside and in constant tension with the genuine kingdoms it inhabited. The papacy is "the *Ghost* of the deceased *Romane Empire*, sitting crowned upon the grave thereof."[34] Its existence is dreamlike, founded as it is upon the ruins of that pagan empire. And yet, though the content of dreams is imaginary, the dreams themselves are real enough. So it is with the papal kingdom of fairies. The church succeeded in establishing a rigid separation between clergy and laity, a distinction that was entirely unknown to the early Christians. It wrested legal control of the clergy away from civil sovereigns by establishing its own canon laws distinct from the civil laws of states and declaring clerical exemption from the latter. It consolidated its independence of civil sovereigns by introducing compulsory taxes, or tithes, subjecting the people to a second tribute beside that which they owed the state.[35] With its own officials, laws, and revenues, the power of this ersatz state was every bit as real as that of any civil commonwealth. By accumulating and consolidating power over the centuries, the church became a mortal enemy to commonwealths, threatening everywhere to "reduce all Order, Government, and Society, to the first Chaos of Violence, and Civill warre."[36]

Yet the basis of the Catholic church's power was never entirely secure. For the ultimate foundation of this weighty structure consisted of fantastic myths and superstitions:

> To this, and such like resemblances between the *Papacy*, and the Kingdome of *Fairies*, may be added this, that as the *Fairies* have no existence, but in the Fancies of ignorant people, rising from the Traditions of old Wives, or

[34] *Leviathan*, ch. 47, p. 712 [386].

[35] *Leviathan*, ch. 44, pp. 631-633 [336-337]; ch. 46, pp. 697-698 [376-377]; ch. 47, pp. 706-708 [382-383].

[36] *Leviathan*, ch. 36, p. 469 [232].

> old Poets: so the Spirituall Power of the *Pope* . . . consisteth onely in the Fear that Seduced people stand in, of their Excommunication; upon hearing of false Miracles, false Traditions, and false Interpretations of the Scripture.[37]

The continued domination of this Christian hierarchy was contingent upon maintaining the ignorance of Christians. This dependency was the Achilles' heel of papal power. As long as men could be kept in a condition of ignorance, it had nothing to fear. Once the glimmerings of science and enlightenment began to appear, however, the basis of that power would begin to dry up and blow away.

The church's introduction of the frivolous and obscure philosophy of scholasticism into the universities, as well as its resolute opposition to any genuine philosophy or science, were accordingly parts of a calculated effort to maintain the basis of its own power. The "frequency of insignificant Speech" of which Hobbes complains at the beginning of *Leviathan*[38] was a product of deliberate clerical design. The aim was to keep men in ignorance and confusion by substituting the appearance and trappings of a philosophy for the real thing. "Lastly, . . . the frivolous Distinctions, barbarous Terms, and obscure Language of the Schoolmen, . . . serve . . . to make men mistake the *Ignis fatuus* of Vain Philosophy, for the Light of the Gospell."[39] The ultimate purpose of this substitution, as Hobbes pithily explains, was to "*take from young men, the use of Reason*."[40] The church positively cultivated superstition and irrationality; for its continued power over ordinary Christians, which enabled it to maintain a degree of control rivaling and sometimes exceeding that of civil sovereigns, was dependent upon this active suppression of reason. It is no wonder that genuine philos-

[37] *Leviathan*, ch. 47, p. 714 [387].

[38] *Leviathan*, ch. 1, p. 87 [4].

[39] *Leviathan*, ch. 47, p. 708 [383].

[40] *Leviathan*, ch. 47, p. 713 [386], emphasis added.

ophy and science lay uncultivated for so many centuries. The universities were ostensibly founded to promote learning. Their real purpose, however, was to hide truth, and to do so in a way that would confound even its most determined seekers.[41] If the power of civil sovereigns was at least in principle founded upon the presumption that their subjects would seek to pursue their own interests, and especially their self-preservation, by rational means, that of church leaders was dependent upon confounding this pattern of action by maintaining the superstitions and irrationality of those subjects. The power of the church could be preserved only by the active suppression of science and truth, and even of the human capacity for reason itself.[42]

Once the real structures of power by which the Catholic church maintained its position had been consolidated, no other power on earth could challenge it successfully. The myths propagated by the Catholic clergy held men in an almost hypnotic grip. Indeed, the strength of this grip was so great that it calls to mind that possession by spirits in which the clergy sought to make its victims believe. In reality, they were possessed not by spirits, but by "spirituall men." Once established, any effort by a civil sovereign to resist this power was bound to fail: "But when the people were once possessed by those spirituall men, there was no humane remedy to be applyed, that any man could invent."[43] In fact, past attempts by civil sovereigns to break the hold of Christian mythology over the imaginations of their subjects had not merely proved unsuccessful. They had backfired, leading to an effect opposite to that for which they had been intended: "the Impatience of

[41] "Which Insignificancy of language, though I cannot note it for false Philosophy; yet it hath a quality, not onely to hide the Truth, but also to make men think they have it, and desist from further search." *Leviathan*, ch. 46, p. 702 [379].

[42] *Leviathan*, ch. 46, p. 703 [380].

[43] *Leviathan*, ch. 47, p. 709 [384].

those, that strive to resist such encroachment, before their Subjects eyes were opened, did but encrease the power they resisted."[44]

This point is important, and deserves to be emphasized. However timeless and universal Hobbes considered the principles of his political philosophy, at no time during the long era of Catholic ascendancy could those principles, by his own account, have been implemented in practice. Those who had attempted to implement similar principles "before their Subjects eyes were opened"—before the first glimmerings of reason and enlightenment began to break through the darkness of medieval superstition—had ended by sapping their own authority even further. The only previous opportunity to cleanse the cultural foundations of sovereign authority of superstition and irrationality had occurred toward the beginning of the Christian era, when clerical power had not yet established firm roots. Thus

> the Emperours, and other Christian Soveraigns, under whose Government these Errours, and the like encroachments of Ecclesiastiques upon their Office, at first crept in, . . . may neverthelesse bee esteemed accessaries to their own, and the Publique dammage: For without their Authority there could at first no seditious Doctrine have been publiquely preached.[45]

Similarly, William the Conqueror was grievously mistaken, at the beginning of his rule over England, to pledge not to infringe the liberty of the church.[46] Once made, these mistakes could not be put right by later sovereigns. They created openings in which the church could establish its own independent

[44] *Leviathan*, ch. 47, p. 709 [384].

[45] *Leviathan*, ch. 47, p. 709 [384].

[46] *Leviathan*, ch. 29, p. 364 [168].

power. Sovereigns might have resisted that establishment in the first place, and are culpable for failing to do so:

> But I blame those, that in the beginning, when their power was entire, by suffering such Doctrines to be forged in the Universities of their own Dominions, have holden the Stirrop to all the succeeding Popes, whilest they mounted into the Thrones of all Christian Soveraigns, to ride, and tire, both them, and their people, at their pleasure.[47]

Once the power of ecclesiastics had become established, however, there was nothing civil sovereigns could do to overcome it.

Even so, the impregnability of Catholic power was not enough to ensure its permanent survival. For the church could never rid itself of the weakness inherent in its own foundation. Ultimately it was founded upon superstition, fantasy, and deception. This foundation could be maintained as long as the people could be kept in ignorance. The church had done everything in its power to maintain that ignorance, but it could not last forever. The same pagan doctrines upon which ambitious clerics had erected the power of the church were bound eventually to bring it crashing down.

"[A]ll formed Religion," Hobbes argues, "is founded at first, upon the faith which a multitude hath in some one person." It follows that when men lose their trust in the wisdom or sincerity of their religious leaders, they begin to suspect their own religion as well. But what causes men to lose trust in their leaders? One cause, Hobbes declares, is "the enjoyning of a beliefe of contradictories." By amalgamating the pagan superstitions of the Greeks and Romans with the new doctrines of Christianity, however, the Catholic church had fallen into this fault. Another is "the doing, or saying of such things, as ap-

[47] *Leviathan*, ch. 47, pp. 709-710 [384].

peare to be signes, that what they require other men to believe, is not believed by themselves." Yet the injustice, cruelty, and avarice of clerics belie their warnings that such vices cannot go unpunished in the next life. Still another cause is "the being detected of private ends." But the worldly benefits that have redounded to both the Catholic and the reformed churches are manifest to anyone who troubles to examine their history. The doctrines of Christianity had been syncretic and corrupt from the very beginning. As the Church became larger and more powerful, the ambitions of its leaders and the corruption of its doctrines could only increase. Finally they became so blatant that they could no longer be concealed.[48]

With the unveiling of these faulty joints in its internal structure, the entire edifice of organized Christianity began to crumble. The first stage in its fall was the Reformation, in which the yoke of papal power, the "third and last knot" upon the liberty that had been enjoyed by the first Christians, was cast off. In England this stage in the dissolution of organized Christianity was brought to completion by Queen Elizabeth. The second stage, in England at least, was the triumph of presbyterianism over episcopacy. The power of bishops was broken and returned to councils or presbyters like those which had held supreme ecclesiastical power in the early Christian centuries. The third and final stage in this collapse came upon the heels of the second:

> And almost at the same time, the Power was taken also from the Presbyterians: And so we are reduced to the Independency of the Primitive Christians to follow Paul, or Cephas, or Apollos, every man as he liketh best.

This stage, reached in the tumult and aftermath of civil war in England, closed the circle of Christian history. The first knot to be imposed upon Christian liberty was the last to be dissolved.

[48] *Leviathan*, ch. 12, pp. 179-183 [58-60].

This was the knot that had subjected the consciences of men and women to the decrees of their own assemblies. Now, for the first time since the earliest years of Christianity, the liberty of conscience that had been enjoyed by the first Christians had returned.[49]

New Wine into New Cask?

The emergence of radical religious freedom in England during the 1640's evoked an equivocal response from Hobbes. As an ideal, he was drawn toward religious independency and freedom of conscience.[50] Perhaps one reason for his attraction was the extreme heterodoxy of his own religious views, which he might have been forbidden to express in normal and more repressive times. Hobbes was also keenly aware that the vitality of philosophy and science was dependent upon freedom of thought, which had been stifled by Catholic theologians and philosophers for centuries. He was sharply critical of the Inquisition, arguing:

> There is another Errour in their Civill Philosophy . . . to extend the power of the Law, which is the Rule of Actions onely, to the very Thoughts, and Consciences of men, by Examination, and *Inquisition* of what they Hold. . . .[51]

These sensitivities lay behind Hobbes's insistence throughout *Leviathan* that the thoughts and consciences of men neither should nor can ever genuinely be subjected to the control of human laws, whether ecclesiastical or civil.

But Hobbes's political concerns would not permit him to endorse any truly general freedom of belief. Over and over again

[49] *Leviathan*, ch. 47, pp. 710-712 [384-385].

[50] *Leviathan*, ch. 47, p. 711 [385].

[51] *Leviathan*, ch. 46, p. 700 [378]. Hobbes criticizes the inquisition of Galileo in implicit but obvious terms a few paragraphs later, on p. 703 [380].

in *Leviathan* he argues that opinions are the true immediate causes of human actions. The strength of commonwealths ultimately resides in the opinions and beliefs of their members. Genuine and general freedom of belief was likely to sap this strength. For, as I have had occasion to note, Hobbes also argued that a belief in "Powers invisible, and supernaturall," as well as sundry other superstitions, "can never be so abolished out of humane nature, but that new Religions may againe be made to spring out of them, by the culture of such men, as for such purpose are in reputation."[52] This observation is by no means a veiled announcement of Hobbes's true views about the basis of a rational commonwealth, as at least one commentator has suggested.[53] It is instead a warning that an enlightened, rational cast of mind is not necessarily self-sustaining, and cannot be relied upon to perpetuate itself without the active support of those who determine the form and content of public instruction. Hobbes did not share the assumption of those ecclesiastical authorities who believed that the most inward thoughts and opinions of men could be coerced, but he also had little in common with the naive optimism of the later historical Enlightenment. Even if the struggle between enlightenment and superstition were won by the forces of reason, their victory would never be so secure that their enemies could be forgotten.

Hobbes interpreted the emergence of virtually complete religious freedom in his own time as a return to a primordial condition of chaos, a much more thorough "state of nature" than any which might be brought on by an ordinary political breakdown. His eagerness to demonstrate the need for absolute sovereignty often leads him to write as if every breakdown of sovereignty were equally absolute. This conclusion even seems implicit in the very structure of his political argument, which is constructed around a central antithesis between absolute sov-

[52] *Leviathan*, ch. 12, p. 179 [58].

[53] Eisenach, *Two Worlds of Liberalism*, p. 29.

ereignty and absolute chaos. But this implication of his atemporal, analytical argument is sharply at odds with the conclusions implied by his account of the origin and history of Christian faith and ecclesiastical power. The relentless theme of this account, to which Hobbes returns again and again, is that the crucial factor in the institution of any commonwealth, determining from the very outset whether in the long run it will succeed or fail, is the character of the cultural and intellectual foundations upon which it is constructed, the state of mind of the subjects who constitute its "matter." This powerful emphasis upon the importance of intellectual culture—of the degree to which the thoughts and actions of subjects are governed by reason or by irrational superstitions—suggests a significant modification of the antithesis between order and chaos implied by Hobbes's analytical argument. In spite of that argument, his interpretation of history indicates that a sharp distinction must be drawn between ordinary political breakdowns, on the one hand, and any collapse that involves the cultural infrastructure of political authority, on the other. Political breakdowns are indubitably dangerous and liable to be destructive. But they cannot be equated with a situation of absolute cultural upheaval and collapse, which leaves every man free to do "whatsoever seemeth good in his owne eyes."[54] This situation of complete "ethical chaos," as one interpreter has described it,[55] is what Hobbes thought had come into being in his own time, and what he attempts to capture in the striking language of his portrait of the state of nature.

For Hobbes this complete cultural upheaval was in effect a return to the condition of the primitive Christians, before ecclesiastics had begun to assert their authority and gain that control over the human imagination which they had exercised so

[54] *Leviathan*, ch. 46, p. 686 [370]. Hobbes also applies this phrase to the time in ancient Jewish history between the death of Joshua and the crowning of Saul, in ch. 40, pp. 506 [253] and 510 [255].

[55] Riedel, *Metaphysik und Metapolitik*, p. 185.

effectively throughout most of the Christian era. It thus presented an opportunity unlike any that had occurred in more than a millennium. As in those very early times, England was, in Hobbes's view (which was undoubtedly shaped by those powerful eschatological currents in the thinking of his contemporaries to which Pocock has rightly called attention[56]) undergoing a cultural revolution—a period of dissolution in social ties and ethical norms as well as in political authority more absolute than anything ever previously experienced by his fellows. For Hobbes, this absolute dissolution brought England to an historic crossroads.[57] He had no reason to doubt that a sovereign would emerge to quell the disorder into which England had fallen in the 1640's. Fortune would eventually allow someone to gain the upper hand and seize control. A new commonwealth would inevitably rise from the ruins of the old; by the time Hobbes completed his book, it had already begun to do so.[58] It made no difference to him that this new commonwealth would be based, in effect, upon conquest. The previous regime, like most other commonwealths in the world, had had similar beginnings.[59] Hobbes was not very concerned about the identity of the new sovereign, either. The important thing was that there should be some definite sovereign to rule the country; who that sovereign might be was a matter of no great moment.

[56] Pocock, "Time, History, and Eschatology," p. 161.

[57] This argument is similar to Eisenach's assertion that the English civil war had created an "historical moment" of opportunity in Hobbes's eyes (*Two Worlds of Liberalism*, pp. 42, 66). But Eisenach, like most of Hobbes's interpreters, focuses too narrowly upon the effects allegedly created by the civil war on Hobbes's thinking, and underestimates the importance of his interpretation of ecclesiastical history, as well as the distinction between political breakdown and cultural upheaval implied by that history.

[58] Hobbes alludes to the civil war as an ongoing event at several points in *Leviathan*: ch. 3, p. 95[9]; ch. 18, pp. 236-237 [93]; and ch. 19, p. 251 [101]. In his Review and Conclusion, however, he speaks only of "the disorders of the present time" (p. 728 [395]), reflecting the fact that although the new regime was not yet fully established, the civil war itself was over.

[59] *Leviathan*, Review and Conclusion, pp. 721-722 [391-392].

But this comparative indifference to the origins and identity of the new sovereign contrasts sharply with Hobbes's deep concern about the design and foundations of the commonwealth that sovereign was to rule. The collapse of clerical control over the human imagination did not mean that the danger to commonwealths posed by superstition and irrationality could be considered a thing of the past. Far from it. Though its mechanisms of control were in a state of disarray, the Christian faith itself remained as strong as it had ever been, and the seeds of superstition out of which it had arisen could never be wholly eliminated. There was nothing to prevent new religious leaders from drawing upon them again, as the Catholic church had done in the past, to pose new challenges to civil authority. This prospect was of the deepest concern to Hobbes, as he makes clear in the closing paragraph of his main text:

> It was not therefore a very difficult matter, for Henry 8. by his Exorcisme; nor for Qu. Elizabeth by hers, to cast them out. But who knows that this Spirit of Rome, now gone out, and walking by Missions through the dry places of China, Japan, and the Indies, that yeeld him little fruit, may not return, or rather an Assembly of Spirits worse than he, enter, and inhabite this clean swept house, and make the End thereof worse than the Beginning? For it is not the Romane Clergy onely, that pretends the Kingdome of God to be of this World, and thereby to have a Power therein, distinct from that of the Civill State.[60]

Clerical power was at a low ebb, but it had not been stamped out. It could never be destroyed forever, given the nature of the human imagination and the gullibility of most men. New, ambitious clerics, whether Catholic, Protestant, or of some yet unheard-of faith, would arise in the future, peddling their superstitious doctrines to an unsuspecting people. These men, and

[60] *Leviathan*, ch. 47, pp. 714-715 [387]. This passage is a deliberate imitation of Matthew 12:43-45, which Hobbes cites in ch. 8, pp. 145-146 [39].

the ignorance upon which they preyed, posed a constant danger to all commonwealths, which could easily gnaw away at and ultimately destroy their foundations if they were not carefully watched and prevented from doing so.

The only way to ensure against this calamity was to identify its potential sources and do everything possible to destroy them, or at the very least to inhibit their growth. For Hobbes the root of this danger was not clerical power as such. Clerical power was more accurately portrayed as a manifestation than a cause of flawed political foundations. Nor were the doctrines of traditional Christianity the true root of the problem. Hobbes mounts a scathing attack upon some of those doctrines in *Leviathan*, but the aim of his attack is not exclusively to refute those doctrines. It is misleading to interpret the Scriptural and historical argumentation of *Leviathan* as *simply* an attack upon the power of Catholic and Presbyterian clerics, or as an attempt to refute some of their theological claims. The true object of this argumentation is more fundamental. That object is the ignorance and superstitious inclinations—or, in short, the irrationality—of ordinary subjects. The best way to ensure a commonwealth against danger was to root out that irrationality as thoroughly as possible.

The state of absolute cultural flux that had arisen in his time presented Hobbes with what seemed to be a rare, indeed historic, opportunity to attempt this eradication. In a revealing metaphor, he hints that the disintegration of clerical power had opened men's eyes, finally, to the raw ambitions that had lain behind the hierarchical structure of ecclesiastical authority:

> And for the remedies that God should provide, [for "possession" by "spiritual men"] . . . wee are to attend his good pleasure, that suffereth many times the prosperity of his enemies, together with their ambition, to grow to such a height, as the violence thereof openeth the eyes. . . .[61]

[61] *Leviathan*, ch. 47, p. 709 [384].

The visual metaphor is significant, for it suggests an important parallel with Hobbes's own undertaking. English subjects were ready, he believed, both to accept new doctrines to govern their political thinking and to re-evaluate the entire web of relationships by which they were connected with other human beings, and even with the world itself. They were prepared, in short, to reinterpret both themselves and the nature of the universe they inhabited. This readiness would last, however, only as long as their memories of the absolute upheaval so recently experienced remained vivid. On political doctrines in particular he argues that

> there be few now (in *England*,) that do not see, that these Rights [of sovereignty] are inseparable, and will be so generally acknowledged, at the next return of Peace; and so continue, till their miseries are forgotten; and no longer, except the vulgar be better taught than they have hetherto been.[62]

The opportunity to institute a fundamental change in men's interpretations of their own existence, to bring about an essentially enlightening transformation of the way in which they understand and act, would not long remain open. "The vulgar"—ordinary subjects—would have to be taught much better than they had hitherto been, and not on points of political doctrine alone. Their entire outlook, those perceptions of the world which determined whether or not they would act rationally—and hence be receptive to the claims of civil power—would have to be transformed. Their wild, unbridled imaginations would have to be controlled, their ignorant, superstitious fears be calmed, before secure foundations for a new, rational commonwealth could be laid.

The new doctrines needed to effect this transformation were contained in *Leviathan*, and in a form so vivid and powerful that Hobbes could actually dare to hope that this work might at

[62] *Leviathan*, ch. 18, p. 237 [93].

least initiate the movement of cultural and ideological change that was required. At the end of *Leviathan* Hobbes suggests that his work was written "without other designe, than to set before mens eyes the mutuall Relation between Protection and Obedience."[63] But this statement is by no means accurate. It describes the upshot of Hobbes's political argument, construed in a narrow sense, fairly enough. But Hobbes aimed to do more in *Leviathan* than demonstrate the relationships of right and obligation that should obtain in a commonwealth, or to show the grounds upon which these relationships arise.

Three paragraphs earlier he defends the "new Doctrines" offered in his interpretation of Scriptures by arguing that

> in this time, that men call not onely for Peace, but also for Truth, to offer such Doctrines as I think True, and that manifestly tend to Peace and Loyalty, to the consideration of those that are yet in deliberation, is no more, but to offer New Wine, to bee put into New Cask, that both may be preserved together.[64]

This deliberate evocation of the words of Matthew 9:17 reveals[65] the true scope of Hobbes's aims in *Leviathan*. Christianity had been flawed from the earliest times because its first "Doctors" had poured its "new Wine" into the "old empty Bottles of Gentilisme." Now a rare, perhaps unique, opportunity to reshape men's most deeply held beliefs about themselves and the world had arisen. It could not be allowed to pass. For those beliefs in turn shaped men's actions, and ultimately determined whether they would conform to those rational patterns which could provide the foundation for a new commonwealth of

[63] *Leviathan*, Review and Conclusion, p. 728 [395-396].

[64] *Leviathan*, Review and Conclusion, p. 726 [394].

[65] "Neither do men put new wine into old bottles: else the bottles break, and the wine runneth out, and the bottles perish: but they put new wine into new bottles, and both are preserved."

uniquely secure design to emerge from the ruins of political and cultural collapse.

Thus, two essentially distinct but intimately intertwined aims are pursued in Hobbes's *Leviathan.* The first and, to modern readers, vastly more familiar of these two aims is to demonstrate, once and for all time, the grounds and extent of the rights of sovereignty, and of the obligations of subjects, in any commonwealth on earth. The distribution of rights and obligations that should obtain in any commonwealth could be demonstrated, in his view, by rigorous philosophical reasoning. Like *The Elements of Law* and *De Cive* before it, *Leviathan* attempts to offer such a demonstration. But any interpretation of that work which fails to see beyond this aim is radically incomplete. For the second and no less essential aim of *Leviathan* is to initiate a cultural transformation, a process of enlightenment by which Hobbes hoped to lay the foundations for a new kind of commonwealth. That commonwealth would be fundamentally—in the literal sense—unlike any that had ever before existed, including those ancient commonwealths in which, by his account, political authority had gone unchallenged for so many years. For it would not, like them, be founded upon myths and superstitions. Its subjects would be moved by their own self-interest, pursued rationally and without the distorting effects to which myths, superstitions, and other forms of irrationality must inevitably lead. The commonwealth envisaged by Hobbes in *Leviathan* would be truly everlasting because its foundations would, for the first time in history, be truly rational. Those rational foundations would have to be created before that commonwealth could be brought into being. The creation of those foundations is the very core of Hobbes's political aim in *Leviathan*.

Epilogue

HOBBES IS generally credited with offering a new vision of man and society that breaks sharply with an older, traditional view. The old view subordinated man to a larger, cosmic order of things governed by its own eternal laws. The highest ideal for humanity was the attainment of harmony with this eternal order. The way to this harmony was through the highest part of man's soul, reason, which was defined as a means to understanding of the eternal and the divine. The ends of human life were prescribed by nature and could not be understood without reference to the larger community to which each individual belongs. The concept of man and society expressed in Hobbes's political philosophy is in many respects the antithesis of this traditional view. His concept implies that the universe is a collection of objects external to man, not a cosmic order of which humanity is one subordinate part. Human fulfillment consists less in the attainment of harmony with that world than in the achievement of ascendancy over it. This ascendancy can be established by each person individually through the use of reason, understood as a faculty of calculation, to gain control over at least some small sphere of activity. Man is a fundamentally egoistic being whose actions are designed to promote his own self-interest, which each individual defines in his own way. Far from being prior to the individuals who compose it, political society is a creation of those individuals, who are bound together by their desire to remain as free as possible to pursue their own, privately defined ends, and especially by their desire to avoid death.

It is often argued that the concept of man which lies at the core of this new vision was merely a mirror of the reality of human nature as Hobbes perceived it, and that for this reason that concept can never provide an adequate basis for an enduring political philosophy. At least two distinct versions of this thesis have attained widespread currency. The first is that the concept was drawn from a "possessive market society," which English society is said to have become by the seventeenth century, and that the inadequacy of Hobbes's vision is a consequence of the fact that its applicability is limited to such a society.[1] The second is that his concept of man is in fact an accurate representation of many enduring features of human nature, and that the flaws in his political philosophy derive from its failure to challenge men to become better and more virtuous beings than they are inclined to be by nature. Neither of these claims is entirely false, but both are misleading. Hobbes's new view of man as a rational egoist was not merely a representation of reality as he saw it. On the contrary, it was a carefully constructed model of man as Hobbes believed he would have to be in order to live in a peaceful and lasting political community. The overwhelming impression which emerges from a consideration of *Leviathan* as a political act is that Hobbes saw a deep discrepancy between this model and the reality of men as they existed in his own time. To judge from observation alone, men were essentially ignorant, superstitious creatures. Ignorance and superstition were so deeply ingrained in their characters as to render them fundamentally irrational. Far from being sanguine about the prospects for his vision of political society, Hobbes was in fact deeply concerned that the irrationality of his contemporaries would pose an insuperable obstacle to the realization of that vision.

There are grounds for believing that Hobbes's vision corresponds closely to certain features in modern societies. The im-

[1] C. B. Macpherson, *The Political Theory of Possessive Individualism: Hobbes to Locke* (Oxford: Clarendon Press, 1962), esp. pp. 61-68.

portance in political discourse of the concept of civil society, which began to come into use very soon after he was gone, and the enduring appeal of Hobbesian styles of analysis in contemporary social science, testify at least to the plausibility of this vision as a description of those societies. If such a correspondence does exist, however, it cannot be regarded simply as a product of Hobbes's shrewdness as an observer of his own times. His vision had to be brought into being through a change in the men and women who were to compose it. This change could not be accomplished merely by persuading people that absolute political authority is necessary to the preservation of peace and their own lives. What was needed was a more fundamental change, a transformation that would recast the human psyche into the mold of rational egoism Hobbes had created for it. If his vision has to some extent been realized, that realization is at least in part a product of deliberate efforts—including that of *Leviathan* itself—to reshape the human psyche.

This observation should have a significant bearing upon our assessment of the Hobbesian vision and the moral and political world it helped bring into being. Hobbes's political philosophy has been criticized for a host of alleged weaknesses and failures. It has been charged with plunging us into an abyss of moral and political subjectivism by breaking with the "rationalism" of classical political philosophy, which rested upon the assumption that the ultimate source of all ethical and legal standards lay in an eternal natural law. It has also been indicted for creating a framework of political discourse that excludes from the outset any real recognition of the importance of political community as well as for imposing excessively narrow constraints upon the development of human individuality.[2] Any or all of

[2] See, respectively, Strauss, *Political Philosophy of Hobbes*; Wolin, *Politics and Vision*, ch. 8; Macpherson, *Political Theory of Possessive Individualism*, esp. ch. 6.

these charges might seem to be lent some encouragement from the picture of Hobbes's political aims painted in the foregoing pages of this book. For perhaps the central conclusion to be drawn from this picture is that the Hobbesian vision of man and society is far from "natural." Hobbes did not portray man as he is. He depicted what as he hoped man would become. Those who find his world too confining can derive some solace from the thought that there was a time when that world had not yet come into being, and that the passing of that world is well within the realm of possibility as well as imagination.

But a note of caution is in order, too. We need not accept Hobbes's own vision of political society to recognize that many of the pitfalls he was trying to avoid are real enough, and should be approached only with great circumspection. It should not be assumed that the revival of natural law or political community, or the further development of human individuality, can be effected without producing unwanted side effects. There is much talk today, for example, about the limitations imposed upon our understanding of politics and society by the congenital failure of modern Western thought to recognize the irreducible importance of myth as a factor shaping the thoughts and actions of all men and women, however "advanced" the societies they inhabit may be. If the consequence of this talk is to improve our political understanding, then it is unimpeachable. But another possible consequence might be the rehabilitation of myth itself. We should be extremely wary of any such result, for reasons Hobbes's political philosophy makes clear. The common charge that he failed to appreciate the role of myth in politics is at least in one sense misdirected. Hobbes was deeply impressed by the role myth had played in politics in the past and was continuing to play in his own time. The fact is, however, that he considered myth a product of egregious ignorance. Such ignorance, he thought, is incompatible with any genuinely rational political society, which must be founded upon an enlightened populace.

Was this view misdirected? Perhaps. Hobbes equated enlightenment with adoption of an understanding of the universe as a collection of material objects governed by mechanical laws of motion and acceptance of a concept of the self as a radically mortal being for which no evil greater than death is conceivable. To many people today these understandings will seem outmoded and parochial. There is no reason for us to accept them in the versions formulated by Hobbes. Yet some of the phenomena he identified as products of ignorance and superstition were precisely that. In seeking to broaden our concept of human rationality—our self-understanding—we should not abandon altogether the line he tried to draw between the rational and the irrational, even if we do decide to shift or redefine that line. If the vision of man and society Hobbes proposed is hostile to the need for political community or too confining to allow for the full development of human individuality, we should nevertheless remember the ills he was attempting to escape by formulating that vision.

Select Bibliography

THIS BIBLIOGRAPHY includes all primary sources used in the preparation of this book and all secondary sources cited in my footnotes. Readers interested in a comprehensive bibliography of works by and about Hobbes published during the past century should consult William Sacksteder's fine *Hobbes Studies (1879-1979): A Bibliography* (Bowling Green, Ohio: Philosophy Documentation Center, Bowling Green State University, 1982).

Primary Sources

Collections of Hobbes's Works

The English Works of Thomas Hobbes of Malmesbury, 11 vols., and *Thomas Hobbes Malmesburiensis: Opera Philosophica quae Latina Scripsit*, 5 vols. Sir William Molesworth, ed. London: John Bohn, 1839-1845. The most comprehensive edition, but often marred by textual flaws.

Philosophical Works of Thomas Hobbes. Howard Warrender, ed. Oxford: Clarendon Press, 1983-present. A critical edition with extensive scholarly apparatus. Two volumes have appeared to date: vol. 2, *De Cive*, The Latin Version (1983); vol. 3, *De Cive*, The English Version (1983).

Editions of Individual Works by Hobbes

"The Autobiography of Thomas Hobbes." Benjamin Farrington, ed. In *The Rationalist Annual*, 1958. London: Watts and Co., 1957, pp. 22-31. A modern prose translation of Hobbes's *Vita, Carmine Expressa.*

Behemoth; or, The Long Parliament, 2nd ed. Ferdinand Tönnies, ed. London: Frank Cass and Co., 1969.

Critique du De Mundo de Thomas White. Jean Jacquot and Harold Whitmore Jones, eds. Paris: Vrin, 1973. The first publication of a lengthy and important scientific manuscript Hobbes composed in the early 1640's.

A Dialogue between a Philosopher and a Student of the Common Laws of England. Joseph Cropsey, ed. Chicago: University of Chicago Press, 1971.

The Elements of Law, Natural and Politic, 2nd ed. Ferdinand Tönnies, ed. London: Frank Cass and Co., 1969.

Leviathan; or, The Matter, Forme, and Power of a Commonwealth, Ecclesiasticall and Civill. C. B. Macpherson, ed. Harmondsworth, Middlesex: Penguin, 1968.

Leviathan; or, The Matter, Forme, and Power of a Commonwealth, Ecclesiasticall and Civill. W. G. Pogson Smith, ed. Oxford: Clarendon Press, 1909.

The Life of Mr. Thomas Hobbes of Malmesbury. London: A. Crooke, 1680. An anonymous translation of Hobbes's *Vita, Carmine Expressa.*

"The Life of Thomas Hobbes Of Malmesbury." J. E. Parsons, Jr. and Whitney Blair, trans. *Interpretation* 10 (1982), pp. 1-7. A translation of Hobbes's *Vita, Carmine Expressa.*

Man and Citizen. Bernard Gert, ed. Garden City, New York: Doubleday, 1972. The text of Hobbes's translation of *De Cive*, known as *Philosophical Rudiments Concerning Government and Society*, together with a translation of selections from *De Homine.*

Sir William D'Avenant's Gondibert. David F. Gladish, ed. Oxford: Clarendon Press, 1971. Contains an accurate edition of "The Answer of Mr. Hobbes to Sir Will. D'Avenant's Preface before Gondibert."

Thomas White's De Mundo Examined. Harold Whitmore Jones, trans. London: Bradford University Press, 1976. A translation of the Jacquot and Jones manuscript, *Critique du De Mundo de Thomas White*, above.

CORRESPONDENCE

Aubrey, John. *Brief Lives*, 2 vols., Andrew Clark, ed. Oxford: Clarendon Press, 1898.

Brockdoff, Cay, Baron von. "Fünf ungedruckte Briefe von Jean Pierre de Martel an Thomas Hobbes." *Hobbes-Gesellschaft Veröffentlichungen* 6 (Kiel, 1937), pp. 7-23.

Cohen, Bernard I. "A Lost Letter from Hobbes to Mersenne Found." *Harvard Library Bulletin* 1 (1947), pp. 112-113.

de Beer, G. R. "Some Letters of Thomas Hobbes." *Notes and Records of the Royal Society of London* 7 (1950), pp. 199-205.

"Ellis Papers," folio 4. British Library Additional Manuscripts 28,927.

[Great Britain] Historical Manuscripts Commission. *Report on Manuscripts in Various Collections*, vol. 7, p. 401. London: His Majesty's Stationers, 1914.

———. *Thirteenth Report, Appendix, Part Two: The Manuscripts of His Grace the Duke of Portland*, preserved at Welbeck Abbey, vol. 2, pp. 124-130. London: Her Majesty's Stationers, 1893.

Hall, A. Rupert and Marie Boas Hall. *The Correspondence of Henry Oldenburg*, vol. 1, pp. 74-76, and vol. 9, pp. 329-330, 374-375. Madison: University of Wisconsin Press, 1965 and 1973.

"Letters from Foreign Correspondents." Hobbes Manuscripts in the Chatsworth Collection of the Duke of Devonshire.

"Letters to Thomas Hobbes, 1656-1675." British Library Additional Manuscripts 32,553.

Tannery, Paul and Cornélis de Waard. *Correspondance de P. Marin Mersenne*, vol. 6, pp. 311-312, and vol. 10, pp. 588-591. Dijon: 1960 and 1967.

Thompson, Francis. "Lettres de Stubbe à Hobbes." *Archives de Philosophie* 12 (1936), pp. 99-106.

Tönnies, Ferdinand. "Contributions à l'Histoire de la Pensée de Hobbes." *Archives de Philosophie* 12 (1936), pp. 81-89.

———. "Hobbes-Analekten I" and "Hobbes-Analekten II." *Archiv für die Geschichte der Philosophie* 17 (1903-1904), pp. 291-317, and 19 (1905-1906), pp. 153-175.

———. "Siebzehn Briefe des Thomas Hobbes an Samuel Sorbiere." *Archiv für die Geschichte der Philosophie* 3 (1890), pp. 192-232.

Other Primary Sources

Bacon, Francis. *The Advancement of Learning*, Arthur Johnston, ed. Oxford: Clarendon Press, 1974.

Blundeville, Thomas. "The True Order and Methode of Wryting and Reading Hystories," Hugh G. Dick, ed. *Huntington Library Quarterly* 3 (1940), pp. 149-170.

Cavendish, William. "Essays Addressed to His Father," in Friedrich O. Wolf, *Die Neue Wissenschaft des Thomas Hobbes*. Stuttgart–Bad Canstatt: Friedrich Frommann, 1969.

Descartes, René. *The Essential Writings*, John J. Blom, ed. New York: Harper and Row, 1977.

Erasmus, Desiderius. *Desiderius Erasmus Concerning the Aim and Method of Education*, W. H. Woodward, ed. Cambridge: Cambridge University Press, 1904.

———. *The Praise of Folly*. New Haven: Yale University Press, 1979.

[Great Britain] Historical Manuscripts Commission. *Twelfth Report, Appendix, Part Two: The Manuscripts of the Earl Cowper, K. G.*, preserved at Melbourne Hall, Derbyshire. London: Her Majesty's Stationery Office, 1888.

Hale, Sir Matthew. *Reflections by the Lrd. Cheife Justice Hale on Mr. Hobbes, His Dialogue of the Lawe*, in W. S. Holdsworth, *A History of English law*, vol. 5. London: Methuen, 1924.

"Hobbes: Translations of Italian Letters." Hobbes Manuscripts in the Chatsworth Collection of the Duke of Devonshire, E.6.

Horae Subsecivae: Observations and Discourses. London: Edward Blount, 1620.

Quintilian. *Institutio Oratoria*, 4 vols., H. E. Butler, trans. Cambridge, Mass.: Harvard University Press, 1953.

Sidney, Sir Philip. *A Defense of Poetry*, J. A. Van Dorsten, ed. Oxford: Oxford University Press, 1966.

Secondary Works

CRITICAL STUDIES OF HOBBES

Ashcraft, Richard. "Ideology and Class in Hobbes' Political Theory." *Political Theory* 6 (1978), pp. 27-62.

Ball, Terence. "Hobbes' Linguistic Turn." *Polity* 17 (1985), pp. 739-760.

Brandt, Frithiof. *Thomas Hobbes' Mechanical Conception of Nature*. Copenhagen: Levin and Munksgaard, 1928.

Eisenach, Eldon J. "Hobbes on Church, State, and Religion." *History of Political Thought* 3 (1982), pp. 215-243.

———. *Two Worlds of Liberalism: Religion and Politics in Hobbes, Locke, and Mill*. Chicago and London: University of Chicago Press, 1981.

Gauthier, David P. *The Logic of Leviathan*. Oxford: Clarendon Press, 1969.

Gert, Bernard. "Introduction" to Thomas Hobbes, *Man and Citizen*, Bernard Gert, ed. Garden City, New York: Doubleday, 1972.

Goldsmith, M. M. *Hobbes's Science of Politics*. New York and London: Columbia University Press, 1966.

Hamilton, James Jay. "Hobbes's Study and the Hardwick Library." *Journal of the History of Philosophy* 16 (1978), pp. 445-453.

Hood, F. C. *The Divine Politics of Thomas Hobbes*. Oxford: Clarendon Press, 1964.

Hungerland, Isabel C. and George R. Vick. "Hobbes's Theory of Signification." *Journal of the History of Philosophy* 11 (1973), pp. 459-482.

Johnson, Paul J. "Hobbes's Anglican Doctrine of Salvation," in *Thomas Hobbes in His Time*, Ralph Ross, Herbert W. Schneider, and Theodore Waldman, eds. Minneapolis: University of Minnesota Press, 1974, pp. 102-125.

Kemp, John. "Hobbes on Pity and Charity," in *Thomas Hobbes: His View of Man*, J. G. van der Bend, ed. Amsterdam: Rodopi, 1982, pp. 57-62.

Krook, Dorothea. "Thomas Hobbes's Doctrine of Meaning and Truth." *Philosophy* 31 (1956), pp. 3-22.

McNeilly, F. S. *The Anatomy of Leviathan*. London: Macmillan, 1968.

Macpherson, Crawford B. *The Political Theory of Possessive Individualism: Hobbes to Locke*. Oxford: Clarendon Press, 1962.

Mintz, Samuel I. *The Hunting of Leviathan*. Cambridge: Cambridge University Press, 1962.

Oakeshott, Michael. *Hobbes on Civil Association*. Berkeley and Los Angeles: University of California Press, 1975.

Ong, Walter J. "Hobbes and Talon's Ramist Rhetoric in English." *Transactions of the Cambridge* [England] *Bibliographical Society* 1, pt. 3 (1951), pp. 260-269.

Peters, Richard. *Hobbes.* Harmondsworth, Middlesex: Penguin, 1967.

Pitkin, Hanna F. *The Concept of Representation.* Berkeley: University of California Press, 1967.

Pocock, John G. A. "Time, History, and Eschatology in the Thought of Thomas Hobbes," in *Politics, Language, and Time.* New York: Atheneum, 1973, pp. 148-201.

Polin, Raymond. *Hobbes, Dieu, et les hommes.* Paris: Presses Universitaires de France, 1981.

———. *Politique et Philosophie chez Thomas Hobbes.* Paris: Presses Universitaires de France, 1953.

Raphael, David D. *Hobbes.* London: Allen and Unwin, 1977.

Reik, Miriam M. *The Golden Lands of Thomas Hobbes.* Detroit: Wayne State University Press, 1977.

Riedel, Manfred. *Metaphysik und Metapolitik.* Frankfurt: Suhrkamp, 1975.

Robertson, George Croom. *Hobbes.* Edinburgh and London: William Blackwood and Sons, 1910.

Ryan, Alan. "Hobbes, Toleration, and the Inner Life," in *The Nature of Political Theory*, David Miller and Larry Siedentop, eds. Oxford: Clarendon Press, 1983, pp. 197-218.

Sacksteder, William. "Hobbes: Philosophical and Rhetorical Artifice." *Philosophy and Rhetoric* 17 (1984), pp. 30-46.

Saxonhouse, Arlene W. "Hobbes and the *Horae Subsecivae.*" *Polity* 13 (1981), pp. 541-567.

Schwartz, Joel. "Hobbes and the Two Kingdoms of God." *Polity* 18 (1985), pp. 7-24.

Sherlock, Richard. "The Theology of *Leviathan*: Hobbes on Religion." *Interpretation* 10 (1982), pp. 43-60.

Skinner, Quentin. "Conquest and Consent: Thomas Hobbes and the Engagement Controversy," in *The Interregnum*, G. E. Aylmer, ed. London: Macmillan, 1972, pp. 79-98.

Springborg, Patricia. "*Leviathan* and the Problem of Ecclesiastical Authority." *Political Theory* 3 (1975), pp. 289-303.

Strauss, Leo. "On the Basis of Hobbes's Political Philosophy," in *What Is Political Philosophy?* Glencoe, Illinois: The Free Press, 1959, pp. 170-196.

———. *The Political Philosophy of Hobbes.* Chicago: University of Chicago Press, 1952.

Tarlton, Charles D. "The Creation and Maintenance of Government: A Neglected Dimension of Hobbes's *Leviathan*." *Political Studies* 26 (1978), pp. 307-327.

Tuck, Richard. *Natural Rights Theories: Their Origin and Development*. Cambridge: Cambridge University Press, 1979.

Warrender, Howard. *The Political Philosophy of Hobbes: His Theory of Obligation*. Oxford: Clarendon Press, 1957.

Watkins, J.W.N. *Hobbes's System of Ideas*, 2nd ed. London: Hutchinson, 1973.

Whelan, Frederick G. "Language and Its Abuses in Hobbes' Political Philosophy." *American Political Science Review* 75 (1981), pp. 59-75.

Wolf, Friedrich O. *Die Neue Wissenschaft des Thomas Hobbes*. Stuttgart–Bad Canstatt: Friedrich Frommann, 1969.

Wolin, Sheldon. *Hobbes and the Epic Tradition of Political Theory*. Los Angeles: Clark Memorial Library, 1970.

———. *Politics and Vision*. Boston: Little, Brown, 1960.

Other Secondary Works

Aurner, Nellie S. *Caxton: Mirrour of Fifteenth-Century Letters*. London: P. Allan, 1926.

Bennett, H. S. *English Books and Readers: 1475 to 1557*, 2nd ed. Cambridge: Cambridge University Press, 1969.

Boas, Marie. *The Scientific Renaissance, 1450-1630*. New York: Harper and Row, 1962.

Bundy, Murray Wright. "The Theory of Imagination in Classical and Medieval Thought," *University of Illinois Studies in Language and Literature* 12, nos. 2-3 (1927).

Eisenstein, Elizabeth L. *The Printing Press as an Agent of Change*, 2 vols. Cambridge: Cambridge University Press, 1979.

Frank, Joseph. *The Beginnings of the English Newspaper, 1620-1660*. Cambridge, Mass.: Harvard University Press, 1961.

Haller, William. *The Rise of Puritanism*. New York: Columbia University Press, 1938.

Howell, Wilbur S. *Logic and Rhetoric in England, 1500-1700*. New York: Russell and Russell, 1961.

Knappen, M. M. *Tudor Puritanism*. Chicago: University of Chicago Press, 1939.

Ong, Walter J. *Ramus, Method, and the Decay of Dialogue*. Cambridge, Mass.: Harvard University Press, 1958.

Pollard, A. W. and G. R. Redgrave, eds. *A Short-Title Catalogue of Books Printed in England, Scotland, and Ireland and of English Books Printed Abroad, 1475-1640*. London: The Bibliographical Society, 1946.

Schaaber, Matthias A. *Some Forerunners of the Newspaper in England, 1476-1622*. Philadelphia: University of Pennsylvania Press, 1929.

Skinner, Quentin. *The Foundations of Modern Political Thought*, 2 vols. Cambridge: Cambridge University Press, 1978.

Stone, Lawrence. "The Educational Revolution in England, 1560-1640." *Past and Present* 28 (1964), pp. 41-80.

Thomas, Keith. *Religion and the Decline of Magic*. Harmondsworth, Middlesex: Penguin, 1973.

Trimpi, Wesley. "The Ancient Hypothesis of Fiction: An Essay on the Origins of Literary Theory." *Traditio* 27. New York: Fordham University Press, 1971.

———. "The Quality of Fiction: The Rhetorical Transmission of Literary Theory." *Traditio* 30. New York: Fordham University Press, 1974.

Yates, Frances A. *Giordano Bruno and the Hermetic Tradition*. London: Routledge and Kegan Paul, 1964.

Index

Library of Congress Cataloging-in-Publication Data

Johnston, David, 1951-
The rhetoric of Leviathan.

(Studies in moral, political, and legal philosophy)
Bibliography: p. Includes index.
1. Hobbes, Thomas, 1588-1679. Leviathan.
2. Hobbes, Thomas, 1588-1679—Contributions in political science. I. Hobbes, Thomas, 1588-1679. Leviathan. II. Title. III. Series.
JC153.H66J64 1986 320.1 86-4967
ISBN 0-691-07717-7